Choose Life!

Living Consciously

in an

Unconscious World

Beverly M. Breakey

ASHAR
PRESS

SAN JOSE, CA

Published by: Ashar Press
                 Post Office Box 54130
                 San Jose, CA 95154-4130 U.S.A.
                 1-877-342-7427
                 http://www.asharpress.com

First Edition 2000
PRINTED IN THE UNITED STATES OF AMERICA

Cover design by Peri Poloni, Knockout Design
Cover image by Annabelle Breakey Photography; Model: Monique Strauss
Layout, design, and book production by Phelps & Associates LLC
Copy editing by Karen Stedman of PenMark; Proofreading by Sonja Beal
Illustrations by John Wilkins
Grateful acknowledgment is made to the following for permission to reprint material:
• Center Press, from Stanley Keleman, excerpt from *Love: A Somatic View*, © 1994, Center Press, 2045 Francisco St., Berkeley, CA 94709.
• S.L. Feldman and Associates for the partial line from the Joni Mitchell composition, *Big Yellow Taxi.*
• Dave Severn for the excerpt from a speech given on the World Wide Group, LLC stage.
• Jane Wagner, writer for Lily Tomlin, for a one-liner spoken from stage.

Names and identifying characteristics of people used for this publication have been altered. Any similarities of the names or characteristics of any living persons are purely coincidental and not intended by the author. This publication is designed to provide accurate and authoritative information in regard to the subject matter covered. It is sold with the understanding that the author/publisher is not engaging in rendering psychological, medical, spiritual direction, legal or other professional services. If expert assistance is needed, the services of an appropriate professional should be sought.

Cataloging-in-Publication Data
(Provided by Quality Books, Inc.)

Breakey, Beverly M.
        Choose Life! : living consciously in an
    unconscious world / Beverly M. Breakey. -- 1st ed.
        p. cm.
        Includes notes, resources and index
        ISBN 0-9674738-0-2

        1. Self-actualization (Psychology)   2. Conduct
    of life.   I. Title

    BF637.S4B74 2000   158.1
                             QBI99-1668

*This book is dedicated to the memory of my mother,
Jean Brown Segall, who loved to write
and inspired me to do likewise.*

"I call heaven and earth to witness against you today,
that I have set before you life and death,
blessings and curses.

Choose life,
that you and your descendants may live..."

From the book of Deuteronomy, 30:19
The Holy Bible, Revised Standard Version

Table of Contents

Following an Unqualified Leader • Authority Figures • Asking for Affection • Religious Rigidity • Making Waves • Decisions • Political Power • But Isn't Anger Bad? • This Doesn't Involve You • Control • Is Money the Root of All Evil? • What Is It About "No" You Don't Understand? • Commitments • Overwhelmed • Discomfort

Some Things Never Change • Actions Should Be Congruent with the Highest Belief Held • A Whole Is Greater Than the Sum of Its Parts • Everything Affects Everything Else • Consciousness Demands a Willingness to Listen and an Ability to Hear

Table of Contents

Table of Contents

Foreword

I am writing this in the aftermath of the death of John F. Kennedy Jr., in a plane crash near Martha's Vineyard. Accompanied by his wife and her sister, Kennedy was piloting the private aircraft at night to join his family at the wedding of one of his cousins. Because evidence of the crash came in bits and pieces in the following days, the drama of the event held the nation spellbound as the media replayed the tragic history of the Kennedy clan since the death of Joe Kennedy, Jr. as a pilot in World War II.

The mystique of the Kennedy clan, dating back to the Camelot days of John F. Kennedy's presidency, was heightened by the tragedy of his assassination and the death of his brother and political heir-apparent, Robert Kennedy. Part of the mystique has been the capacity of the family to support one another in their grieving and to emerge from such tragedies like a Phoenix from ashes with renewed vigor and continued commitment to public service. No whining. No asking, "Why us?" No bitterness that they seemed to be under a family curse. Regardless of our assessment of their political leanings, no one has ever questioned their courage in the face of adversity, their faith in a God of justice and mercy and their commitment to public service.

This family as a collective unit is a wonderful example of choosing life. There are exceptions, of course, like the death of one of Robert Kennedy's children from a drug overdose, but for the most part members of this family demonstrate the qualities that Beverly Breakey identifies as characteristic of those who choose life. They are visionaries and activists. They are people of faith and hope. Exposed to excessive media attention, they are able to establish boundaries as individuals and a family and still remain engaged in public life. Above all, they exude a positive attitude toward life, even when crushing adversity presses in on them. These are the qualities that cause so many people to identify with this family as they now grieve their most recent loss.

We need models of people who choose life, but we also need descriptions of their characters and qualities. Beverly Breakey provides us with both in this book. Her clear and nontechnical descriptions are supported by example after example. She cites relevant research and provides background information, such as the etymology of words and the cultural context of particular practices to assist the reader in grasping the significance of what she is describing. Her style is personal and engaging. It is as if she is speaking to you directly, encouraging you to move away from being a bystander to choosing life.

Beverly is the embodiment of everything she describes and promotes in the following pages. In her presence you can feel the energy and positive attitude that she brings to every relationship and every task that she's engaged in. She has had extensive experience in health promotion through a faith-based wellness program located in a Lutheran church in San Jose, California. The material is this book is the product of her experience in choosing life and encouraging others to do so in workshops and personal counseling.

The model for choosing life that I suggested at the beginning of this foreword was an extended family rather than an individual. That was intentional. No man, no person is an island, as John Donne said many years ago. You can't choose life all by yourself, no matter how hard you try. You need the support of others, if not your family then friends, colleagues or a faith community. And above all, you need the support of a higher power, whatever name you give to the source of all life and power. My prayer for you is that with such support and the guidance of this practical manual, you will find the balance and harmony that comes with a way of life that is holistic and life affirming.

–Tom Droege, Senior Scholar, Interfaith Health Project, Carter Center, Atlanta, Georgia.

About Tom Droege

Tom Droege is a Lutheran pastor and educator whose area of expertise is faith development and the relation between health and spirituality, with a particular focus on the implementation of health ministries in congregational settings. After a career of teaching and research in practical theology at Valparaiso University, he joined the Interfaith Health Program (IHP) at the Carter Center in Atlanta Georgia. He held the position of associate director of the center from 1992 to 1998 and currently serves as the Senior Scholar and editor of the IHP newsletter, *Faith and Health.*

Tom has authored numerous books and articles on faith development, grieving and health and spirituality. His most recent book, *The Healing Presence,* is a source book of thirty guided imagery exercises in health and healing. It is available from Educational Media Corporation at (800-966-3382).

Acknowledgments

With great humility and appreciation, I wish to honor the following people who so generously supported me throughout the course of this project...

Pat Williams, a lovely English lady, who tirelessly protected the Queen's English in my behalf,

David Birdsall, whose creative engineering mind showed me where I wasn't making sense,

Marilyn Wilson, a gentle spirit, whose delightful humor and editorial gifts allowed me to delve once more inside myself to create that added change,

Laynee Wild, who urged me through the publication process and told me she was through with being a bystander,

Jane Hegrat, for her editorial comments and encouragement,

The World Wide Group, LLC, for the positive consistency of their mentoring program and resources which have been an ongoing source of inspiration for me,

My precious family, friends and co-workers, whose stories are woven into the tapestry of this work,

Karen Stedman, copy editor and Janice Phelps, book producer, who were the best cheerleaders a writer could ever have,

Jack Lundin, long time friend and mentor whose wit and creative spirit permeate the essence of this work,

Lastly, to my husband, Richard, who believed in me and insisted that I share the following wisdom with the peoples of the world.

To the Reader

If you are reading this I admire your curiosity. Did the title stir a dream in you, a little hope perhaps? You are probably the type of person who has already worked on your self-esteem and personal growth. It is my hunch that if you are awake enough to have picked up this book, you are looking for more. I applaud you.

This book teaches healing: healing yourself, healing your life, and healing your world. You may not believe you are an especially courageous soul. I believe you are. Let me help you to strengthen your vibrant self, thereby enriching your life and everyone's you touch.

We can choose to live anywhere along the continuum of human consciousness. Some of us are barely awake. We exist marginally, putting one foot in front of the other until it's time to go to bed. Others of us scurry around so much we are like hamsters on a treadmill. Too many of us have settled into a comfortable rut, convinced that life is just fine.

No matter where we are on life's path, we must challenge ourselves to seek more. Giving up is not an option. Choosing to stay put is tolerable and safe, but not an option either. It means we are succumbing to the role of *bystander to life.*

I invite you to choose life: to take tiny steps forward in understanding yours and other people's humanity so that you and the world may be healed. I want you to be a *participant in life.* The following chapters will tell you how to become one.

Lechaim, Life!   —*Beverly Breakey, San Jose, California*

xix

Chapter One
Participants and Bystanders

Never give up, but give in gracefully from time to time.

How would you like to remember yourself? By that I mean, take your current wisdom and experience, pick whatever chronological age you want, and start your life anew. This sounds idyllic doesn't it? It is actually more realistic than you think.

How many times have you looked back and said, "If only I knew then what I know now!" Stop that! You made the best decisions you could based on your knowledge and experience at the time. Let it go.

Now, here is a magical secret. You can take your present wisdom and re-live great portions of your life as if you are doing it for the first time. For instance, if you are fifty years old and have the good fortune of falling in love, simply imagine you are fifteen. Chances are you will be acting like a fifteen-year-old anyway, and the beauty is this: at fifty you don't care what other people think.

If you are making a mid-life career shift, fantasize that you are twenty-two years old, just starting your first job. Can you sense the excitement? Don't you feel invincible? The fantasy is magic. The feelings are real.

Each time you do this, years will melt from your body, mind, spirit and emotions. Love your past for the lessons it has given you, but don't hover there. Turn and greet your future by facing forward. Adopt an attitude of adventure and tolerance for the mistakes you are about to make. This is choosing life.

I invite you to make this choice and discover some aspects of living you may have forgotten. Health and wholeness mean more than eating well and getting plenty of exercise. They involve waking up, taking a look around, and saying, "I will." When you choose holism (the big picture) as a way of life you give up being a *bystander* and become a *participant.* Everything appears to change. People will look at you and say, "Now, there goes a person with their lights on!"

One of the first things you need to know is that you possess an untarnished blueprint. One of the most amazing aspects of this blueprint is that, no matter how you live your life, there is within you an intrinsic drive to get back to that original. Wouldn't you like to become the full potential of your unique design? It is possible. Moreover, chronological age doesn't have anything to do with it.

Participants in life learn how to live with change. Just like the rest of us, they suffer when they lose jobs, friends, family members and communities. (They do not, however, attempt to suffer in silence.) They share their pain with at least one good confidant. If they have a spiritual faith they do all they can about the situation and turn the rest over to God. They know that this particular brand of suffering is life-generating even though it feels like death. It is, in fact, a type of death. Any ending is, but each ending births a new beginning.

Endings and beginnings are nothing more than the natural cycling of our lives. In fact, they let us know we are alive. Just as a forest fire cleanses the soil, sanitizing and preparing it for healthy new growth, we, too, reorganize after every change. Participants know that growth only occurs if there are downward as well as upward cycles. They have faith that each upward phase will take them higher than before. (Fig. 1)

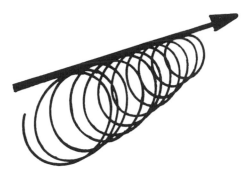

Figure 1. Participants believe the cycling phase will take them higher than before.

Waking Up

How do you define yourself: by name, profession or accomplishment? Are you satisfied, or do you wish your life were happier, richer, easier? When was the last time you allowed yourself to dream, really dream about places to go and people to meet, intimate love and family connectedness? Is your daily work challenging? Are you productive and well paid? Do you have the time, energy, and inclination to expand your creativity? Are you growing the spiritual part of you? Are you full of life, gracious and receptive, yet generous and loving?

From our first breath to the last, life happens to us in unexpected ways. When we lose track of the realization that we have choice, we lose spiritual consciousness. We become what I call bystanders to life. There is too much to do, in too little time, without enough money. We forget about dreaming because we can't bear the thought of one more disappointment. Motivational books, tapes and seminars inspire us for a time, but they will not awaken us from indifferent living.

You may, in fact, be a bystander and not even know it. The good news is that you can find out and reclaim your participant-in-living status. If you already know life is passing you by, you can improve it. There are places to find healing and ways to cope with change. People will help you when you learn where to look and whom to ask. You can open fresh venues for pleasure and deepen your relationships. The basics of choosing life and living consciously do not require any special gifts or intelligence.

Looking Around

Because we live in a cyclical universe we are constantly in flux, moving from one aspect of a continuum to the next. Just as day flows into night, we, too, transition from wakefulness into sleep. We move from feeling up to feeling down. At times we must assert ourselves, at others we withdraw. We give and we receive. We retreat inside ourselves but are soon thrust out again by some natural and irresistible force.

Within our bodies millions of cells expand and contract all by themselves. Each is a tiny replication of universal pulsation. We have no choice in the cycles of natural law and this is a frightening thought. The more rigid we are the more we depend on control to feel alive. Herein lies one of life's paradoxes.

As members of humankind we forget we are cyclical creatures. We resist change and yearn for the non-stressful state of homeostasis. We overlook the fact that homeostasis represents a resting place; a temporary calm impervious to the impending winds of change. It is a region where questions await answers and problems sit unsolved. It seductively masquerades as peacefulness and we desire it.

When life's inevitable stresses disturb our slumber we may feel afraid or angry. We think, "What am I supposed to do now?" Remember, this is not the time for doing, it is the time for being, waiting and dreaming.

· Being means accepting that change is occurring and we will be affected by it.

· Waiting means being patient and inviting the process of shifting out of our familiar way of doing things.

· Dreaming means engaging our creativity through some quiet presence and support.

· Doing comes later.

We live in physical bodies on a physical planet and our life experiences register in every cell. Opportunities to solve problems and create a new reality surface every day through touch, laughter, music and beauty. In essence, we are spiritual creatures. It is through confession, forgiveness and faith that we renew hope. Our choices are endless, limited only by our own conditioning. We can learn how to create healing moments of quiet presence in the midst of life's greatest storms. We can learn how to live in community with others by choosing to give and receive hospitality. The first stage of creation is wishing and dreaming, yet we often lose sight of its importance because we let the circumstances of life choose us instead of choosing life.

We do not choose our bodies, emotions or our inherited temperaments, but we do choose how we live with them. We are born with a brain and we choose how to develop our minds. We either nourish our physical form or ignore and abuse it. We possess a human spirit and we choose to nurture it or let it atrophy. We learn and we un-learn. We sense and we feel. We live as participants or as bystanders every second of every day.

I Am Not a Bystander; or Am I?

Resistance to change is an important clue that bystander behavior is settling in. Inactivity breeds its own type of stress, a weightiness that impedes our choices and creative expression. Remaining in a non-active state beyond its point of renewal soon becomes an effort. We become restless yet resistant to change. We stifle our inclination to wish and to dream, for dreams proceed from ideas, to verbal expressions, and then to actions. Because we don't know what to do we shut down our creativity and hope the urge to change will go away. Are you working in an impossible situation? Are you in a disastrous relationship? Should you sell your house and move to a more manageable condominium? Would your life improve if you altered your diet? This paradoxical push/pull invokes panic because we forget that throughout each phase of every cycle we have choices and can make changes.

Bystanders are people whose deep-seated fears and acquired knowledge interferes with choosing life. Their emotional postures are flat and circular: flat because they lack vitality and circular because they remain stuck in a type of holding pattern. (Fig. 2) Their consummate energy resists the rhythms of change. They may even be successful in the eyes of the world, but their life experience lacks freedom. Money, plus time and satisfying intimate relationships, are seldom theirs. The successful image of a bystander is often linked to prestige and power rather than joy and happiness. Most importantly of all, they have forgotten how to dream.

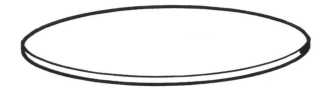

Figure 2. A bystander's emotional posture is flat and circular.

Julie's Story: Waking Up

Julie was a woman in her mid-fifties. After a long marriage she divorced, returned to school and became a professional designer. She helped her two children through college and after they left home she focused on her career. Life was good. She had friends, a nice home, her own business and more money than most.

A lingering thought hovered in the back of her mind: She would like another try at marriage. This notion was really a dream that Julie was suppressing for a variety of reasons. Long ago she had given up on singles activities because the participants appeared so desperate. "I'm certainly not one of those," she assured herself. The capable men she met and admired were either gay or already in relationships. "Could I be overlooking something? I've listed all the features and attributes of this ideal person, just like the books tell you to. Well, where is he? It doesn't work."

Once she had read a survey of professional women who married after building their careers. It showed that within one year the lifestyle of these women had deteriorated by fifteen percent. "I'll just stay put," she thought. "After all, it is a good life. I'm going to stop thinking about it. If God wants me single, then I'll be single. No New Year's resolutions this year."

On January 4, it happened. A gentleman sat next to her at a meeting and before long they were exchanging ideas, stories and business cards. A friendship quickly developed, followed by a budding romance. Intellectually they were a good match. Each had an entrepreneurial spirit. They laughed and played together, delighting in their deepening camaraderie.

One day he asked her if she was the content type or the want more type. When she replied, "I'm really satisfied with my life," he exploded. "That's what's wrong: I can't find a dream in you anywhere."

Julie catapulted into shock. She didn't know what he was talking about. Why was he reacting like this? Had she really forgotten how to dream? No, she'd always been a visionary. At the tender age of six she knew she would become a wife, a mother and have a career, too. At age eleven she could see herself as a medical missionary. In her mind it was as good as done.

She had accomplished most of her goals. Marriage and family upstaged the medical missionary dream but it didn't matter. After all, marriage was a mission of sorts. She was happy with friends, church, children and a home. What she didn't know was that a lifetime partnership requires on-going evaluation and accommodation for change. Parents leave a marital legacy to their children. Healthy and unhealthy patterns will continue unless steps are taken to stop them.

Because of the way they were raised, Julie and her first husband needed professional help to mould a flexible relationship. She was willing to pursue it but he refused. The couple became polarized, and the children began withdrawing into their individual worlds. Healing under these circumstances needed a miracle. None came. Julie held tremendous remorse for the failed marriage. Had it caused her to settle for a dreamless life?

Anger filled her now. "How dare he criticize me? Who is he anyway? Why, I'm good in all of society's accepted ways; a little too serious perhaps, but so what?" For three days she struggled with her bitterness. She prayed. She took long walks. She continued to have defensive conversations with herself.

Finally she felt a softening in her emotions as anger yielded to sorrow. "Of course, he's right. I don't dream. I function. Accept it. This really is an incredible gift because now I can do something about it. I can choose life and I have an idea that this man will show me how." In nine months they were married.

You Know You Are a Bystander If…

The biggest problem with being a bystander is that so often we don't recognize it. Like Julie, we may suppress our dreams with rationalizations. Those vague yearnings so easily dismissed as unrealistic or impractical, often signal the very direction we should be taking. It is crucial to grasp these dreams and share them with an honest friend. Such a person will usually see possibilities where we cannot. They can also help us brainstorm about transitional steps. "A new job in Atlanta? Wonderful! What's stopping you? Oh, your mother is in a nursing home here. You can go. There are ways to maintain your connection with her. Let's make a list of them."

Possibilities bring change and impending change can paralyze our creativity. It is also important to heed the big signs that signal stagnation. We may become depressed or physically ill. Some of us lose our jobs. We can sustain work injuries or crash our cars. Life cycles. If we don't cycle with it, we find ourselves being re-cycled by it.

The following is a list of questions related to some of the more subtle indicators of being a bystander. They suggest that you have settled for less than you should in your choices for living fully. Avoid rationalizing your responses. A quick yes or no will suffice.

1. *Do you choose to follow a leader even though you are better qualified?*

2. *Do you prefer that authority figures, including physicians, tell you what to do?*

3. *Do you believe you should not have to ask your spouse or loved ones for affection?*

4. *Do you embrace a religious philosophy that teaches morality through fear of punishment and requires blind obedience?*

5. *Do you avoid making waves at all costs and prefer to play it safe?*

6. *Do you let others make all the big decisions, while you become indignant about the small ones?*

7. *Do you believe you have no political power?*

8. *Do you believe anger is bad?*

9. *Do you believe your daily choices affect only you?*

10. *Do you have the need to be in control of situations and relationships?*

11. *Do you believe profit is bad?*

12. *Do you have difficulty saying no, or do you automatically say no?*

13. *Do you hesitate to make commitments in fear of making a mistake?*

14. *Are you overwhelmed much of the time?*

15. *Did answering any of these questions make you uncomfortable?*

If you answered yes to any of the above it means that you may not be choosing life as fully as you could be. Contemplate the following discussion of each question to further your insight, then make a mental note to come back to them after reading the remainder of this book.

1. Following an Unqualified Leader

There are times in life where we discover that in many areas we know more than our appointed leader. This is a dilemma for us as well as the leader. We can probably stick it out for a short time, but eventually the incompetence will be impossible to disregard. It will eat away at us, compromising our performance as well as our health.

If the leader is unable or unwilling to hear our concerns, two choices remain: we can remove ourselves from the situation or initiate actions to get rid of the leader. Neither choice is easy and should never be approached in isolation. Change here is inevitable. Ask yourself, *"What outcome behooves the greatest good for the greatest number involved?"* Make a decision, get support and move forward. Don't give up but realize that you may have to give in gracefully. [1]

2. Authority Figures

Other than in emergencies, don't let authority figures dictate what you should do. Ask for their knowledge and experience; you decide on the action. Learn to listen to your own wisdom. It is better to follow a hunch than to blindly follow a leader. That leader may not have your best interests in mind.

True authority is never bossy or controlling. It is confident and welcomes debate. Be on guard for people who presume their beliefs to be absolute. Beliefs are not necessarily truths. A paternalistic attitude masquerades as one that takes care when it is really taking control.

3. Asking for Affection

Believe that you can have whatever you want in life and then create a plan to get it. This involves asking for help. Practice learning how to ask, when to ask and ways to respond should you hear, "NO." People have varying levels of love-ability. If you want the people in your life to be more aware of your needs for affection you must teach them how to demonstrate their love. We all want love to be expressed in a particular way, and we expect others to automatically know what that is. "When I come home from work I know that you love me when you give me a quick kiss and leave me alone." "When I come home from work I know you love me if you pull up a chair for me and ask me what my day was like." Find out what pleases your loved ones and tell them what pleases you. Negotiate and compromise when there is a conflict. [2]

4. Religious Rigidity

Don't mistake rigidity for strength. Fear, intimidation and withholding human love do not bring us closer to God. You must choose how and where you get your spiritual nourishment. Organized religion can feed you or it can make you sick.

5. Making Waves

Most people don't relish confrontation. Its reputation ranges from uncomfortable to *frightening*. We don't like to be the confrontor or the confrontee. We will avoid it even though we may detest the behaviors of others. When an electrocardiogram measures the rhythms of a healthy heart, the print-out is lined with peaks and valleys. When the heart begins to die, the peaks and valleys disappear and are replaced with a flat line. Living as a bystander resembles a flat line.

Avoidance damages the human spirit. A little bit of our character dies when we ignore something we shouldn't. Character building begins with honesty that is a learned attribute. When honesty is revered and rewarded, it comes naturally, even if it means admitting a wrongdoing. It is also the most important ingredient in any relationship.

People who have difficulty being direct and don't know how to confront others become mired in vicarious behaviors. Some avoid decisions in fear of being offensive or making a mistake. Most of us are offended at regular intervals, and we get over it. We also make mistakes, and seldom are they fatal. Life goes on and hurt feelings heal.

Others deal with their own uncertainties by becoming cleverly political, waiting for the tide to turn in a particular direction so they can align with the popular side. These folks usually isolate themselves from offers of friendship, must have control and live in a vacuum of denial. Sometimes they explode inappropriately. At other times they behave like pyromaniacs, playing one person against the other just to watch the fireworks.

These are examples of bystander behavior, play-actors at life. Learning to confront is merely a skill. Failing to do so disorganizes the body, the mind and the spirit. It erodes trust and ruins relationships.

6. Decisions

Allowing others to make the big decisions for us demonstrates our own lack of self-regard. Ask to be part of the decision-making process on large issues, otherwise you may find yourself making a big fuss over small matters. This applies to any system whether it be marriage, work, organizations or in the marketplace. Children need adults to make decisions for them. Adolescents begin making their own decisions and usually have to painfully learn from some of their poorer ones. Adults should know that they bear the consequences for their decisions and that life usually doesn't end from poor judgement. It adjusts and goes on.

7. Political Power

Each of us has the power to drive corporate change. We can act individually or collectively, but we must know that we can affect policy. Consumer power lies easily within our reach; simply don't buy products that are unhealthy for you or for others. Manipulating government policy is more complex. Government, like any large organization, is made up of people just like us who succumb to pressure and influence. Speak up. Don't be afraid to engage with another human being whose opinion differs from yours. If you cannot convince him or her to shift a belief, then agree to disagree.

8. But Isn't Anger Bad?

Anger is a powerful human emotion. Its purpose is to cleanse the human spirit. Unbridled anger is destructive while healthy anger is a passionate revelation of how you feel about something. Anger masquerades under many pseudonyms: irritability, frustration, sarcasm, rage, animosity, wrath, fury, hostility and exasperation. Because anger so often leads to violence, we have dubbed it *bad.* Learn to recognize your own anger. Discover that venting in the moment brings refreshing aliveness to an argument. Clean anger dies quickly. Don't let anger smolder inside of you. It has a way of leaking out subversively or blasting others inappropriately.

9. This Doesn't Involve You

Systems, large and small, have similar characteristics. A family is a system, so is a corporation. They have distinct personalities and behave in particular ways. One cardinal characteristic of a system is that everything that goes on within it affects each member of the system. In a family, each member becomes accustomed to the behaviors of the others. When one changes, each has to adjust to that change. If Mom decides to wear her hair differently, each family member adjusts whether he or she likes it or not.

Systems function best when there is honesty among members; the whole system participates in the pain as well as the pleasure. A husband, who hides financial worry from his wife in order to protect her, betrays the honesty of their relationship and the integrity of their marital system. He also denies the synergistic potential for them to solve the problem together. The strain takes its toll on the other family members who sense something is wrong but are told, "Everything is fine." The couple's unhappiness affects the relationships they have with friends who also sense something is wrong. We may believe we can isolate ourselves but, in truth, we cannot. We all live together on a very small planet. We are as interdependent as a giant weaving: pull one strand and the other strands must adjust.

10. Control

The need to control situations and relationships stems from our own inflexibility. It gets us into a great deal of difficulty because we are looking through our own lenses of life experience. Others see life differently. Bystanders stand stubbornly within their own line of vision. They are unable or unwilling to take their lenses off, even for a minute, to try on a different perspective.

When we fail to understand or accept the behavior of others it is much simpler to ask them to change than to hear their viewpoint. If we do, we may have to give up some or all of ours in behalf of the greatest good. Rigid people need to control situations and relationships for this reason: fear of change.

11. Is Money the Root of All Evil?

Money is not evil. Greed is evil. Selfishness is evil. Money derived from profit, which is honestly earned and generously shared, is merely one aspect of life's bounty. Profit is generative. It creates opportunities for work and play, giving and receiving, all of which are healthy aspects of choosing life.[3]

12. What Is It About "No" You Don't Understand?

Bystanders have trouble saying "no" because they fear the point of controversy with another person. They would rather say something that sounds like "yes" and then avoid the issue all together. This is a dishonest response based on fear. It jeopardizes the relationship. "No, I don't want to," is good enough. We don't have to rationalize or explain our reasons, but we do need to honor our own and another's integrity.

Another bystander tactic is to automatically say "no" when invited to think about something new. These folks rush to their own pre-judgment and opinions rather than soliciting the facts. Once more their fears have taken over forcing them even deeper into their entrenched zone of familiarity.

13. Commitments

Bystanders dislike commitment. They view a commitment as a jail sentence rather than an opportunity to give and receive on a deep level. A commitment to a relationship, a career, an idea or a cause will demand passion. Bystanders lack passion. They hum through life on middle C, never knowing the agony or the rhapsody of choosing life. When we anticipate and experience our emotions deeply and fully, we are truly alive.

14. Overwhelmed

This is a disease of the nineties. Never in the course of history have so many people felt their life slipping into an abyss of stress and pressure. Feeling overwhelmed more days than not is a principal warning that you are fast becoming a bystander. You may believe you have no choice, but you do. Pay close attention to this sign. Get help immediately. Remember that you are viewing your situation through emotional lenses. Your situation may seem hopeless to you, but it is not. Others will help you. Every challenge has a solution, in fact, usually more than one.

15. Discomfort

If answering any of the above questions on page nine makes you uncomfortable, then you need to heed your discomfort for it signals something awry in your life. Don't perpetuate the bystander credo that *ignorance is bliss.* There is a difference between ignorance and ignoring. Ignorance is a pure lack of information and understanding. Ignoring is a conscious act of avoidance. It may even be termed *stupidity.* Use the suggestions in the following chapters to determine where you can change. Treat discomfort as a gift; a shove that will propel you out of aggravation into consolation. Choose life by asking questions and associating with lively people. They are waiting to help you. Reaching out is your first step, listening to what they say is the second and taking action is the third.

Choosing Life Means Becoming a Participant

If you were shipwrecked and getting into a lifeboat, all your perspectives would change. Can you imagine such a situation and how you would value survival as never before? When you are given a second chance by choice or by force, the options remain the same: you can drift or you can paddle. The following is a list of behaviors common to life's participants.

1. *You can be either a leader or a follower and embrace holism as a way of life.*

2. *You respectfully gather information from authority figures and use it wisely.*

3. *You pursue a spiritual path: a daily practice of quiet presence and the seeking of great wisdom from God, sages and contemporaries.*

4. *You voice your likes and dislikes, first to yourself and secondly to others. You process your hurts while learning to forgive yourself and others.*

5. *You refrain from basing your actions only on opinions.*

6. *You strive to understand other cultures and other people's ideas and opinions. You work toward healing yourself, your community and your world.*

7. *You question, stepping back from issues long enough to gather more information before acting.*

8. *You continually renew your hope by finding the positive in people and situations.*

9. *You act, sometimes on faith.*

10. *You respect your uniqueness which is a culmination of ancestry, acquired learning and experience.*

11. *You enjoy yourself and share your talents generously. You are hospitable.*

12. *You ask for affection and learn to enjoy sexual and non-sexual touch.*

13. *You practice integrity in even the smallest matters.*

14. *You add music to your daily routine for a variety of reasons.*

15. *You bring people into your life who will laugh with you.*

16. *You confess your mistakes and accept help.*

17. *You wish and you dream, alone, with other individuals and corporately.*

18. *You beautify your environment.*

19. *You give some of your working skills away.*

20. *You develop your creativity and playfulness.*

21. *You vote.*

22. *You get angry and get over it quickly.*

23. *You listen to the early warning signals of your body and your intuition.*

24. *You can see beyond your own pain to hear the pain of others.*

The following chapters offer you a metaphorical lifeboat. They will uncover fresh insights for living richly and lovingly. Lifeboats have life jackets, paddles and oars. If you had a choice, wouldn't you use them all?

Begin charting your course for living consciously in this rather unconscious world. There is no time like this moment to begin. Choose life!

Chapter Two
Holism, A Way of Life

Pain, suffering, health and learning can and do co-exist.

D o you think of yourself as pure and holy? You should! The English word *whole* comes from the ancient word *hael*, which means *without blemish*. This infers that for something to be whole it must be perfect. This is fine if we are talking about a piece of fruit. But what about a person?

The word *holism*, on the other hand, comes from the Greek word *holos*, which means *in its entirety*. One derivative of holos is *holy*. Holism anticipates an acceptance of the entirety. Conflicting conditions within you, such as warmth and coldness, illness and health or happiness and sorrow, are merely gradients along a continuum. The path of life flows back and forth along it. Each aspect contributes to your wholeness, even the warts. Isn't it a relief to know that you are pure and holy even though you are not perfect?

Intellectually, we humans like to believe that we are in relative control of ourselves most of the time. Consider this: how much of your physiology are you aware of? Do you realize that you are a marvel of complexity? Your body continually replaces its cells, adjusts its oxygen/carbon dioxide ratio and simultaneously engages in thousands of other intricate activities. If you were to replicate its myriad functions on a map it would cover the walls of a huge office building. Here is a paradox: Only when one little part malfunctions do we really give the whole system much thought.

When something goes wrong with our physical, mental, emotional or spiritual state, we suffer. Suffering gets our attention. Perhaps our physical form becomes too acidic and as a result, it develops a duodenal ulcer. Pain in our gut gets our attention. Our minds can be so preoccupied with a relationship problem that we can't focus at work. When the boss calls us in for a talk, it gets our attention. Our emotions can become immersed in grief when someone we love dies. If we are awake to life we suffer. We are whole and with blemishes. Still, we are pure and holy.

Suffering itself brings temporary imbalance to the human system. It represents disorganization of the mental and emotional aspects of us. It cannot destroy us, however, when we remember that we are whole beings rather than random pieces of creation. We are part of the greater cosmos. We have within our very blueprints the natural instinct to reorganize. We are already holistic, and, when we work with our natural rhythms, we regroup and flourish. Choosing life, as a conscious participant, is another way of saying, "I embrace holism as a way of life."

During the past decade, Western societies have become familiar with the terms *body, mind, spirit and emotions.* These characteristics aptly describe the human organism from the standpoint of its parts. Yet a person is not just an accumulation of physical or behaviorally fixable parts. The wholeness of a person includes spirituality, happiness, relationship to the environment, creative expression, hopes, dreams and other aspects of living that give it the juice of life. How can we manage our wholeness? How do we transcend physical pain, mental anguish and emotional turmoil? How do we set our human spirit free so that it can soar above the adversities of life? We do it by living by the principles of holism.

Principles of Holism

The development and maintenance of individual and group holism is governed by holistic principles. These are relational laws that have stood the test of time. Their causes and effects remain constant, regardless of era or circumstances. Some of the most salient holistic principles are:

1. *Some things never change.*
2. *Actions should be congruent with the highest belief held.*
3. *A whole is greater than the sum of its parts.*
4. *Everything affects everything else.*
5. *Consciousness demands a willingness to listen and an ability to hear.*

Principle 1. Some Things Never Change

An excellent example of holistic law is the famous Ten Commandments. They can be found in one of the oldest parts of the Holy Bible, the book of Exodus. This group of rules for daily living addresses each person's relationship with God and with other people. Who can argue with such basic mandates as "Don't lie, steal, covet or curse. Place your belief in the one God and don't make gods out of things. Don't disrespect your parents, murder or adulterate your marriage vows." The words contained in these commandments are estimated to be three thousand years old, yet, they are as appropriate today as they were then.

There is one more commandment. Where the nine that are cited above address behaviors done to others and to God, this one affects a behavior we direct toward ourselves. It relates well to choosing life because it illustrates an uncanny wisdom about humanity. This law commands us to rest one day out of every seven. It is easy for the majority of us to refrain from killing anyone. How easy is it for you to take one day each week to rest and play? The "I'll wait until ..." excuse is an illusion. It lies! Don't wait. Choose life!

We must remember the cyclical laws of nature to which we are permanently connected. Quiet presence is not a luxury, it is a necessity. In this day and age, where having and doing more is deemed the better way, we cannot afford a complacent attitude about taking regular time out. The days zoom by and before we know it another year has past.

Working with our natural rhythms requires a commitment to choosing life, an organization of schedules, and a rediscovery of how to play. It is time to get excited about doing nothing!

Physical laws are also constant; they just appear to change. Our breadth of understanding unfolds with each scientific discovery. We once believed the world was flat and that what went up always came down. Now we know that the earth is round and we can transcend its gravitational field. Because of this expanding knowledge, the laws of physics are not as timeless as are those governing human relationships. Rational, systematic thinkers would have us believe that reality is grounded only in pure science. Holistic thinking makes allowances for change while holding sacred the inalienable truths of time.

Principle 2. Actions Should Be Congruent with the Highest Belief Held

Humans must develop certain characteristics in order to choose life. Consider the quality of integrity. The temptation to employ it, or not, presents itself every day. Suppose you are walking along a busy sidewalk when you happen to look down and spot a gold bracelet. You pick it up. It is just your size. What do you do next? The choice is entirely yours. You can pocket it for yourself or run an ad and try to find the owner.

Acting with integrity takes time and practice. There is a law of holism that covers situations such as this. It states, "Always do what is right according to your highest conscious belief." A little of our human dignity erodes each time we deny our consciousness.

Continuing with the bracelet example, it is not only we who are involved. There is the person who lost the bracelet, the people we question about it, and those for whom we are role models. We are never completely isolated in our choices. Integrity stands for "doing what is right."

Most of us have good intentions, but we don't want to take the time needed to follow through with them. However, if we make integrity a serious priority in our every day living, we will make room for it. The mental, emotional and spiritual rewards for such behavior are immense. You will find that there will be time enough for all your activities when you put integrity first.

There are several other positive qualities of good character that we must be continually developing. Honesty, accountability and teachability are some of the best. They begin in our relationship with us and spread to all of our associations. You will find kindness, tolerance, and patience at work in healthy relationships. Consistency is essential in child rearing. Humor, courage and gratitude are other hallmarks of life's participants. Each of these human qualities fortifies the laws of holism. They cannot be legislated. They are choices.

Choosing to embrace positive qualities elicits personal growth which in turn brings increasing levels of awareness and consciousness. Participants strive to understand and integrate all aspects of themselves. This quest begins the moment we smile our first smile, and ends with breathing our last breath. Even dying yields discovery and mastery. Wholeness is not a state that one arrives at and then stops. Learning, failing and maturing are ongoing, and they occur simultaneously. Far Eastern philosophers bestow the name of *sage* to those who attain a high level of awareness, harmony and maturity. Their wisdom is born from a lifelong desire to risk, learn and grow. Sages are participants.

Principle 3. *A Whole Is Greater Than the Sum of Its Parts*

A summation of the parts belonging to any person is always going to yield a unique individual. Even within typologies there are exceptions. The magnificent complexity of the human organism deserves the designation of holy.

As humans we share several physical similarities, but even identical twins have differences. No two pair of blue eyes are exactly alike even though they both qualify as being blue. When we add mental, emotional and spiritual idiosyncrasies to the physical, we come up with an infinite number of possibilities.

A similar correlation can be made to groups regardless of their size. A summation of all the characteristics in a family or even a culture will produce a group personality. Families may be regarded as standoffish or friendly, private or gregarious. Societies may be considered liberal or conservative, militaristic or socialistic. These generalized qualities are much broader than the personalities of individual members in either example. When circumstances threaten the stability of any group, leaders will emerge to cope with it according to *their* beliefs. Each time the group personality changes the outcome will be different.

Principle 4. Everything Affects Everything Else

Another holistic principle deals with the interconnectedness between all peoples. Like it or not, we share one planet and one solar system. We have one God. We share one global climate, environment and economy. Occurrences in Asia impact Americans indirectly if not directly.

Even when we desire it, we cannot completely isolate ourselves. Although the human body appears to be made up of solid matter this is not completely true. Matter is composed of molecules that are always in motion. The skin of the body is permeable to many types of molecules and, therefore, the human body cannot end at the skin. Physically and energetically we extend outward. How else can you explain turning around to discover someone looking at you from across a room?

When Albert Einstein revealed his Theory of Relativity he gave us clues as to the importance of relationships in all of life. The branch of physics known as *quantum mechanics* concerns itself with the behaviors of very small things, such as the particles that make up atoms. These tiny particles move so rapidly that they actually engage with whatever is near them. Indeed, everything is affected by everything else. [1]

Principle 5. Consciousness Demands a Willingness to Listen and an Ability to Hear

Even though many of the rules for living do not change, circumstances do. Each of us must adopt a means for coping with the many pressures of daily living and the changes they bring. In choosing life, participants adopt a holistic framework for growth and change. The principles of holism form the foundation from which this framework is built. As we grow in conscious living, these principles allow us to see beyond our immediate personal situations to the greater scheme of things.

Decisions we make today will affect the rest of our lives. Not only will they affect us, but everyone whom we influence. The Amazon rainforests are not in a Chicago suburb, but they affect Lake Michigan weather. We are not isolated from that which is at a distance. Participants take a proactive stance on ecological salvation. Bystanders mock attempts to save the rain forests or living creatures within the ecological network.

Participants make daily choices by first asking, "How will the outcome of this decision affect others? If I don't floss between my teeth, who will that hurt but me? Neglecting my teeth may cause cavities. Repairing cavities costs money. Money is in limited supply. If I have to spend money at the dentist's office I can't spend it elsewhere. I had better floss."

Most of us live in a pressure cooker of complex systems and paperwork. Prioritizing our daily tasks is as necessary as breathing. We are continually juggling our time between doctor appointments, lines at the post office, commuter traffic, the kids' homework, congregational meetings, work demands, and the thousands of other activities that routinely occur. Emergencies throw our packed schedules into chaos, leaving us panting to catch up. How do we choose life amidst it all?

Planning ahead eliminates much of the daily urgency. If you don't know how to plan, find people who do and have them advise you. Commercial systems with calendars, task lists and reminders are very helpful. Planning begins with the broadest dreams and filters down-ward to the smallest chores. It allows you to move toward your dreams consistently while still caring for you and your daily responsibilities. Built into these plans are times for creativity and play, rest and renewal, intimacy and romance, as well as community service. Choosing life in this way allows us to be productive and satisfied.

Progress in consciousness is made through a process of duplication and involvement rather than single-mindedness. We must replicate actions and ideals that are basic to human survival and to the greatest good for all. Others will assist us and in turn we can assist others. The premise is not complicated. A suitable addition to the fifth principle of holism would be: "The wise will counsel all who have a willingness to listen and an ability to hear."

Holistic Practices

Once we understand the five holistic principles, we can use them as a foundation for daily decisions. When we view life holistically, we embrace its entirety. To do so is to become conscious, a lively partici-pant, full of joy and excitement. It means choosing life.

Resolving Conflict Holistically

Individuals develop their attitudes and ability to make choices based on their beliefs about living. Each person copes with challenges according to his or her particular values and rules. When an individual's rules con-flict with society's laws, change is inevitable. Participants are strong individuals who proactively resist injustice. Bystanders react passively to it or not at all. Participants who choose life and desire to live consciously seek first to resolve conflict through discussion and consensus. Except in situations of crisis, conflicts are best resolved when there is some agree-ment between each party. Unhealthy bystander methods of coping with conflict include running away, avoidance, domination and manipulation.

Too often, when we have a disagreement with another individual or an organization, we place ourselves in an adversarial position. This is a polarized arrangement that states, "I am right therefore you are wrong." It leaves no room for reconciliation. Many times we are afraid that if we yield our *right* position we lose something vital. Loss is equated with failure. The only apparent solution is cutting off all association with the adversary.

Holism teaches that even though we have divergent views we are still part of a greater whole. Any dispute can be resolved if there is an earnest desire to participate in discussion with the goal being a consensus. We begin by finding some place of common agreement. It can be as broad as, "We are all one species," or "We all want freedom from oppression and a high quality of life." Bridging differences involves a willingness to negotiate and to keep on negotiating until each side believes it is not losing.

Often we both want the same results, but disagreement arises from the process of getting them. Bystanders balk at negotiation, participants thrive on it. It is a stretch to listen to another's point of view first. It is an even bigger stretch to be able to comprehend what we hear. It rarely happens in one sitting. When there is an intention to reach a consensus, however, healing will invariably happen. We grow when we participate. We stagnate when we alienate.

Holism and the Physical Body

Our physical form has a basic constitutional design made up of solids and liquids. The solids provide our shape and the liquids provide our chemistry. Social factors such as economics, parenting and stress will influence our shape and chemistry, but they do not alter the basic design. When we embrace holism we accept our physicality and take care of it. This is just one aspect of choosing life.

Illness in an individual body can be viewed as disorganization within the system. The human organism is, by design, a self-organizing one. It adapts to its environment and possesses innate healing chemistry. It strives to correct itself, and given adequate support it usually will. Adequate support for the physical body includes support for the mental, emotional and spiritual bodies as well.

The wonders of modern medicine have increased our length of life and speed of recovery. There is, however, a cost to the integrity of the physical system because of this progression. Far too often health care consumers ignore the practices that keep the body functioning at optimum performance. Aspects of holistic living such as nutrients, clean air and water, rest, confession, positive attitude, intimacy, creative expression and play are too often deemed luxuries rather than necessities.[2]

Holism and the Mind

Each person's mind influences his or her physical form in profound ways. This phenomenon dictates the attitude we bring to living, which in turn manifests our personal resourcefulness and success. It plays a significant role in our physical health, our emotional well-being and our relationships.

What we believe to be true is the foundation for the way we behave. If you believe that when you become chilled you may catch a cold, you will probably take extra precautions against chilling. It is the belief that drives the behavior. If you don't hold that belief you will keep warm merely for comfort. The notion of catching a cold won't enter your mind.

The way we behave is the person we become, the one whom others know. If you understand your body well enough and if you are wise, you will take the precautions necessary to prevent it from catching colds. You maintain these behaviors for a reason. You have become a person who understands his or her body in the cold-catching department and acts accordingly.

The person we become drives the manner in which we try to shape the world around us. Since we have learned how to prevent colds, we will want to teach those whom we influence how to prevent colds as well. Even if we don't say a word about it, our children and peers will see us taking the time to dress warmly before venturing out into inclement weather. Unless we live in absolute isolation, we continually exert influence over those around us.

It is our attitudes or beliefs that we need to shift when life is not working out the way we planned. A change in belief eventually results in a change in behavior. If we believe that we are successful human beings we will behave successfully and we will prosper. If we believe we are failures, voices hidden in the recess of our mind will say things like, "I don't deserve this job; it's too easy," or "I can't stay in this relationship; it's going too well."

Even though we feel uneasy about these messages, they are perpetual and we will continue to sabotage work and relationships until we confront them. Our *dis-ease* serves as an early warning device. It too has a voice. It says, "Something is really wrong here. I don't know what it is exactly, but it resembles a toothache. It nags and nags, won't go away and seems related to job loss and loneliness."

Beliefs are so powerful that we will sabotage the truth rather than change them. Bystanders will attempt to bring others down to their level and surround themselves with other bystanders, just to prove that they don't need to change. Watch how people who overindulge in food love encouraging others to order that extra dessert!

Can practicing successful behaviors with consistency and discipline affect a negative belief? Absolutely! The key is a strong intent to shift the belief and a willingness to practice appropriate new behaviors until it does.

Going it alone is an act of the strong will. Some people are good at invoking the strong will, but there are additional ways to change a behavior. Why not use your skillful will by engaging others to help you? They will gladly share your struggle and your success. Ask people you trust to give you regular encouragement, and to *tag* you when you falter.

One thing you can easily do on your own is to dress as if you have already reached your goal. Smart sales people wear business attire while making cold calls. It boosts their self-image and allows them to deflect repeated rejection. When you think of yourself as if you are already using your new behavior you have almost mastered it. Your body will get the idea and change its posture. Your emotions will play along and trigger positive feelings. Your spirit will shine and success will follow.

The human mind is a tool. It can lead us toward our intended dreams or away from them. Holism requires us to first examine our own behaviors when things go awry and then look at others. Only by using the totality of this information can we discern what is true. Bystanders blame others when things go wrong. Participants uncover the beliefs behind their own behaviors and work toward changing both.

Holism and the Emotions

We are provided with a set of emotions by virtue of our existence. Emotions are part of our innate chemical biology. They are not many, just love, fear, anger and sorrow. Unlike emotions, feelings are numerous. Choosing life requires learning how to experience and express a full range of both.

Feelings are rooted in the basic four emotions, and each can be traced to them. We are born with the capacity to love, but someone must teach us how to be compassionate. Compassion is but one expression of love; tenderness is another.

Fear is partly instinctual and partly learned. A healthy function of fear teaches us to look both ways before crossing a busy street. An unhealthy example would be the suspicious neighbor who bars her windows because she believes you might steal her jewelry. A California child calmly gets under her desk when an earthquake hits. The adults in her life have taught her not to fear, but to act safely. Midwestern children learn not to fear thunder. They are taught that it's just a big noise. The California child will have nightmares for weeks after a thunderstorm, and Midwesterners of all ages hate earthquakes.

Anger affords us a reaction to life's injustice and abuse. It resembles fire; burning away the deadwood of envy, resentment and jealousy to make way for new growth. It serves as a clearing for fresh thought and reconciliation. Sub-sets of anger are frustration or irritation.

Sorrow provides us with a response to pain and a process for healing. When we are experiencing sorrow we may say we are sad, downhearted or blue. Tears help to wash away the body's chemical reaction to trauma. The more we are able to lean into our sorrow and feel it fully, the quicker we heal.

Feelings and emotions allow us to experience life and express ourselves to others. They should not be feared or avoided, but respected and felt. Bystanders avoid passion, participants relish it.

In choosing life we examine the degree of excitement and passion in our relationships. Emotions are in each of us. Sometimes they just need to be coaxed out of hiding by a trusted friend or mentor. Feelings are learned expressions, variations of the emotions. We develop them by associating with others who have learned them well. Sometimes they are appropriate, at other times they are not. Learning to know the difference is one of the choices we make. It represents choosing life.

Holism and the Human Spirit

We choose life when we acknowledge that we are spiritual creatures linked to a greater cosmos, or to God. Tending the human spirit is something we usually allocate to religious endeavors. *Religion* infers the seeking of God. Owning up to one's spirituality implies believing that God exists.

What we are seeking, then, is a rich relationship with the divine. Holism regards our alliance with God as a cyclical process. We come closer and we drift, come closer and stray again. The more we revere and respect the holistic laws of creation, the more holy we become. The closer our walk is with God, the more we are blessed. However, we are not blessed as an end in itself, but to be a blessing to others.

Our spiritual self is the force that glues us all together. It is the inde-scribable vigor that connects us to others and to God. Spirituality is closely linked to both our creativity and sexuality. It gives us life. It nourishes the body, the mind and the emotions. When the human spirit is alive and well the rest of the organism can function at its best.

Caring for the human spirit is not an isolated activity. It goes beyond a healthy regard for the physical, mental and emotional aspects of us. It encompasses not only our relationship with God but with all of life. Everything affects everything else.

The spiritual gifts we share with others are intangible. The willing-ness to listen and the ability to hear is one such gift. Wisdom is another. Yet another is the gift of healing. No monetary value can be placed on any of them. We develop our spirituality when we accept and use these gifts. This is an important aspect of choosing life.

Participants in life are healthy givers of intangible gifts. One such gift is the influence we exert over others through our behavior. As mem-bers of the human species, we like to think we are evolving to higher and higher levels of consciousness. This means more than becoming a better person; it means becoming a caring and conscious human being, a participant. Choosing to love others as we love ourselves involves doing just that: loving ourselves, not in a self-serving or self-indulgent way, but as a symbol of self-respect.

Some of us have a long way to go when it comes to self-care. It stands to reason that we should eat what nourishes us, drink what hydrates us, learn work skills that financially support us, build rela-tionships that sustain us, and make time for play to refresh us. We, as a species however, are not always reasonable.

There are four arenas of living that can support the human spirit. One is the work we do for a wage and, in addition, the work we give away. If we employ our skills only in exchange for money, then money is all we have to give. It is the combination of work and service that nourishes the human spirit.

We are also spiritually fed through the intimacy, mentoring and companionship from our various relationships. A participant in life prizes relationships and learns life's most important lessons from them.

Another salient aspect of living is our path of spiritual growth. A participant pursues avenues that lead to God and the greater meanings of life. Many seek spiritual connection through organized religion. Others search the fields of philosophy, poetry, anthropology and astronomy. Those who choose life automatically choose this quest. They know that truth and reality are not limited by the tangible.

Lastly, creative expression and play complete our formula for balance. Humans are by nature inventive creatures and will apply their creativity to all areas of living. It stands to reason that we should spend some time being playful and spontaneous in order to develop this part of us. Rest and relaxation are aspects of creativity and play. Together, these endeavors provide the spiritual refreshment that empowers us for working and learning.

Western society is becoming a workaholic culture. There is a widening gap between those who work much of the time and those who have learned not to work. The human system is not designed for continual production, nor is it designed for non-production. We cycle. We need self-respecting work and play. The weekly Sabbath is an excellent design for overall time management, as are numerous mini-Sabbaths each and every day.

As participants who choose life we need to include these four ingredients of spiritual nourishment into our self-care plan: work and service, intimacy and relationships, spiritual growth and creativity and play. Only by effectively caring for ourselves can we teach others how to do the same. Whether we realize it or not, we do influence those around us. If we respect ourselves enough we will make nourishing choices in each of these areas with increasing regularity. This is choosing to live fully.

Another spiritual goal is learning to create a balance between caring for ourselves and caring for others. If we care only for ourselves we will spiritually stagnate. If we care only for others, we will limit our human potential. Some of each nourishes the human spirit and provides a healthy balance between the two. Selfless giving, the kind without a price tag, expands our capacity for loving exchange. However, if we expend all of our energy in giving, we skew the balance of exchange; everything is going out, and with the exception of praise, nothing is coming back. Gratitude does not satisfy our love hunger. It merely assuages it for a time. Healthy giving and receiving creates a synergistic quality between two people known as *intimacy*. A beautiful giver is also a willing receiver.

Holism in Health Through the Ages

The idea of physical health being managed by the mind is not new. During tribal days, village healers developed their craft based on experiential wisdom. Before prescribing any treatment they counseled their patients to satisfy debts and settle disputes. They would ask, "Are you holding any grudges against anyone? Are you worrying about something? Are you angry with someone? Is there someone who has harmed you for whom you seek revenge?" They understood that emotional burdens disrupt bodily functions. There were no lab tests or X-rays to prove it. They just knew. As keen observers they relied on oral teachings plus understanding gained through experience. Theirs was an age when the body, the mind and the spirit didn't each have a title and a job description. People were understood within the context of their wholeness.

During these times coexistence meant survival. Each person was responsible for the community and the whole community was responsible for each member. Societies were small enough that people could relate to each other's needs as well as to the goals of the entire group. Health and spirituality were woven into a pluralistic belief system involving morals, justice, wisdom, confession and healing. Natural laws were revered in prayerful awe. Healthy relationships were not a luxury. They were a necessity. Interdependence was easy to identify and was accepted by all.

As regional cultures developed, each produced a life philosophy based on relationships and commitment. There were three levels of relationship: the one with the self, the one with other individuals and the one with the community and spirit world. Hinduism taught respect for an ideal way of life. Taoism stressed man's relationship with nature and all living things. Paganism sought to explain the relationship of humans with gods and nature. Islam and Buddhism focused on total surrender to God. Confucianism defined the Five Constant Relationships as stabilizing forces in a society. Judaism laid its roots in a desire to understand God's meaning for humankind. [3]

Three health care models arose from these great religions. The Far Eastern or *Chinese* system maintains that disharmony within oneself and the greater cosmic order has a direct correlation to illness.[4] This is also true for the Middle Eastern, Ayurvedic system.[5] Each Eastern health paradigm proposes that we should get our thoughts and beliefs in order so the physical body can be its best.

In the Western European system or dictum people believed that disease occurred because the gods were angry. This belief led to an attitude of personalized victimization that persists in present day European and English language: *fallen ill, came down with, victim of,* and *stricken with.* Of the three models only the Western system has moved from pluralistic to reductionistic, from holistic to rational and scientific, from homeopathic to allopathic.[6]

Paradigm shifts are both gradual and profound. They involve changes in beliefs and concepts that define how we should behave and who we wish to become. Western health beliefs actually began shifting as early as 2000 BC. Until that time the peoples who lived in what is now known as southern Europe believed man's destiny to be at the mercy of the gods. It follows that keeping the gods happy was the best way to ensure health and prosperity. Confessing one's mistakes, healing broken relationships, and obeying community law seemed pleasing to the gods. At that time these behaviors held no credence in their own right; rather they were intrinsic to the capricious relationships between people and their deities.

Apollo was an ancient god responsible for many aspects of life, one of which was medical treatment. However, medicine was low on his priority list. The goddess, Hygeia, held power over health and healing. She favored cleanliness and human integrity. People understood that if they nurtured their relationships by mending their differences she would grant them good health. For centuries her stature went unchallenged, mostly because, when lived out, these tenets proved true.

During the next millennia, ferocious invaders plundered and raped much of Europe. The common people lived in fear and their focus shifted toward survival. Warriors became society's heroes. Male gods rose to power and gradually, Hygiea's influence dwindled. Eventually she was forgotten and replaced by her father, a son of Apollo named Aesclepius. This was all part of the transition away from whole person wellness and toward male dominance and paternalism within health care.

In much of Europe, Greece in particular, society began organizing itself into specialties called Guilds. The Guild for health care and physician training was known as the *Sons of Aesclepius.* One faction of this group stubbornly maintained that health was not deity-dependent but resulted from nourishing food, massage, clean air, fresh water, good living habits and a pleasing environment. Within this faction was a young physician who vigorously supported these standards. His name was Hippocrates (460 to 377 BC). He is credited with elevating the field of medicine to a scientific discipline. Today we refer to him as the *Father of Western Medicine.*

Scientific Model Prevails

Liberal thinkers of this era began espousing a theory of two types of energy: matter, which moved by itself, and inert slow energy, which was moved by the gods. People began shifting away from the idea of being controlled by unpredictable god-like forces. Power of the individual was gaining popularity, especially among those who enjoyed authority and control. This birthing of dualism was pivotal for health care because it eroded the spiritual and relational aspects of health and healing. The relationship between matter and spirit was severed. Holism in health relinquished its place to the beginnings of a scientific model.

As time went on, Eastern and Middle Eastern medical systems maintained their integrated cultural and healing beliefs while Western thinking became more and more abstract. Most Europeans accepted the newer model as superior. It was sophisticated, intelligent, scientific and *right*.

In subsequent years, respected scientific thinkers, Copernicus, Aristotle and Descartes, introduced to the West even broader reductionistic theories of separateness. The human being was compared mechanistically to a clock that simply winds down and wears out. Human intelligence was credited as being wise, while the body was viewed as greedy, lustful and impulsive. Spirituality was labeled *superstitious* or *religious*. Unfortunately for Western medicine, the healing concepts of clean living, moral behavior, confession and forgiveness also fell into disfavor, at least within the scientific community. This evolving tragedy continues to perpetuate a medical system without a soul.

In the mid-1800s, Louis Pasteur, a French chemist, theorized that the basic elements required for life, such as amino acids, could be found in both human and animal blood. He also postulated that these building blocks can co-exist in different forms and that they change in the presence of bacteria. Pasteur was certain he had found the reason why people became sick. In order to prove his theory he conducted extensive, meticulous research. He used yeasts as the bacterial component and the fermentation process as the changing medium.

Hearing of his work, a group of brewers and vintners approached him to help solve a problem they were having with spoilage. "Why does one barrel of wine turn sour while another from the same harvest remains clear?" they asked. "We need a way of preserving our wine and beer without altering its appearance or its taste."

This was a great opportunity for Pasteur to further his original work. Could the same bacteria, which cause disease in humans and animals, also spoil the vintage? Pasteur went on to prove that heating wine or beer to 57.2 degrees Celsius would preserve it as well as retain its flavor, color and clarity. This method, called *pasteurization,* not only saved the wine industry but the dairy industry as well. Pasteur went on to develop immunization, a revolutionary gift to humankind. His work led to many other discoveries that further demonstrated the relationships between microorganisms and disease. The *Germ Theory* was born; one cause, one cure. It sealed the fate of Western medicine for years to come.

One of Louis Pasteur's closest friends was a physiologist named Claude Bernard. For years the two held an ongoing debate over the causes of illness. Pasteur's discovery that heat kills certain types of microorganisms reinforced the popular belief that man could manipulate matter. Here was proof that humankind was in charge after all, not the things of the spirit.

Claude Bernard argued that what goes on inside the human system contributes just as much to illness as the invading bacteria. He referred to the body's ability to prevent illness as its *milieu interior,* or internal environment. "How can you explain," he would say, "why in a family of five, three get the pox and two don't?"

The contributions of Louis Pasteur are well remembered, but who recalls Claude Bernard? Yet the story goes that on his deathbed Louis looked into the eyes of his lifelong friend and said, "Claude, I believe you were right." Pasteur's words were lost, however, in the ensuing popularity of the Germ Theory.

A century-and-a-half later, amidst all of our preventive vaccines and chemical cures looms the unalterable truth: We have become careless with our milieu interior, our spiritual/mental/physical system and our wholeness. It is time to restore integrity to ourselves and to humanity. It is time to choose life.

Holism in the Treatment of Illness

Treatment, as we know it in the West, is designed for speedy cure. This philosophy conflicts with holism. Reorganization of the full human system is a slow process. Adapting to physical, mental, emotional and spiritual changes will not occur over night.

Attitudes and beliefs play significant roles in the treatment of illness. A fighting spirit and a positive outlook will entice the best from one's caregivers and the most from one's immune system. Passive people can learn to assert themselves. Patients should not be *patient*. Having something to live for, like a book to complete or a trip to take, will boost the system. Those who believe in the power of prayer and who establish a relationship with God can transcend amazing health challenges.

An often overlooked aspect of treatment is the creation of a support system. Adequate support extends beyond professionals to include friends, family and spiritual directors. Each is of vital importance in meeting the human needs for medical skill, confessor, confident, listener, advocate and friend.

It takes courage to look beyond traditional treatment. Sometimes it is important to take stock of where we *aren't* going. We can choose therapies that complement the natural healing process and traditional management. Patients must realize that they are employers. Medical professionals work for them. They should question every aspect of treatment and get second or even third opinions when it is warranted. Information is powerful. Health libraries and the Internet offer vast research on every malady.

Patients need to learn assertiveness so they can question the medical experts in a businesslike manner. This is where advocates can be of great benefit. They can help to organize a list of questions before doctor appointments. They can go along and record the session. They can research community resources such as support groups and referral services.

Character building is just as important in the healing process as are medications and surgery. Why? Because every life event, including illness, offers opportunities to adjust our beliefs, change our behaviors, become better people, and create a better world. This is how we choose life.

Modern day physicians rarely assess their patients for mental, spiritual or emotional pain. If there is no medication to prescribe or surgery to perform, Western medicine is at a loss. There is nothing wrong with eradicating symptoms, but why continue ignoring the relationship between emotions and cellular disorganization? When the physical body is burdened with unresolved emotional conflict, a toxic residue persists long after the infection heals.

There are countless medications that effectively suppress guilt, shame, anger, fear and hurt. Emotions and feelings are the health barometers of the whole system. Quelling them as a crisis intervention is understandable, but counseling should be encouraged at the same time. Suppressing symptoms, in order to feel better, while ignoring the underlying strife, is wrong.

Medical practitioners must begin to work with mental and spiritual health providers. Cognitive, or *talk therapy,* does not work for everyone. Many people respond more positively to the languages of art, music, movement, creative writing and touch. The Hippocratic oath taken by all Western physicians pledges, "Above all, do no harm." Healers have choices in how they help their patients choose life or suppress it.

The quick eradication of symptoms by chemical means results in two negative consequences. First, it short-circuits the body's innate healing ability. The body has a vast internal pharmacy to handle most of its problems. The brain supplies enzymes and hormones that suppress pain, dilate blood vessels, and produce feelings of well-being. It choreographs other organs to secrete anti-inflammatory substances and energizers. Powerful chemicals, with multiple side effects, will weaken the body's native effectiveness by intercepting its natural response to disorganization.

Secondly, when cure comes quickly we are robbed of creative healing time. As much as we dislike it, restricted activity is an opportunity to evaluate our lifestyles and relationships. Even more importantly, we can rekindle respect for our bodies and rededicate ourselves to their care. Too often we only contemplate the value of something when it is taken from us. As Joni Mitchell sings in *Big Yellow Taxi:* "Lord, it always seems to go that you don't know what you got till it's gone...."

Guilt, anger, resentment, envy, shame and stubbornness all become stored in the body's tissues. With every thought a muscle fires. Muscles firing in rapid succession establish a state of ongoing readiness called the *stress response.* Thoughts impress electrical impulses upon our hormones that in turn trigger feelings. Feelings influence receptors in the white blood cells. White blood cells fight disease. We are indeed complex and intricate creatures. Our thoughts and beliefs as well as our behaviors that follow them do affect our health.

The internal milieu of the human organism is delicate and easily disorganized. Even so, it tolerates monumental abuse while cleverly adapting to it. But it has limits. It warns us with pain, infection or depression, otherwise known as disorganization. Rather than heed these messages we complain about them; then we strangle the messenger with artificial compounds made up of long, unrecognizable chemical chains that disorganize other body systems. We mask these warnings without making lifestyle changes that would allow our delicate systems to operate with ease. The bottom line is we don't always do what's right.

Emotional and cognitive disorganization emits early warning signals. When our memory slips we panic and think, "Do I have Alzheimer's Disease?" Much of Western society continues to shroud mental illness in shame. Paradoxically, we are *less* likely to seek help for an emotional problem than for a physical one. Our tendency is to worry about it instead, thereby compounding its burden in the body. More often than not it takes a life-halting experience for us to evaluate our lifestyle and relationships.

One woman tells how she knows she is setting herself up for an upper respiratory infection when she loses her car keys. Her internal dialogue goes something like this: "I've misplaced those keys for the third time this week. I must be out of balance. Am I trying to do too much? Yes, I'm working too many hours. I'd better slow down. Last fall I did the same thing and lost a week of work because of the flu. That really slowed me down. I'll make a conscious choice about it this year. It's time to take an extra day off."

How do you care for your health holistically? Do you settle your differences with others, thereby releasing some of the burdens in your body? Do you get help when problems defy solutions? Are you a good steward of you body, giving it healthy nutrients, clean water and clear air? Do you allow it to rest? Do you take it out to play? Do you exercise and strengthen it? Do you listen to its warning signals and take appropriate action? If you do, then you are really choosing life. You are a true participant. Congratulations! [6]

Holism in the Workplace

The figure of a circle symbolizes holism. A circle has no end, just infinite possibilities. Hospitable people like to sit at round tables. Management models are rarely circular. They are also rarely hospitable.

Movement in a circle can be clockwise, counterclockwise, in and out, up and down or forward and backward. Movement in a hierarchy is downward with a little lateral leeway. It is extremely limited from a humanistic perspective. Wholeness represents several forces in constant motion. Everything tends to be connected to everything else. Problems are not viewed as isolated and solutions are created synergistically.

Linear thinkers have a great deal of difficulty with this. They may thrive on activity but lack the ability to delegate or involve others. They tend to do everything themselves, working harder and longer to reach their goals. Eventually they burn out and wonder what happened.

A holistic manager is able to link subsystems within the context of the whole so that the whole becomes a bounded system of linked components. Systems can be open and closed relative to their environment. They tend to be self-enhancing, self-confirming and self-limiting. Evaluation is ongoing so that each aspect of the system stays rooted to the mission.

A business is a system. As a system, it has a certain ambiance. This may be described as whatever thought, feeling or notion is conjured up when one hears its name. It is what a person understands to be the sum of the most familiar perspectives. These are not all the perspectives, however. A marketing image is an impression, but a response from an experience is unique to individuals.

A leader within a holistic system empowers each member within it. There is no hierarchy as such. Individuals begin to think of themselves in a newer, less linear way. Their contributions are acknowledged and creativity is encouraged. There is, however, a much greater payoff for working in a holistic system. It is the synergy that arises from the group effort. Because members are continuously involved in the whole, their individual efforts appear to be much greater than they are. In other words, the whole is greater than the sum of the parts.

Activity within a holistic group is recognized to be rhythmic and cyclical, a microcosm of the larger system. Change occurs continuously and is not limited by cause and effect. Even if a product fails it is not viewed as an end but rather a beginning. Healthy systems always regenerate when given adequate resources and support. Individuals within such a system do not waste time on placing blame but rather on regrouping, capturing assets, pooling ideas and moving on. Big egos and power struggles will not survive.

Within the workplace there is an ongoing need for teachers. The relationship between teacher and student is based on the holistic notion that the observer becomes the observed. The teacher demonstrates a willingness to learn from the student, encouraging challenges and philosophical questions. Knowledge is power insomuch as it is used for the greater good of all. When knowledge is wielded *as* power it invites divisiveness.

Businesses close every day. Others start up. Those that fail usually do so because of out-dated management and a lack of leadership. The performance of a business system depends more on how its parts interact than on how they act independently of each other. When a system loses its ability to reshape in response to the constant energy that flows through it, rigor mortis sets in. The thought that a system can build to a point and remain fixed is a myth. There are no fixed systems, only systems of relative stability.

A holistic business system deals with dichotomy and invites opposing points of view. This offers an opportunity to better understand the whole. Effective leaders want to know the weaknesses and opposing forces to their ideas. They are able to integrate them into their own plans and thereby increase the strength of the system. Any system must be strong enough to adapt to negative and positive forces that are internal as well as external.

Holistic leaders advocate power sharing at the group and individual levels, which enhances cooperation between them. People who work best when allowed to work independently are given tasks suited to their skills. They are brought into the entire group on a regular basis for feedback and evaluation. There is no fear attached to individuals having control as long as there exists interdependence and cooperation. The key to the success of the whole is the functioning of all the subsystems in an adaptive relationship with each other while incorporating all the system laws.

In a holistic business system, specialists are given a great deal of autonomy because of their high levels of self-discipline and responsibility for relationships and communication. Specialist titles do not indicate more or less power, but differing responsibilities.

What will happen to the corporate ladder? It will disappear. In a holistic system there is so much job satisfaction that people have no desire to change jobs unless they see an opportunity to become a specialist in another area.

Rewards are linked to the success of the whole as well as to individual performance. They are not attached to power or position. Leaders will still be leaders and followers will be viewed not as subordinates but as specialists of equal value to the whole system.

How is success defined holistically? It is the ability of a system to remain focused and flexible. It shapes and is shaped by the changing needs of the marketplace. It has a circular management structure that empowers individuals to work to their highest potential. It has infinite possibilities because it incorporates the positive aspects of the negative energies that influence it. It grows in a contained manner with its subsystems linked together in support of laws of the whole.

Holism in the workplace is being forced into existence because of a global economy and communication technology. Business leaders of the new millennium will be those who understand and welcome it. They will be choosing life in the workplace.

Holism as a Way of Life

Holism as a way of life must be central to our work, our relationships, our creative expression and our spiritual growth. It is as old as time and as new as we allow it to be. Choosing to live as a participant means living holistically. Just as with the circle, the opportunities are infinite. Why not choose life, so that you and all whom you influence may live?

We embrace holism, or a holistic lifestyle, when we intend to live in relationship with others and still grow in the direction of our highest potential. Couples with several differences rarely have boring marriages. Uniqueness introduces strength to humanity for it is through diversity that living becomes exciting.

Participants in life thrive on paradox and variety. They revere living fully, vivaciously and vigorously. We must remember that the word *holistic* is derived from the same root as the word holy. Herein lies the essence of choosing life. When we honor life as sacred and holy we respect it, care for it, enjoy it and protect it. We refute the idea of sameness and homeostasis.

Living holistically involves self-care and growth of the physical, mental, emotional and spiritual aspects of ourselves. What we do between the events of illness or other dramas in life is every bit as important as the learning we achieve while we are disorganized.

When we choose the role of a participant we assume that we will grow. This is because we open ourselves to being vulnerable with other individuals. We undertake a relationship with the divine. Growth accelerates dramatically when it occurs within the context of such relationships. In holism we learn to relate even to our enemies. We learn from them, and rather than conquering them we walk a path toward consensus with them.

A holistic way of life goes beyond being the best we can be to becoming a positive influence on others and a good steward of the earth's resources. Participants in life seek holism. You can begin right now. Choose life!

Chapter Three
Community

*It is through the joys and struggles of community
where we learn the relationship skills to Choose Life.*

People and redwood forests have something in common: They thrive because they live in communities. Despite a shallow root system, redwoods defy wind and storm to survive for up to 3000 years. Mature trees drop their seeds so that the seedlings emerge in a perfect circle known as a *fairy ring*. Their shallow roots entwine forming a strong substructure that provides both sustenance and support. Thus, survival depends on group strength and cooperation.

People, too, need the kind of strength that comes with connectedness. If we pretend to avoid societal dilemmas we merely delude ourselves. We cannot thrive in isolation. Joining with others offers synergistic solutions to apparently insurmountable problems. The strength of a group, be it one family or a neighborhood, provides stability to face the storms of life.

Healthy families and communities possess a sense of belonging. Each supports the other and together they uphold the whole. Individuals discover how to establish and respect each other's boundaries. They learn how to communicate. They put down their roots and form a network of goals, standards and philosophies. Choosing life means participating in the joys and the struggles of living in community.

Belonging

Each of us is born into some sort of family. For better or worse, this family is our first experience of community. It has roots. It forms a crucible for our initial desires and lessons. As early as eighteen weeks following conception, while our subtle stirrings are still obscure, we can hear. Think of it! Sound vibrations, especially those created by musical tones, can penetrate that fluid world inside the womb. The tiny fetal heart responds to rhythms by speeding up or slowing down. What do you suppose it does with other sounds: dogs barking, kids yelling, sirens screaming? How much does community affect the developing fetus? We hear of parents reading and singing to their unborn children. Surely these precious little bodies thrive within an environment of love and laughter before birth as well as afterward.

A newborn is a soft elaboration of a prior liquid state, a vulnerable receptacle for each of life's vibrations. For nine months the mother's body serves as a partial filter for the pulsations of sound, light and temperature. At the ripe moment the fetus is pushed and squeezed through an impossibly small space into the waiting community. It is one of shockingly bright lights and dry air. These new sensations startle the semi-soft body. It stiffens and cries out in protest. Then, soothed by gentle hands and wrapped in cozy cloth, it once more softens and relaxes.

This rhythm of startle-and-relax is a basic introduction to living in community. When infants are startled too frequently their growth and development is thwarted. When they are nourished, physically, mentally, emotionally and spiritually, they thrive. This is how our life experiences begin, and in the beginning we have no choice.

Human babies are the most dependent creatures in the animal kingdom. They must be held and cuddled in order to survive. The *holders of babies* have the most meaningful job in the community. They are among the front line participants in life and, as such, have several important duties to perform.

Holders must embrace babies snugly lest they experience the fear of falling. Animal and human babies share this innate fear and both must be protected from it. Infants must also be kept warm and dry so their little bodies do not tense and shiver. They need all their calories for growing.

An infant's delicate eye structures require gradual accommodation to light rays. Hospital nurseries typically use lights that are much too bright for newborns. Moreover, they emit their noxious glare twenty-four hours a day. This disturbs a baby's sleeping/waking rhythm, so they often have difficulty falling asleep when they go home. Some children require a night light for years. Parents can counter this situation by gradually increasing environmental light during the day and introducing contrasting visual images. Place black and white mobiles near the changing table, the crib and wherever baby gazes.

Baby holders must also learn to distinguish between a hungry cry and a lonely one. When family members perform these essential tasks, human babies get a good start in life. It is their earliest learning and it teaches trust. They are on their way to becoming life's participants. If the first community fails the infant, negative changes begin to occur in the physical form, the emotions and the human spirit.

Yearning to Belong

Crying reflects a child's verbalization of need. When a child cries its whole body swells and expands with yearning. If this yearning goes unnoticed the child's emotional state changes to anger. Its cry takes on a very different tone as its body hardens with rage. If this anger cry is ignored the child's body weakens and collapses. Its cry dissolves into a tragic whimper.

Repetitions of this sequence leave an indelible message in a child's physical and emotional memory. This message is the foundation of a belief that says, "When I want something I ask for it. If I don't get it I get mad. When I get mad, I get loud. I stay loud as long as I can, demanding that someone hear me. If no one answers I say 'What's the use'?

Then I give up. The day may come when I won't even bother getting mad. I may even stop asking." This state of collapse accompanies us into our future until we encounter a different life experience: one that teaches us that we can ask, we can be heard and there are people in the community who will help us.

When an infant is left to cry itself to sleep it embodies the experience of emptiness. The baby cries because it has not learned to tolerate separation from its caregiver. It has not developed an ability for self-soothing. Parents can teach babies gradual detachment without the experience of emptiness. It involves leaving the infant alone for two, five, then ten-minute intervals with comforting reassurances in between. Gradually, the baby gathers its blanket and toys and goes to sleep. It has learned to tolerate separation. Instead of learning "My people abandon me and leave me feeling empty," the child learns, "I can be apart from them and still feel safe. I belong."

Learning to Belong

Each of life's stages must be experienced within community for us to learn and to grow. The family is a mini-community, a strategic learning center for our first gathering of knowledge. Knowledge is conceptual and experiential, intellectual and embodied. It is an integrated imprint, a type of compass that guides us through each life passage from birth to death. This compass influences how we respond to life's rhythms and vibrations, its rainbows and tornadoes. Our community members teach us how to respond based on their own uniqueness. This is how we learn to make choices.

In addition to conceptual and intellectual learning, our physical forms and innate temperaments provide us with a hormonal chemistry that is designed to surge through our bodies producing feelings and emotions. These feelings and emotions become active or remain dormant tandem with the way they were encouraged or suppressed in our earliest years.

As we grow, our communities extend from family to neighborhood, from school to peer system, from college, military or Peace Corps to the workplace and from local to global society. During each stage we have physical, mental, emotional, spiritual and social growing to do. We progress from dependence to independence and on to interdependence. We learn to choose life or to hide from it. We discover how to agree with some aspects and ignore the rest. We learn to be proactive participants or inert bystanders. The people of our communities shape everything we come to know. We both influence and are influenced by them.

Nobody masters life's entire script during the first chronological run-through. However, what we do not learn as children and adolescents we can acquire later. There is always hope when there is an intention to grow.

We have each encountered the adult who whines like a helpless toddler. A forty-year-old who pouts or has temper tantrums is at best annoying and at worst unbearable. Fortunately for all concerned, these unpopular learned behaviors can also be un-learned. Once adults recognize that their life is out of kilter they can seek help and create change. Behaviors are like clothes: They can go out of style and be cast off like rummage. People who learn to be trusting and positive lead rewarding lives. The minute you decide you want to be different you are already changing. A genuine desire to improve your relationships signals the first stage of belonging. You are choosing to participate. You are choosing life.

Abandonment

The opposite of belonging is abandonment. This, too, can be learned during childhood. Small versions of abandonment occur each time a child does not get what it wants. The child feels betrayed by being refused. Appealing to a young child with logic and reason does not soothe angry feelings. A firm, no-nonsense "no" with a simple explanation provides a structure the child can learn to accept.

It is the nature of the child to try and manipulate the adult into a change of heart. Adults do children no favors when they capitulate on a regular basis. It gives the message, "You can have whatever you want if you persist." Weak parenting throws a child into a very unforgiving world. They have difficulty with authority and relationships until they learn the meaning of "no."

Do I Really Belong?

Some children have mellow temperaments and they challenge adults less than those who test life through physical experimentation. Three-year-old Eric decided that going for a spin in the clothes dryer would be fun. He convinced his five-year-old sister to turn on the dryer once he was securely inside. It wasn't fun. Screams brought his mother running to the scene. What should Mother do now?

Going for a ride in the dryer seems perfectly logical to a three-year-old. If Mother punishes him for this experiment he becomes confused. He is simply following his three-year-old desire to discover how something would feel. Because of his age he lacks judgment and reason, the cognitive ability to envision the consequences of tumbling around inside a clothes dryer. When Mother yells "What do you think you're doing?" Eric's mind does not make the leap to understanding; he must be guided there. All he perceives from the rebuke is that his attempts to learn something have been thwarted. Mom is interfering. Mom is bad. He pushes her away with vehemence. If Mom reacts in anger he feels betrayed. Where is the loving Mom he can trust? He cannot understand her exasperation. He feels hurt and confused, emotionally abandoned and betrayed.

To prevent such experiments from getting an F, Mom has to make wise behavioral choices. Emotional responses of fear and frustration are natural reactions. We do not choose to have them. They just emerge. Expressing them appropriately teaches children that powerful emotions are an important part of living. What parents can choose are the feelings and behaviors they attach to these emotions. Blaming, shaming, and battering are not innate to humans. These are learned behaviors and we choose to use them or not. To hit a child or not is a choice. Children are like sponges, soaking up their experiences without benefit of critical thought or reasoning. However, the adult brain *is* fully developed. It allows the parent a choice of stepping back from the situation, thinking about it and choosing an appropriate behavioral response.

In emotional situations it is the adult with the reasoning mind who must take charge. In the dryer incident an initial outburst of fear or anger is likely. After all, one would hope that a child would not think to do something like that.

Following the outburst it is time to express relief that no one got hurt. Words, gestures and feelings can tumble out simultaneously. A hug is an effective indication of "I'm so glad you are safe. You are so valuable to me. I love you and don't want you to be hurt." The next step is to establish a rule for future reference. "No more climbing in the dryer, it's dangerous." Then distract the child with another activity and let go of the incident. By taking charge the adult teaches many valuable lessons:

1. *Emotional expression is natural and healthy.*
2. *Risking and exploring have consequences as well as rewards. They are not forbidden.*
3. *There is a rule for everything but it takes time to learn them all.*
4. *You belong here even when Mom is scared and angry.*

All communities strive for safety. It doesn't just happen. Every member must be both a teacher and a student. Individuals need to grow and experiment. New ideas and creative suggestions require a forum.

Societies are becoming increasingly complex. It is incumbent upon us to be creative so that all of our problems don't get passed on to the next generation. If we open our consciousness and consider the wildest dreams, we will discover the solutions. Do you recall the old story about Pogo, the comic strip philosopher, who went to the swamp looking for the enemy and all he found was himself? People must be encouraged and never demeaned for ideas.

Belonging Begets Consequences

Every action has a consequence. Children have so much to learn. It is staggering to realize how many natural laws they must assimilate. As children learn these laws they also learn the consequences of breaking them. "No hitting your brother" is a simple straightforward rule teaching the natural law that when one person intentionally harms another there will be a painful consequence to that person in body, mind and spirit. If the parent hits the child to "teach him a lesson," she negates the very lesson she is trying to teach, which is "Do not hit, it leaves scars."

Mis-takes

Children's bodies are still very soft and sensitive to the vibrations around them. They are naturally empathic. They can both see and feel the painful reactions they impose on others. However, they lack the cognitive reasoning to comprehend all the consequences of their actions. They want to belong, and they have a tremendous amount to learn. Family members must be conscious about setting limits. If the family's acceptance is dependent on strict compliance, children are sure to fail. They are not dogs, and home is not obedience school. Mistakes must be tolerated with love that is laced with teaching geared to the child's level of understanding. The child is a person. A behavior is nothing more than an activity.

Expanded Influences of Belonging

Children take the familiar as gospel truth and until adolescence, the family continues to be their most believable resource. They know they belong to the family. To a lesser degree, they also belong to their class at school and to their neighborhood.

When children's spheres of community influence extend into the classroom, they want to bring their newfound education home to test its validity. Kindergartners revel in "bathroom talk." The degree of reaction they get when they try their new vocabulary at the dinner table sets the tone for establishing personal boundaries. "We don't use that word at home or anywhere else. Understand?" These increased opportunities for learning are enhanced or stifled by the family members. New rules are constantly being created to deal with the contradictions in behavioral standards between home and school. The simpler the rules, the easier they are to follow. Children don't want or need lengthy sociological explanations. That comes later.

Another challenge that faces school-age children is learning to work in groups away from family influences. In doing so children expand their experience of belonging and increase their operational reference.

As children enter adolescence they gravitate toward their peers and away from the family. They shed yet another set of experiential clothing, the one of *family* as *unquestionable resource*. While moving through adolescence, a teen's choices remain rooted in family experience even though there is a powerful drive to rebel against it. The level of belonging within that family profoundly influences his or her alliances during this tumultuous stage of surging hormones and self-identification.[1]

Support

The more children can trust their family members, the more they know they belong. Tommy, age three, will not eat his breakfast at Grandma's house because it does not resemble Mommy's. However, when older brother enthusiastically attacks Grandma's blueberry pancakes, Tommy takes a bite. His acceptance is based on older brother's experience, not his own. His sense of trust and belonging is linked to the more familiar brother rather than to Grandma.

This sense of belonging is essential to human existence. Without it we are like lonely pieces of clear glass without a reflection. We look everywhere for something consistent and familiar to belong to, for belonging reflects back to us who we are. We cannot know ourselves in isolation. One characteristic of belonging is learning to both give and receive support. We begin choosing life the first time we do something for somebody else.

Throughout our formative and adolescent years we are constantly "trying on" other people's experiences. We mimic conversational styles, fashions, postures and choices. We feel supported by group approval for the way we dress, talk and behave. Fitting in with our peers cements our sense of belonging and teaches us about support. When we understand that we belong to a community, be it family, class, or gang, we assume a foundation of confidence that makes us feel safe. When *we* feel safe we can begin to support others. It is our own sense of belonging and support that are the precursors for successful relationships.

Funny, This Doesn't Feel Like Support

Initially, it is our family members who teach us how to behave within relationships. The old adage, *Action speaks louder than words,* is one of those timeless laws that is so easy for adults to forget. Children take their behavioral cues from the emotional and non-verbal expressions of authority figures. If we are eight years old and babbling at the dinner table, a withering look from Dad can make us stop in mid-sentence. So will a gentle touch to the arm, a shake of the head, a little smile and a finger to the lips. One message says "Stop it or you'll get 'it' later." The other says, "I'm touching you gently to get your attention. I'm shaking my head because I want you to stop what you're doing. I'm smiling because we've talked about this before, and I know you can do better, and I have my fingers to my lips to remind you that it's your talking that needs to stop."

The first message is fast and furious. It gets quick results. The child is subdued through an implied threat. The associated feeling is one of fear. The other message is more complex. It gets the same results; the child stops babbling. But the feeling engendered is one of being loved while being taught.

As we grow up, wordless commands continue wielding their power through our memories. To the adult, a withering look from Dad should lose its punch, but often it does not. We react to it as if we are still eight years old rather than saying, "What does that look mean, Dad? Am I talking too much again?" When we want another person, child or adult, to re-order their behavior, we have choices. We can use fear and intimidation or limit-setting and support. We can remember the power-less child and choose to treat others with belief in their ability to change.

Empathy and Influence, Cornerstones of Support

When two-year-old Jenny hears three-month-old Eric beginning to fuss she goes into action. She pushes a chair over to the kitchen table where Eric squirms in his car-seat. She climbs onto the table and attempts to get Eric's bottle into his mouth.

Jenny is not old enough to have cognitive reasoning. She doesn't think, "Eric is fussy, now what should I do? Oh, I see he's dropped his bottle. I'll give it to him." She does not act from a sequence of logical thoughts; she acts from her own empathic embodied experience. In her brief span of life, Jenny has already learned that being given a bottle of lovely liquid makes her feel good. Hearing the baby fuss brings her some discomfort too. She soothes her own discomfort as well as Eric's by giving him his bottle. When the toddler is praised for this action, she begins to develop a belief system about comforting others. In these subtle everyday experiences we learn to affect others with our own behaviors. We discover that helping others yields personal pleasure as well as approval.

Influencing others by what we say and do gives us a sense of choice and power. We choose to support others, first because it soothes us and second because it improves the quality of our relationships. Belonging allows us to begin seeing ourselves as similar to others but with some dif-ferences. Gradually we stop trying to be like someone we admire because our emerging sense of self feels good to us. Fitting in does not matter as much, and we begin to value our own uniqueness. We see it as something positive. We feel a surge of power and confidence. Next we begin to notice the effects of this outward expression of our power: It is called *influence.*

Sometimes our power frightens us, and we develop an inflated sense of responsibility for it. We may even hesitate to offer a good suggestion for fear of it turning out badly. We can become excessively protective, disallowing others the right to fail or succeed based on their own interpretations.

Too much community control teaches the compliant child to be a victim and the rowdy child to be a rebel. On the other hand, too little control teaches the compliant child dependence and the rowdy child confusion. Adults who use their rightful influence for the greatest good of the child and the community will foster strong individuals who like to care for themselves and others. These adults reach maturity far earlier than those who spend much of their adult life searching for belonging and support.

Unconditional Love

Adolescence is the only time in life when humans can safely and seriously rebel. This is the stage for mock attempts at leaving home and for testing immature wings. While still protected by the nest, teens will challenge its morality and stability. Secretly they want it to hold together but outwardly they try to tear it apart. If discipline has been extremely rigid or extremely lax, their efforts will also be extreme. The harder they try to disrupt the nest, the more diligently the parents must listen to them while maintaining the family standard. As parents forgive the rebellion and reassert order, children begin to develop their inner adult. This in turn leads to consciousness and mastery in the world. They learn respect for divergent views. They learn to overcome recklessness. This is the ultimate support that parents give their children because it goes beyond protection; it demonstrates how to love someone even when they hurt us.

Support is the glue that holds relationships together. It comes in a variety of forms from the simplest smile to the noblest sacrifice. We all need support, or propping up from time to time, especially when we are filled with doubt. Being good at giving and receiving it relates back to the ways we were supported in our earliest communities of family, neighborhood, school or spiritual center. If these communities fail us, we will have no inner support experience from which to draw. All we will have is an idea of what we need. We carry this idea into our current experience, looking for that glue, that approval or acknowledgment, and we keep looking until we find a community that provides it. However, if we have the embodied knowledge that giving and receiving support is beneficial, we bring emotional wealth to our communities. Supportive people understand other people's problems because they can look beyond their own.

Giving and receiving support unifies any community. Humans are conceived because of a relationship and born into a community of many relationships. Belonging and support are two of the roots that bring both strength and sustenance to individuals as well as the whole.

Many people grow up and move away from their communities. This growth dynamic follows the natural law of universal rhythm: expansion and contraction. People move from that which is familiar so they may explore new horizons. It is part of choosing life. From time to time they return, surrounding themselves, once more, with the familiar. They yearn for the automatic sensations associated with belonging and support. For some, this coming home represents another type of yearning: a desire to see with adult eyes what may or may not have been there when they were young.

This expansion and contraction of geographic boundaries mirrors another of our communal roots: our personal boundaries. The phenomenon of relating to other individuals is determined by our sense of ourselves. Where we end and another begins is called a *boundary*.

Boundaries

Personal Boundaries

A boundary is a nonphysical point of interaction, an imaginary perimeter. (Fig. 3) We learn about boundaries from the community members who raise us. From the time of our birth till the day we die our uniquely created boundaries influence the manner in which we relate to all living things and to our communities.

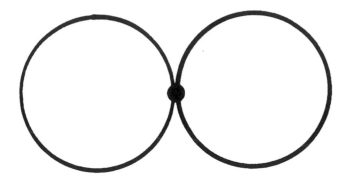

Figure 3.   A boundary is a nonphysical point of interaction.

Overlapping Boundaries

Families who live each day by an abundant commingling of feelings, ideas, information and desires tend to raise children who are steeped in togetherness. (Fig. 4) The members of such families have overlapping boundaries. This is the culture they create and the filter through which they view all other cultures and communities. These family members develop a keen sense of "What's mine is yours." They have an enhanced tolerance for other people's needs and increased flexibility when it comes to sharing.

Exaggerated overlapping of boundaries, however, creates an unhealthy interdependence between family members that breeds reluctance in choice making. In such families there is an implicit assumption that decisions are made through group process. This over-stated assumption creates dependence: a need for approval from the family before making decisions.

Young adults emerging from these families find leave-taking difficult. Not only are they fraught with indecision, they fear making mistakes. They are extremely concerned with having their family members be proud of them. They continue seeking approval from authority figures in the greater communities of work and play. Approval-seeking garners disrespect. Disrespect from others leads to self-contempt and unhappiness, which in turn creates an even greater desire for approval. Sadly, they can never get enough. Only when young people gain some insight into this strangling enmeshment can they choose to disengage from it. To choose life they must abandon the unhealthy teachings of their formative communities and explore new experiences.

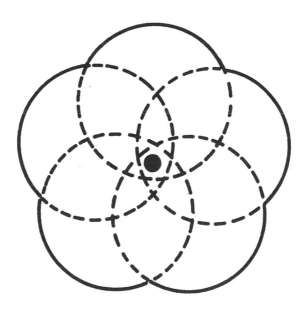

Figure 4. Families that teach togetherness.

Disengaged Boundaries

On the opposite end of the spectrum are families who isolate themselves from their neighbors and teach social restraint. Their children develop in an atmosphere steeped in privacy. Private individuals tend to divide their relationships into two categories, the personal and the public. They carefully protect their polished family life from the tarnish of public view.

The authority figures within these families enforce stern rules about behaving and relating. It's as if they need to keep members within an emotional and physical container in order to tolerate them. Their rules are rigid and their relationships disengaged. Interaction between members is stiff and bereft of intimacy. Open displays of affection and touching are rare.

Independence and individualism are the personality gods of these rigid, disengaged families. Their members have boundaries that are tough and unyielding. Adolescents and young adults who grow up in these families have difficulty developing and maintaining relationships even though they yearn for them. Their training in separateness teaches, "What's mine is mine, what's yours is yours." As they reach adulthood, they become society's pariahs. Eventually they tire of their loneliness and begin reaching out to new communities for belonging and support. (Fig. 5)

Flexible Boundaries

Healthy families possess strong flexible boundaries. Members come together for mentoring and shared intimacy, both joy and sorrow. They also know the empowerment of independence and the richness of individuality. Even geographical distance cannot separate their bond of love, respect and tolerance. (Fig. 6)

Boundaries in the Workplace

Personal boundaries accompany us on life's journey as wordless expressions of our peripheral limits. They impress each person we meet

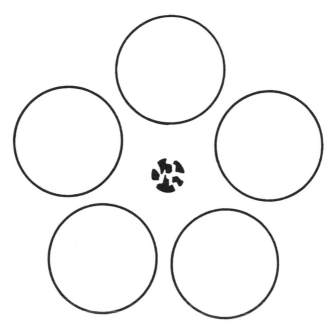

(Above) Figure 5. *Families that teach separateness tire of their loneliness.*
(Below) Figure 6. *Healthy families have flexible boundaries*

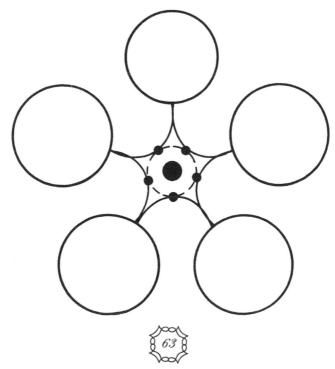

and influence our work. An elementary school teacher reared in a family with overlapping boundaries may have difficulty establishing discipline, but her flexibility will encourage the students to explore new vistas and express their ideas. Another teacher reared in a family that taught separateness will spend more time on discipline and less on freedom of expression. Both teachers will have to learn about boundaries in order to have a well-managed classroom. One will need to tighten while the other will need to loosen. Elementary teachers claim that it takes three years to master this process.

Boundaries in New Relationships

When two people are getting to know each other they engage in the process of testing each other's boundaries, a type of orientation to the relationship. It is an uncomfortable time for the rigid family member and an exciting time for the companionate one.

A person with clear boundaries, be they rigid or elastic, has a good sense of how much he or she will yield. Relationships will flourish when these differences are explored in good conscience and there is intention to understand and negotiate.

Expanding Boundaries

It is in life's laboratory of personal and practical relationships that individuals learn to stretch as well as contain their boundaries. For example, if a dog owner wants unconditional devotion from her Golden Labrador, she must extend her boundaries to care for it. Like it or not, she will cope with fleas, veterinary expenses and spring fever. If rose growers want to bask in the beauty of roses, they will expand their boundaries to include dealing with fertilizer and aphids. If a couple decides to have a baby, their coupleship boundaries must become flexible enough to accommodate sleep deprivation and mounds of laundry. Boundary expansion and contraction is involved in relating to all living things. It is an ever-evolving process called consciousness.

Professional Boundaries

Humans are comfortable with the familiar. It is when we meet someone with differing boundaries that confusion arises. For example, a lawyer and a client engage in a professional relationship. The lawyer provides a legal service to the client and the client pays a fee to the lawyer. These boundaries are clear. Their association is defined. (Fig. 4) However, it is in the more subtle aspects of an alliance where the boundaries can become blurred.

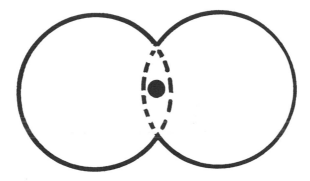

Figure 7. Clear boundaries and intact engagement.

As with all relationships, the lawyer/client relationship must contain the element of trust. For the boundaries to remain clear, the lawyer must act professionally based on her experience and training. The client should bring all pertinent facts to the lawyer based on his best information and understanding. If the client withholds truth from the lawyer, both sets of boundaries weaken and become murky. The lawyer will pull back her boundary because the client withdrew some of his. The association between them changes, and while it is being redefined, confusion prevails. The lawyer struggles to extract the truth from the client, while the client rigidifies his boundary to protect his falsehood. (Fig. 8)

Once they adjust to the new circumstance, their boundaries will clarify, allowing them to proceed with their mutually understood limitation. However, because of the lie they cannot engage fully, and the case may be lost. (Fig. 9)

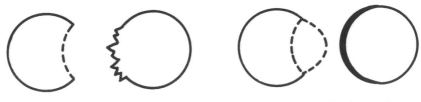

Engaging partially when client lies.

Lawyer seeks the truth.
Client rigidifies the lie.

Figure 8. Boundaries weaken and shift with dishonesty.

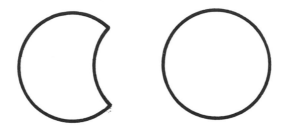

Figure 9. Boundaries clarified but disengaged.

Adjusting Our Own Boundaries

Learning to make adjustments in our own boundaries is paramount for choosing life. Imagine being surrounded by an elastic shield, a permeable membrane over which we have full mastery. We soften and stretch it any time we risk adventure. We dissolve it completely when we wish and dream. We make it thick and resilient in response to environmental stress. It is this place of interaction that allows us the flexibility to withstand pressures and improve relationships, to dream our biggest dreams and recover from devastating loss.

It is a healthy goal to understand our boundaries, accept them without guilt and adapt them to each experience. Often in relationships we expend energy while wishing another person would give up this or that behavior. The boundary or place of interaction between us rubs sharply like fingernails on slate. We are frustrated because we cannot force another person to change his or her conduct.

Supposing your father belches in public. Either he does not know or does not care about the effect this behavior may have on others. It drives you crazy. You cannot force your parent to change, but you have every right to employ some skill in altering his behavior.

We posses the ability to influence others. The kind of influence that is most likely to evoke change begins with us. We can model appropriate behavior. We can choose an unemotional time to discuss the issue and point out the personal benefits that could be reaped from a change. "If you love me you would change," is vague and ridden with guilt. Try to be tactful as well as direct. "You're probably not even aware of this. Do you know that every head in the room turns when you let out one of those public belches. I'm quite embarrassed by it. Do you think you could stop doing it in public?"

When we want to preserve a relationship, we must find ways to be honest without being derogatory. Imagine how your would feel in response to such a request. Wouldn't you prefer to be approached in a kind manner? "You probably don't even realize it, but there is something you do that is ..." (*inappropriate, not right, unbecoming, rude, selfish, or impolite*). Avoid attaching an emotion to your request. Emotion tends to raise the vocabulary ante. Words like *disgusting, foolish,* or *stupid* will attack the person as well as the behavior. You hope for a positive response such as: "I didn't know I did that. Thanks for telling me."

We can choose to be more assertive, less aggressive, more direct, less passive, more empathic and less controlling. Once we shift our focus away from the other person's behavior and toward our own we have taken the first positive step toward altering the boundaries. By giving some careful thought to *how* we will confront we demonstrate a concern for us both.

A compliant homemaker felt helpless and frustrated because for ten years her spouse would not even discuss the idea of new living room furniture. It didn't matter to him that the old couch had a broken spring that was poking through the worn upholstery. The foam padding in the ancient chair had deteriorated so much it shed a sandy substance every time somebody sat on it. The rickety coffee table was scratched beyond repair, and the rug was threadbare. It was good enough for him, and it should be good enough for his family.

One day the young woman's neighbor mentioned that she was replacing her family room furniture. Something clicked. The neighbor's discards were so much better than her pitiful collection. Feeling just a little ashamed but also determined, she asked if she could have it.

Her mind raced to the next step: "How will I get rid of our old junk?" She called a young student who owned a pick-up truck and paid him $35.⁰⁰ to haul it all to the dump. Then she cleaned the living room walls, windows and floor. The room was absolutely empty. When her husband came home he looked around in speechless amazement. Her even tone came as a surprise to them both. The power felt so unfamiliar. "I need $1,500.⁰⁰ to buy paint, draperies and rugs. It will be beautiful." Then she told him about the neighbor's furniture. A new look of respect accompanied his resigned response: "OK." The rigid boundary between them changed because of her inspiration and action.

When we choose a higher purpose for a relationship, such as deepening its intimacy, we begin with ourselves. Our own behavior needs refurbishing before we can expect change in another. If we want more affection, we must become more affectionate. If we want more respect, we must behave more assertively.

Initially, this shifting adds a little stress to the relationship. The other person may barely notice it, but if you persist, and, even better if he or she likes it, a change will occur. These adjustments are inherent to all personal relationships. It is the dynamic through which individuals grow and alliances mature.

Of course, there is always the risk of failure when we initiate change. However, without risk there is no hope for movement. Participants assume a positive outcome whenever they take a risk. Bystanders rarely take risks, and when they do they assume a negative outcome. We have a choice here. Assuming the negative does not help us to prepare for failure, but it does make us miserable in the meantime.

Choose life. Choose to assume the positive result and your courage to change will take wings.

Boundary Formation

The culmination of social experience is just one precursor for boundary formation. Another is our physical shape, our basic constitution and the body that filters and records each life experience.

Bodies come into the world with a genetic proclivity for the distribution of three types of tissue: mesoderm, endoderm and ectoderm. The mesoderm develops into muscles, connective tissue and bones. Its purpose is structure and locomotion. The endoderm grows into the delicate linings of organs and cells. Its purpose is the exchange of fluids and vapors. The ectoderm becomes the skin, brain and nervous system. Its purpose is communication within the system and with the outside world.

Stanley Keleman first described this typology created by William Sheldon and went on to develop his theory of Formative Psychology.[2] In his book, *Love: A Somatic View,* Keleman states, "These are constitutional givens. Although there is no pure type, everyone is born with a predisposition to one or the other of these types.... These types exist not only as a mental image, but as a fundamental urge to be in the world in a particular way."* (Fig. 10)

People who have a large distribution of mesoderm *(Mesos)* per overall tissue volume have squarish, well-proportioned shapes. Their muscular bodies lend themselves to movement and action. They touch and test their environment through physical activity. They remember and rearrange information based on the way they embody it during their physical experiences. ("I remember the day you're talking about. I rode my bicycle down a steep hill and fell off.") They like to work and will act first and think later. Their boundaries are usually in motion.

People with more endoderm *(Endos)* per overall volume have roundish bones and a rounded shape. They engage their world through

* *Keleman, Stanley,* Love: A Somatic View, *p. 24*

feelings and imagery. They like to clarify the emotional aspect of a situation before acting on it. They think in pictures and when trying to express themselves they often find words elusive. You will notice them doodling and sketching in order to communicate. Sharing feelings and emotions with others is important to them and they need to be involved in their communities. Their boundaries stretch outward, ever ready to engage and interact.

People with more ectoderm per overall volume have long flat bones and a more linear shape. *Ectos* like to analyze and they have a keen ability for sensing. They like to ponder and peruse a situation before acting just a little. They hasten through life in small steps even though action must wait for understanding. Because of their quick neural impulses they often are alert and attentive. Their sensory awareness is acute. Their boundaries are taut and cautious.

Our boundaries come right along with us, whether to parties or committee meetings, both naturally occurring phenomena within communities. Since our boundaries are uniquely shaped we strive to maintain some sense of ourselves by conforming to them. We cannot help but view life through these filters of shape and experience. Since the point of interaction between people is at their boundaries, problems can arise when these divergent shapes decide to work together.

If a task is to be done and a committee formed to do it, chances are there will be a variety of shapes and filters among those present. Each will have a particular perspective on how to proceed. The muscular action person will want to get the physical work started. The linear sensing one first needs a clearly defined plan. The rounder feeling person will want the ambiance to be part of the plan and will see no reason why action should start until the plan *feels right*.

Arguments arise because individuals with their unique shapes, temperaments and experiences have their own ideas of the best way to proceed. It's not so much that they choose to be uncooperative, but that they are driven by their own physicality and experience. If the boundaries of each are rigid or fixed, the committee cannot even begin to function.

MESOMORPHIC   ENDOMORPHIC   ECTOMORPHIC

Figure 10. Constitutional givens influence boundary formation.

Agreement happens when each person is satisfied to some extent. Any project needs a plan with input from all the relevant participants. Action people do not like waiting around for plans and planning people are not enthusiastic about getting into action. In order to move forward each must compromise, giving up some aspect of his or her native tendencies in support of the long-term goal. Individuals sacrifice a part of their own boundaries for the good of the project. (Fig. 11)

Figure 11. Each softens part of a boundary for the good of the project.

Committees are little communities. They are successful when individuals learn to flex their own boundaries without fear of losing them altogether. Flexing a boundary allows a person to maintain originality while acknowledging someone else's. How does one learn this?—by choosing to be an energetic participant in the group process, in community life. For some this is natural and familiar, for others it means venturing into new territory. It is through relationships in community where individuals can risk stretching their boundaries. It is how they expand their perimeters, discarding unreliable beliefs and replacing them with fresh new experiences. It is where and how we become participants and choose life.

The root system of any community has one other key element: communication. All of our interchanges with other individuals and corporate systems occur at the boundary. Without healthy communication there can be no belonging or support. Communication requires a willingness to listen and an ability to hear.

Communication

Communities succeed when the individuals in them feel heard. True communication supports the deepest authenticity in each of us. When we know that others want to understand us we believe we are respected and accepted. We know we are participants. If we have difficulty expressing ourselves and are shunned because of it, not only does mis-communication occur but also mistrust. Nothing distorts relationships more. It causes all manner of havoc and mental anguish.

One facet of communication is the verbal exchange of words, the sending and receiving of information. On the surface this appears simple enough. Then why is it that so much information is not received, understood or acknowledged? Is it the sender's fault? Is it an error on the part of the receiver? And whose responsibility is it anyway to get the message across; is it the sender's or the receiver's? (Fig. 12)

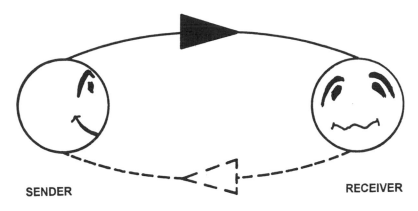

SENDER   RECEIVER

Figure 12. Communication requires a sender and a receiver.

When someone says, "He does not know how to communicate," we get the impression that this individual does not know how to articulate his thoughts. When someone says, "She just does not listen," the implication is that this individual does not know how to interpret what is being said.

Learning how to both articulate and listen is as necessary as breathing if we are to participate in a full life. Healthy interchanges between people affect much more than the intellect; they touch us physically and spiritually. Scathing words cause us to bristle and harden, or cringe and collapse. Loving words cause us to soften and open, to reach out and trust.

Words can be confusing. Someone who talks in images and metaphors seems hopelessly indirect to the person who thinks in a straightforward action-oriented way. It is as if one speaks in Greek, the other in Chinese. Yet we need metaphors and images in our speech to rescue it from tedium. It is the adjectives and adverbs that give communication vitality. However, too many pictures can confuse the message. In fact, the message can become lost entirely. In order to understand, the receiver must orally paraphrase the words until the sender acknowledges they are indeed what were intended.

Feelings are transmitted right along with dialogue. They are more easily discernible during a verbal exchange than with a written one.

When the boss asks, "Where is your report?" The question appears innocuous enough, a clear request for information. If folded arms, a rigid posture and a frown accompany it, however, the message changes from a simple query to an angry demand. Feelings are communicated through gesture, tone and posture commonly called *body language*. The body's voice is far more compelling than words can ever be.

Messages are transmitted via three packages: words, body language and feelings. When the gestures and feelings do not match up with the words the message becomes confusing. It is not logical. We do not understand the person's intention behind the message, and this leads us to mistrust the messenger.

Incongruous messages demand an interpretation. "What is he really saying?" we ask. We would like to believe the words but they pale beside powerful feelings and gestures. We may think, "He is saying he loves me but he's shouting! Is he threatening me? I don't believe he really loves me. I'll bet he hates me. See how angry he is?" Interpretation may be accurate, but it also may not be. Without verifying the meaning and intent, how can we possibly know?

The sender must assume some of the responsibility for message comprehension. This can be achieved by eliciting feedback from the receiver before moving on to another thought. Sometimes senders have the arrogant habit of assuming that once they have spoken their job is done. If the receivers do not hear it's because they either are not listening or are too stupid to understand. It does not occur to them that their sending mechanism might be weak or confusing. Their thinking is something like this: "I told you. It's not my fault you never listen." More often, however, senders simply don't bother to close the communication loop because they are unaware of its importance.

Feedback also comes in three packages: words, body language and feelings. Nodding is a gesture indicating some degree of understanding. Frowning can mean, "I do not understand," "I disagree" or something quite unrelated: "I'm really having a bad day." As the sender we need to evaluate what each response means, and ask, "What's the frown about?", or "Do you disagree?", or "What don't you understand?"

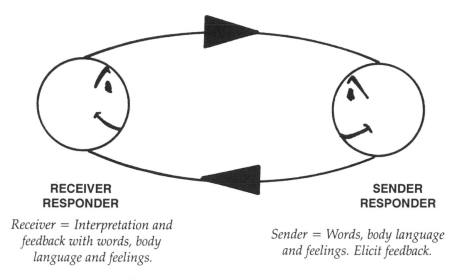

RECEIVER RESPONDER

SENDER RESPONDER

Receiver = Interpretation and feedback with words, body language and feelings.

Sender = Words, body language and feelings. Elicit feedback.

Figure 13. Healthy communication.

It is the receiver's job to give feedback, to acknowledge under-standing through gestures or comments and to ask for clarification as needed. The receiver can say, "Stop just a minute, are you saying you want to rent a movie or go out to a movie?" Sometimes receivers hesi-tate to interrupt because it seems rude. However, it is disrespectful to leave a partially heard message dangling in mid-air. One must then guess at the other half and this usually leads to mistaken interpretation. Each subsequent message will be colored by assumptions that further entangle its meaning.

One of the greatest gifts we can give to another is to both listen and hear. Hearing means doing one's best to absorb all three packages: words, body language and feelings. We have to look at the person who is speaking to see her gestures. We have to listen attentively to hear the words and feel the emotion behind them. Hearing means asking for clarification and making responses that are appropriate before leaving the current thought and moving on to a new one.

This gift of respectful conversing deepens intimacy and strengthens individuals, partnerships and communities. When people feel heard they know they belong. They trust and accept support that allows them the confidence to support others. Belonging, support, boundaries and communication are the roots of any community, be it a family of two or a government of two thousand. They nourish and sustain the essential network for the kind of interaction that allows versatility in each member and solidarity in the whole. Just like the redwoods, strength and growth come from living in community.

Chapter Four
Quiet Presence

I heard you twice the first time.

When American humorist Lily Tomlin stands on stage and says, "For fast acting relief, try slowing down," (Lily actually credits her writer, Jane Wagner with this witty one-liner) everyone in the audience laughs in sympathetic understanding. After all, it makes excellent sense, but first let's ask, "Do we remember how?" Most of us will answer "no," or at best, "Well, I think so, but it's been a while. You see, it conflicts with my scramble to survive. I have bills to pay, night school, my workouts, my family, and oh yes, my week-end job." Deep in the recesses of our minds, a familiar voice keeps chanting, "If you go faster, you will get it all done and then you will have time to rest." The voice lies. In truth, we are never *done.*

If you wind the spring of a watch too tightly, it breaks. So it is with the human system. When we get too wound up we crash, get sick, have a nervous breakdown or become involved in an accident. Rarely do we stop and connect our actions with our illnesses.

Being overloaded with too many activities doesn't allow us the time to really participate in any of them. It is not choosing life. We lose our innate ability to pulsate, and pulsation represents the naturally rhythmic physical state. Every cell and each organ fills and empties. We need to recognize that cells and body systems can only function half-heartedly while in an overloaded state.

There are ways to interrupt this busy-ness that require very little time. When you are wound up carefully you will have ample energy to do all you want to do. A vibrant, pulsing individual makes time for rest and renewal. The rhythmic cycle of action and rest is basic to human existence.

The physical body is a delicate yet marvelous instrument that self-corrects for its own survival. Throughout history it has evolved to greater and greater complexity in order to adapt to its changing environment. During the last decade, however, the rapid increase in sensory stimulation leaves the human organism gasping for space and time.

As a species we are the endangered ones. Our natural resistance to disease is not improving over time. It appears to be more compromised than ever despite abundant food and technological resources. Increasing numbers of autoimmune diseases tell the tale of a downward spiral in cellular integrity.

An assault to each of our individual systems is often more than we can bear. Malnutrition is rampant, even in America. Obesity and eating disorders must be included in this problem. Stress and worry affect the assimilation aspect of our digestive systems. We can eat the most wholesome foods and take the best supplements, but if we are worried we gain a very small percentage of their nutrients. Most processed foods leave long, confusing chemical chains within the cells, lymph and blood. Unrecognized by the body's assimilation and elimination processes, they attach wherever they can and interfere with normal cell function.

Sensory overload disrupts the internal milieu. Continual noise overtaxes the brain's sound filtering system. It loses its sensitivity to sounds so that permanent hearing loss can occur. Hurrying detracts from our sense of taste and our ability to smell. When the information we gather from our environment is harsh and jangled, the receiving body and mind recoil in terror.

Adding to such internal chaos is our pitiful understanding of how computers and other electronic devices affect the body's own delicate electromagnetic fields. We do know that without adequate rest our brains become so charged that the brain waves forget how to slow down. Thoughts race around like mice in a maze.

A Crisis

A middle-aged laboratory technician began having difficulty leaving his work at the lab. Day and night, even though he tried, he couldn't stop his mind from reviewing test results. He had worked in medical labs for twenty-seven years and the last five had been drudgery. He dreaded going in to work, and now, coming home wasn't much fun either. Even his lovely wife and family couldn't distract him from those infernal thoughts. "Did I do that procedure correctly? Did I remember to check on that specimen?" On and on they marched. Sleep eluded him as analytical data raced around the maze of neural pathways in his brain. He became too wound up to function. Finally, he sought medical help.

His family physician gave him a prescription for tranquilizers and placed him on medical leave. It didn't help. He was referred to a psychiatrist who gave him stronger medicine and extended the leave. After three months, feeling groggy but somewhat functional, the man returned to work. After ten days he was back in the laboratory twenty-four hours a day, even while he slept. He was referred to vocational rehabilitation and prepared for early semi-retirement.

We refer to this type of scenario as a *nervous breakdown*. It has nothing to do with psychosis. It has everything to do with sensory overload. Was retirement an unconscious wish on his part? Would this story have a different ending had he enjoyed his job those last five years? Perhaps. Removing him from the work environment and giving him chemicals did not resolve his problem. The complex interplay between the physical body, the thinking mind and the emotional state can become so entangled that a typical physician hardly knows where to begin.

The *relaxation response*, described so well by Herbert Benson in his book by that name, is one of the human organism's self-correcting devices. When we forget how to relax it is because this built-in physiology has been interrupted too many times. The good news is that it can usually be re-learned through techniques such as biofeedback, diaphragmatic breathing, massage and meditation. Even with an unconscious sabotage-factor at play, such as feeling trapped in a job, people can learn how to re-program their relaxation responses. It can be the first step to regaining life as a participant. It is not, however, an end in itself.

To truly choose life, change must occur in all realms: physical, mental, emotional and spiritual. How we work, play, love and create all contribute to our wholeness. They can destroy or uplift us. Before embarking on either career or relationship changes we need to learn how to be quiet. Relaxing in order to rush back into the madness is not really choosing life. Any serious plan for lasting change considers how quiet presence can be woven into an individual's lifestyle.

When there is an acute situation, such as the one with the lab technician, the first goal is to map out a conscious course of combined therapies to resolve the immediate crisis. This may include some social work, counseling and relaxation therapy. Social workers have, at their fingertips, community resources available for almost every human need. Counselors nurture a wounded spirit and provide an environment where any emotion can be safely expressed.

While the emotions are healing, the cognitive mind takes a rest. Memory, focus and motivation go into hiding for a time, allowing the individual to grieve. Eventually, cognition resumes and the person can participate in such activities as reflective thinking and problem-solving. Removing the stress component, such as a job, allows time for an evaluation of the entire situation, the re-grouping of assets and long-range planning. The physical goal is to slow brain wave activity. The mental goal is to remove the brain's need to solve problems and give it a rest. The emotional goal is to lessen the anxiety and fear. The spiritual goal is to give reassurance and restore hope. There is more.

Next, we must uncover the problem lurking beneath the crisis. This stage seeks the individual's insight rather than the physician's. A subconscious wish, such as early retirement, will emerge during skillful counseling. Somatic therapists use a variety of interventions such as art, movement, breathwork, and trance to access secret thoughts and desires. Dream interpretation can also be an effective choice of therapies for this part of the healing journey.

We then move onto the third goal, which is to choose life rather than deplete it. Its dual purpose is resolving the underlying problem while, at the same time, developing healthy lifestyle changes. This stage requires an array of healers and helpers including professionals, confessors, coaches, mentors and teachers. Healing, learning and changing are all occurring simultaneously. Quiet presence is at the heart of regaining and maintaining whole person health. It is integral to the holistic approach for healing any type of disorganization. It is impossible to make a difference until we are able to tell the difference. We cannot tell the difference until we get quiet long enough to feel it.

Some medications force the skeletal muscles into a relaxed state, but the mind can continue to race. Anti-anxiety medications or tranquilizers create an artificially induced state of relaxation but usually have negative effects on the body's liver and nervous system. The price of achieving a quiet state by these methods is much too high. Again, the person isn't present in the process. By acquiescing to the medication-only treatment plan she easily becomes a passive and desperate recipient, unaware of other options. Somatic, or body- oriented therapies, assist the individual to reclaim integration of the physical, mental, emotional and spiritual states.

Presence

Presence is more than being quiet. The term "patient" implies a state of compliant acceptance without active involvement. It may render a cure but it does not elicit healing for the whole person. Presence brings cellular integrity, vitality and verve for living. When you look into the eyes of someone who is present you can see that they are lively and energetic, yet calm and in control.

Being quiet and present at the same time allows the human organism to pulsate in a natural rhythm. The contraction phase is a healthy slowing down of function, which is very different from crashing, collapsing or even sleeping. The healthy contraction phase of the human pulsation cycle is like a flower that closes its petals at night to burst open in radiant beauty with the morning light.

Quiet presence is not a place to stay indefinitely but a place from which we come and go. We seek the quiet place in conjunction with our active cycle, not at its ending. Amidst all our activities and busiest days we need times of tranquility. Our thoughts spur us to action. When thoughts are jumbled and frenzied our resulting actions will be jumbled and frenzied. Two minutes of quiet presence will unravel tangled thoughts thereby allowing order and creativity to emerge.

Creating Quiet Presence

Quiet presence occurs when we create a space in our life for it. The space can be a moment, an hour or a significant period of time. In such a self-losing experience everything feels right and connected. We relax our self-defining boundaries and open to the healing awe of unimagined peace.

When we are in a state of quiet presence we unwind, physically. The organizing and planning aspect of our mind relaxes. Anxiety diminishes. Worry disappears. Creativity flourishes. We are in a state of contentment and tranquility.

All of our body rhythms, except the healing mind, slow down. We are not consciously aware of this cellular activity. We just know we feel warm and lazy, a condition that has become unfamiliar to many a Western workaholic or supermom. We find ourselves in a state of contemplative and uncluttered appreciation.

All of us need periods of quiet presence during the day so our body and mind can refresh and regroup. This rhythmic activity is a life-giving necessity and nighttime sleeping does not guarantee it. Have you ever awakened from a deep sleep more tired than before going to bed? The brain works during sleep. It dreams, problem-solves and processes information. It keeps our basic systems such as respiration, digestion and circulation all functioning. It doesn't care whether or not we feel rested when we wake up.

Cat naps and daytime reveries, however, refresh the whole system. When the physical body reclines, it relinquishes the pull of gravity. Gravity is a continual stress on the muscular and skeletal system. Why not allow yourself to have an anti-gravity break or two during the day? You can escape your corporate office at lunchtime. Go out to your car. Create a comfortable temperature, put on a tape of ocean sounds, and allow yourself to drift. You can teach your brain to awaken you in twenty minutes, but until it learns how to do this, set a small timer. Now you are really choosing life!

Rhythms in Harmony

We think of our body as having one pulse, but in truth it has many. We have heart rhythm, respiratory rhythm, intestinal rhythm, spinal cord rhythm and millions of cells continually filling and emptying. We are one great symphony inherently designed to pulsate harmoniously.

Our physical harmony shares an interchange with our mental, emotional and spiritual selves. Imagine a mother sitting in a rocking chair, her baby cradled in her arms. Can you see her soften in response to the baby's rhythmic breathing and the cadence of the chair? The vibration of her heartbeat comforts the baby. Her body and mind are relaxed. The two are as one. Here is rhythm. Here is intimacy. Here is quiet presence.

Quiet Presence in Grieving

Every system in the universe, even the stock market, has a pulse. Rhythmic contractions give birth to new life. All systems need periods of contraction in order to expand. Tides ebb and flow. Cells shrink and swell. Muscle fibers lengthen and shorten. Bubbles expand and burst. Life and all that goes with it depends on pulsation. At the completion of each phase there is a natural pause before the next phase begins. In choosing life we learn to pay more attention to the pauses.

Pauses are the waiting periods we don't like to endure. They are the places that occur once a change is initiated and before it completes itself. Sometimes they are boring. Often they are frustratingly slow. It is as if we have lifted one foot up and don't know quite where to set it down. We stand teetering with uncertainty until a direction becomes clear. Then we assuredly set the foot down and move on.

There are grieving periods in every life that appear rhythm-less and impossible to navigate. One young woman described such a time. "I feel as though I am at the bottom of a cylindrical pit. There is a ladder to the top but it doesn't reach all the way down. I'm not tall enough to reach the bottom rung and there is nothing to stand on. I feel helpless."

In times of deep grief we believe there is no way to rebound. Yet even within the grieving process there is pulsation, we just don't recognize it. The shock wave of loss numbs the senses and the spirit. Self-control yields to vulnerability. While in this exposed state we are more approachable, more lovable. It is easier to receive caring in times such as these, for we are too stunned to resist it. The physical body is in a state of contraction, but the human spirit and emotions are open to receive comfort. Within the system there is at once contraction and expansion.

When we begin to perceive the pain of loss, part of the physical form increases its pulsation. Hormones that carry feeling sensations course throughout the body creating anguish, sorrow and anger. If we are brave enough to lean into our pain, we will either move on through the healing process, or scare ourselves and return to being numb. This pulsating process gradually allows us to embrace the full reality of our loss. We come close to it and go away, come closer and go away again. This is the pulsation of healing, a healthy type of agony that leaves a minimum of scarring.

Quiet Presence in Aging

Where is there rhythm in the aging process? Vision diminishes, as does memory, mobility and mental acuity. We cannot deny the physical hardening of the tissues, the loss of muscle mass, and the slowing down of organic functions. Newtonian physics compared the human organism to a clock that gradually winds down and stops. This mechanistic view of human life contradicts the universal law of expansion and contraction. We wonder where there can be elasticity in what seems to be a declining phenomenon. We fail to choose life when we view it only from a singular, purely physical perspective.

At the ending of life there can be too much quiet. What do we do with our hours? Television is certainly no solution to the aging mind. We need conversation, music and laughter, children, fresh air and chocolate. We need soap boxes and audiences, students and squabblers. We want to share our years of wisdom and wit. We want to tell it straight because we don't care what other people think, and there is so little time left for the telling.

In the Tahitian culture everybody has a responsibility. The ancient people mend the fishing nets while telling stories to the little ones. They sing and they dance. They are revered as the heads of the community. Senility is rare in Tahiti. These elders have duties to perform and they are expected to fulfill them. Life maintains its rhythms to the end. We can learn from them. If we can only manage is to utter a few words of hope to another human being, we are still choosing life.

Many religions teach of a life after death, a rebirth in another form, a type of life recycling. Another way to view the cyclical aspect of physical death would be the body's natural return to the earth. Still others teach the unending possibility of the human spirit to live and grow even though the physical form weakens and dies.

As humans, surrounded by a pulsating universe, the concept of expansion and contraction makes sense to us. Physical death is a more final form of contraction than any other we encounter. It stuns us with its conclusiveness. Each of us must come to grips with its absolute final-ity, or its next step. Which one is choosing life? Both are. Choosing a belief that proffers a continuing life is hopeful. However, a passionate belief that living ends with this life is one that can also bring peace. Life is an evolving expedition when we choose to live it as a participant. Death is not a failure. It is a rhythmic event in a universal process.

Healing Interludes

The human system has another self-correcting mechanism to slow it down when it gets out of rhythm. We call it illness. According to Bernie Siegel, physician and author, one way to prevent illness is to develop a pattern of using six healing interludes throughout each day.[1] These can be resting, looking out a window, taking a brief walk, pray-ing, deep breathing, meditating, listening to music or doing some type of meditative movement. Siegel's research with cancer patients indi-cates that quiet periods allow the body to regroup and reorganize. One study demonstrates that meditators use health plans fifty percent less than others do and they also have fewer hospital admissions.

People in the Far and Middle Eastern countries consider practices in quiet presence to be essential for life. These highly disciplined exercises prepare them for combat, for healing, for working and for making love. They are designed to elevate the human organism to its highest potential.

Martial arts masters and yogic swami's are some of the most phys-ically fit people in the world. Their power comes from using their minds to master their bodies. Being quietly present allows an integrated type of focus that brings every cell into alignment. The result is exceptional performance. One hour of daily practice in yoga or martial arts is one way of choosing life.

Attentiveness

During quiet times we learn attentiveness. We become present in the present. It is similar to stepping deeply into a forgotten world to examine our old blueprint, fading now with the dust of misuse. There is nothing wrong with the original blueprint. Its design includes a variety of rhythmic activities. Some, like breathing and digesting, are governed by our autonomic nervous systems. They continue in some fashion, with or without our conscious awareness. We have a considerable degree of conscious authority over this system. With practice we can slow our breathing so that all other rhythms slow down as well.

Slowing down allows us to notice our feelings, emotions, bodily sensations, yearnings and dreams. We are fully alive in the present moment and, at the same time, deeply relaxed. Time seems to stand still.

While in this altered state, we can communicate with our bodies, instructing them to heal. We can communicate with our emotions, asking them to swell or subside. We can talk with our problem-solving mind and ask it to find a solution for a current issue. This type of detachment from our usual level of consciousness allows us to create, revive, heal and pulsate. By making time for internal focus we increase our skillfulness in living. We are choosing life.[2]

Clutter

We need quiet presence in order to rescue our delicate cells from overstimulation. Excessive sensory input dulls the senses, rendering them blunt and lifeless. It clutters and confuses our neural pathways. These are designed to sort out sensations so we can respond appropriately. In such a jangled state, they might as well be yesterday's spaghetti. Repetitious pounding in any form causes cells to shrink and stiffen. Too much noise, too many harsh words, too much light, too much spanking; all will diminish cellular integrity and elasticity.

When cells lose their ability to fully expand and contract, they lose vitality. Lost vitality reduces their capacity to ingest nourishment and release by-products of metabolism. Groups of cells, small systems within the whole system, go to sleep. Perhaps it is the heart system that weakens. As a result, the blood and lymphatic circulation will, in turn, slow down. The digestive system may become lazy, resulting in constipation or poor assimilation. Feeble breathing causes low oxygen intake and carbon dioxide output. The body, mind, spirit and emotions become vague and impotent.

To choose life we must be awake and alert, ready to experience the sounds of the sea, the taste of sweet strawberry, the touch of a lover, the smell of fresh grass and the view from a mountaintop. Anything less puts us in the category of bystander to life, a semi-conscious state that is both undesirable and unnecessary.

Overstimulation has a specific affect on people with bright minds. Periods of quiet presence are critical to them. Bright minds that are unable to focus will leap about from subject to subject, starting projects and rarely finishing them, drowning in their own ideas. The thought of quiet presence conjures up in them the fear of boredom. Clutter is preferable to boredom, but even clutter becomes boring after awhile. Quiet presence has infinite possibilities for creative expansion. It is never boring.

When we insulate ourselves with clutter we lose not only our ability to dance but also our desire for the dance itself. Clutter is anything that keeps us from the experience of quiet presence. Television is clutter. Newspapers and magazines are clutter. Chat rooms are clutter. It perpetuates a state of unconsciousness that causes the human spirit to atrophy. We need a certain amount of it to relax our minds, for clutter is mind-less. However, when it replaces quiet presence it behaves like an addictive toxin. In the mind-less state we forget where we are. It is a scary situation to wake up five miles after our freeway exit.

Sensationalized newscasting is clutter. We may think we are being informed when we are really being seduced. Choosing clutter is choosing to be life-less. We have to recognize it for what it is and replace ninety-eight percent of it with active doses of quiet presence.

How then, do we create an uncluttered present? How do we capture precious moments of silent intimacy? What are we afraid we'll miss if we step off the routine merry-go-round before bedtime? What are we reluctant to feel if we confront emptiness?

Risking some time to be quiet brings a marvelous reward. You will find out that being alone with you can be delightful. The deepest you, whom others rarely see, is a delicious secret. Tell yourself, "Well, I love you, and I believe in you. You are just fine. Forget yesterday. It's gone. So what! And let me tell you something else — I'm going to love you tomorrow even more than I love you today. (Today you really did get on my nerves a little. I forgive you.)"

We can create an uncluttered present by shifting our intention and our belief from "I can't," "I don't have time," or "It won't work," to "I can," "I'll just take two minutes," "It's a good thing to do." We can have moments of silent intimacy with others and ourselves. What we miss by taking time out probably won't make any difference five years from now anyway.

Getting to know yourself may pleasantly surprise you. Where you assume emptiness, you may find riches. Try sitting quietly for just two minutes. You can set a timer. Take some slow deep breaths and soften your eyelids. Repeat over and over again, "I love you. I forgive you." Each time you do this, the experience will become more satisfying. You are choosing life. By creating quiet presence in this very simple way, you will begin to have a taste of what it is like to be a participant.

Intention

Just like the pull of gravity, we are pulled by our intentions, be they good for us or not. The sequence of thought-to-action is as follows: "I intend to have a super day today. I'm going to behave as if I'm having a super day even when things go awry. Everyone who sees me will know I'm having a super day. It will make them feel better too." In any situation it is our intention that defines our behavior which in turn influences others. Bringing quiet presence into our harried lives requires that we first intend to do so.

Let us begin by acknowledging that, "I am done with just existing, being a bystander to life. I never seem to get ahead. Most days I don't even feel as though I'm keeping up. The best I can seem to do is ignore this gnawing sense that I am going backwards. There is no time for anything. How can I take time out of my already overly busy schedule to do nothing when there is so much to be done?"

Herein lies the fallacy. Our educated sense of time is an illusion. What we really mean is, "There are only so many minutes in each day, and with my limited vision I don't see how to use them differently." Inserting quiet presence into the day removes the filter that blocks our view. Taking two minutes out of our routine several times each day reaps hours in terms of focus, aliveness and participation. You choose!

Things can change. They will change, but only if we clean our lenses. Most of us have tried working longer, harder and more efficiently. These efforts will garner results for a while but eventually, they too will not be enough. We continue to run out of time unless we include quiet presence in the equation of choosing life.

Intention is a subtle concept. We don't give it enough consideration. Often I will ask someone, "What are your goals? What do you want out of life?" Most people have never really thought about it. The bystanders will be quick to say, "I don't set goals, short term or long term. I tend not to reach them, and then I get discouraged." Interpreted, this means, "I have no hope. I have stopped reaching."

Another type of bystander is someone who is so rigid about reaching a goal that he or she can't make adjustments along the way. We see this in the secondary educational system. Cheryl, age eighteen, may say, "I want to be a nurse." Halfway through the program she begins having headaches, stomachaches and muscle spasms. "But if I stop now, I will have wasted all that time and money." No, Cheryl, you have wasted nothing. To invest with good intention always reaps reward. Listen to your body. It is telling you to try something else. Consider this a gift. You have discovered you belong on a different path. Nursing is not right for you. How could you have really known without some solid investment?

Choosing life means having your intention directed toward fully experiencing anything you choose. I am not advocating wildly flinging yourself from one course to another. Choose a career; set your sail in that direction and give it everything you've got. Observe people who are successful and ask them about the price they paid for their success. In terms of attitudes and behaviors, what did they have to give up and what did they have to acquire? Now you can make an informed decision. Now you have a dream rather than a wish.

Intention is like a seed: you plant it and it grows whether you are watching it or not. Consciously and subconsciously it will continue to direct you. This is why it is essential to choose our intentions with great care. Here is a motto to remember: As I intend, so I behave. As I behave, so I become. As I become, so will I influence others.

Problem Solving

When faced with a problem, we can choose our problem-solving strategy. The human stress response is not completely automatic. There is room for choice when we engage quiet presence. Some of us like to tackle a problem. Others ignore problems that seem to have no obvious solution. Still others take a few moments of quiet presence to step back from the issue and evaluate it. "Does this problem require immediate attention, or not? Do I need more information before I can create a solution? Do I need expert advice?'"

The secret to handling problems doesn't reside in cleverness and experience, although each is important. The key to finding a successful solution to any problem lies in taking some reflective moments to first evaluate the situation.

The way we solve problems is learned. It is a habit, a reinforced mechanism but it can be un-learned. Most of us problem-solve by acting first, reflecting later. We somehow assume that we will get an answer if we make enough noise.

By stepping back and listening, we teach ourselves the fastest, most efficient way of reaching a solution. When we are quiet, a peaceful place opens, breaking the dam of confusion and allowing ideas to flow. It allows us to dream creatively, unencumbered by "how to" details. This technique works whether we have lost our car keys or yelled at the kids.

The first step in problem solving is to set our intention with a positive tone: "I can solve this problem more easily than I think I can." The next step is to take a deep breath and physically lean back in your chair, closing your eyes and assuming a position of quiet contemplation. Keep saying, "This will take less time than I think it will." Empty your mind. Stop going over the issue in its stuck place. That is analogous to fishing around in the same pocket for the keys you know aren't there. Let your unconscious mind have a chance at it. There may be a related situation deep in your memory that will pop up with an answer. The name of someone to help you may emerge. A flash of insight can appear. By creating an uncluttered space of quiet speculation, anything is possible.

Some believe that the only way to solve a problem is with aggression. They like to attack it with a vengeance, shooting all the artillery they can muster. They swear, yell, and shout orders. This technique can be very effective. It raises the blood pressure of everyone within earshot and stirs them to action. Bystanders like to problem-solve this way because it makes them feel powerful. In truth, they aren't powerful, only noisy.

Where aggression raises blood pressure, quiet presence lowers it. People don't die from a normal blood pressure. You have a choice. Why not choose life? It is delightfully easy.

Intimacy

Into-Me-See. We think we know ourselves pretty well. After all, we've inhabited these bodies for a good number of years. Creating quiet presence offers the possibility of an emotionally safe space to go inward. It is easy to do this for ourselves. We simply create a time and a place, then learn how to use it.

Seeing ourselves as others do can be a truly humbling experience. It can even be a revelation. Only through relationship can we discover who we really are. It can lead us to a limitless dimension of intimacy. There is no quicker path to inner experience than the one shared with a trusted friend. This friend may know and share some aspects about us that we weren't ever aware of.

Another person will recognize the beauty and the bane of our personality. Our sabotaging brain has a skewed perspective based on past experience. Without intimately shared experiences of quiet presence, we do not choose life; we choose existence. The operative word here is *choose.* Only we can decide to let another person in closely enough to say, "I believe I am ugly. Please tell me I'm not."

Quiet Gifts

Anne picked up the phone on the second ring and heard the hysterical sobbing and broken words of her mother. Her father was dead. Massive heart attack. The doctor had just left. An invisible hand squeezed her heart. She heard herself saying, "I'll be right there Mom."

She turned a stricken face toward Scott. His concerned question crackled in the still kitchen air. "Do you want me to come with you?" Anne paused and then replied, "No, this is something I have to do alone."

Two hours later Anne returned with Nana, whose white knuckles clutched a small overnight case. Later she recalled, "Scott had made up the sofabed in the family room. There was a fire in the fireplace and the fragrance of hot apple cider greeted us at the front door. I never loved him more than in that moment. He knew what I needed."

Times of wordless sharing are peak experiences that help shape our lives. A surge of emotion flows through the cells, marking the memory with indelible love. They are the most intimate of encounters, sometimes physical, sometimes not; sometimes they are still and at other times active. Always, they demonstrate a majestic quality of human understanding and acceptance. It is with these moments of passionate stillness that we feel life according to our pure design. At such times we are in the very center of the universe, intimately connected to it and to God.

Receiving

Have you ever listened to the breathtaking quiet of snow falling? It is an exquisite sensation: soft, wet flakes brushing your face like the gentlest of lovers. You will feel loved in that experience. Now contrast this with the electrified quiet of the Aurora Borealis. Icy greens, yellows, and pinks spraying a star-studded sky. Your senses pulse with excitement, as you stand awestruck by nature's beauty.

Quiet magnifies each experience. If we pay attention to it, all of our senses open to receiving the impact. When we are cluttered we close off from life, love and pleasure. When we are quietly present we open to the riches that are all around us. We become receptive, interesting and alive.

Discovering our own wonderfulness is an exciting adventure. It leads to self-respect and confidence. It lets us receive praise and respond to it with genuine pleasure. Our spirit smiles. We become more content with being by ourselves as we realize a loving spirit resides inside our body. This respect of the self emanates from every pore, from the way we walk and the tone of our voice. People notice us, are drawn to us and look to us for inspiration. We have more to give because our spiritual tank is full.

Making It Happen

Achieving quiet presence is a delightful, cost effective, efficiency-based concept. In case you believe you can't take the time or spare the energy, let me assure you that you not only can, but your life will improve because you did.

Whenever you begin something new you must acknowledge how you like to learn. Are you a physically active person? Do you like to work with your hands and body? Then look for your moments of quiet presence while you are moving or doing something physical that requires little concentration. Gardening, ironing, changing the oil in the car or washing the car are all excellent work activities that require little concentration. You can focus your intention to dream or problem-solve while jogging or driving. Don't waste this time. Use it to create some quiet presence. The mind is all too willing to wander around in useless meandering. Pick a subject and dream about it.

Are you a feeling-oriented person who thinks in pictures and images? What helps you to create a state of quiet presence: candlelight, firelight, music, comfort food? Time constraints may relegate these full-blown experiences to late evenings and weekends. During the day you merely have to dip into your memory to re-create the sensations of quiet presence in your imagination. It is easy for you. It takes moments. Just close your eyes and go there. Breathe deeply and you will engage your relaxation response on a cellular level.

Are you the kind of person who likes to engage your alert mind with more than one activity at a time? Are you easily distracted by changes in temperature or sudden noises? You probably will access your state of quiet presence while being warm and cozy. You will focus most easily while alone and away from sensory stimulation. Your visionary mind will happily grasp a dream and build it to splendid proportions.

Whatever your unique style, learn to reach deeply inside yourself and yield to that place of quiet presence. It is there. You will recognize it by the calmness that engulfs you. A stillness emerges that you will soon come to recognize as a place of healing. Your body softens. The tension leaves your face, especially around the mouth and eyes. Your creative mind becomes hyper-alert. Your memory discloses the whereabouts of lost articles. That nagging problem now has a solution.

When you recognize the sensations of being in a state of quiet presence you can develop your skills at accessing it. Expand your natural abilities by learning something new. If you are the physically active type don't try to sit still and meditate. Go out and walk instead. If you are feeling oriented and like people around you, don't withdraw to a quiet place. Go to a coffee shop and order a large hot mug of your favorite blend. If you are quick-minded and busy don't try to finish. You will never finish. Make yourself stop, then go out and sit in the sun for ten minutes. Know your personal style, your constitutional learning needs, and accept them.

Once you have mastered recognizing and accessing a state of quiet presence, you will begin to hear a still small voice speaking to you. This is the voice of knowing. Some say it comes from God. Others say it comes from an accumulation of human experience. Still others credit it to intellectual insight and genetic coding. The significance of hearing this voice, be it in words, images or sensations is that it is truth. Truth requires unfettered honesty. It is anchored in more than human experience or thought. Truth is divine in nature. It is universal and crosses all human boundaries. Truth comes to us swiftly and surely in moments of quiet presence. Now is the best time to choose life by embracing its stillness and its passion. Surrender to that inner voice. Just as the stars wait for darkness, the still small voice waits to speak. The first time you hear it you will know it. In that moment you will have chosen life.

Chapter Five
Wishing and Dreaming

How do I make the stars come back?

F ran heard wailing coming from the children's bedroom. "Darn," she muttered, rubbing her eyes. The digital clock came into focus the same time her feet hit the floor. It was 5:30 in the morning! Melanie must be having a bad dream. Pulling her robe close she shivered her way down the hall. It was definitely Melanie. She could tell by the volume.

When she opened the door a lump caught in her throat. There stood her three-year-old, with red face and soggy nose pressed to the window. "Mommy, make the stars come back!" Fran picked her up, Melanie's arms and legs instantly capturing her body. Stroking moist curls away from the troubled face, Fran comforted her daughter, "They will. They always do."

Children readily accept consolation. Give them some loving touch, or intrigue them by distraction. Then they are off to play, imagining the stars coming back just as Mother predicted. Children dream during the day and the night. They can't tell the difference.

By the time children reach adolescence their brains are fully grown and able to accommodate reason. Disappointment becomes a complex kaleidoscope of hormones and emotions. Teens resent their budding awareness and their awakening consciousness. "Why can't you just tell me what to do? What do you mean I'm supposed to weigh the consequences? It's not fair. It's too hard. Give me answers not questions."

With this dawning of reason, life suddenly seems so un-reasonable. Teens are caught between longing for a child's black and white world and being completely grown up. Much of the time they would just as soon skip this stage altogether.

Young adults dream of lasting love, independence and careers. They dream of earning money to buy material goods and rapid promotions to buy even more. Once they have mastered social, economic and sexual responsibility, their life settles into a routine. Too quickly they begin to doze off into a financially overextended lifestyle. Their dreams of romance and adventure fade. They lock themselves into their houses with security systems, television sets and modems. Outside activities revolve around their children and an occasional sporting or cultural event. They enter the world of the bystander. They forget how to choose life.

The stresses of middle adulthood are like sedatives. Faced with increasing financial burdens and aging parents, middle adults sink into a state of survival, living from one paycheck to the next. They go into dream deprivation, shrink-wrapping them to fit their present circumstances. When asked, "If you had an abundance of time and resources, how would you use them?" the reply will be, "I'm afraid to think about it because it hurts too much," or "Why get your hopes up?"

If we stop dreaming we lose our perspective, period. A person without a dream is a person without a vision. Without vision we have no future. Without a future we are souls without hope.

Getting Your Future Back

Children get their futures back with a comforting touch and a promise. Adolescents travel a more complicated course; they need a loosening of the reins and at the same time, a securing of the nest. Young adults must work on their coupleship and all their other relationships. Middle adults have to consider an expansion of knowledge and often, a shift in career.

Each stage has its unique wake-up call characterized by discomfort and confusion. If we ignore these challenges, we stay in jobs we hate or relationships that cause our spirits to atrophy. We become sleepwalkers. This is the realm of the bystander where dreaming subsides and finally disappears. However, if we pay attention to the distress, we can use it to our advantage. Discomfort can be a seed sown at a juncture in the road of life. We can choose to travel the road that has one big rut in it, or we can wake up and choose the bumpy road of life.

There is a profound story in the Bible about a young man named Jacob who committed a terrible sin.[1] Jacob was a twin, the second born along with his brother Esau. Their mother, Rebekah, loved them both very much. As with all mothers, she could see where they were headed in life. She knew Jacob would be the leader of the two, the one most capable of expanding the family business. Rebekah also knew that according to Jewish law, Esau, the first-born, would inherit everything. Still, Rebekah dreamed of the time when Jacob would make them all rich.

The day came when the boys' father, now frail and blind, lay on his deathbed. He called for Esau so he could bless him and bequeath the estate. In a skillful maneuver, Rebekah disguised Jacob as Esau, duping the father into blessing the younger of the two. Jacob went along with the deception and this is where he made his mistake. When Esau discovered their trickery, he flew into a rage. Jacob, being no match for his brother's violence and strength, hid himself until the next day. Bidding Rebekah good-bye, he gathered a small herd of sheep and fled to a faraway region.

Jacob was a skillful farmer and within a few seasons he had tripled his wealth. His success continued, but it brought him little joy. Repeatedly he asked himself, "What good is wealth if you are hated by your family?" He knew there could be no peace without forgiveness, and he could not forgive himself. Could God forgive him? Could anyone forgive him? He longed for reconciliation with his mother and brother.

Jacob was a devout Jew. Through daily prayer he began to hear God's voice urging him to do the right thing: "Return to your country, and to your kindred, and I will do you good." Fearful and ashamed, yet hopeful, Jacob set out for home.

One night, as Jacob slept alone in the darkness, a stranger appeared. He pounced on Jacob as if to kill him. In a writhing, buckling contest they wrestled for supremacy.

Jacob sensed that this was no ordinary assailant. Solitary attackers don't suddenly appear, especially when you are travelling with a large group. He knew God was either testing him or punishing him, and somehow he must prevail. The contest continued throughout the night. Finally, the man (or was it an angel?), recognizing Jacob's determination, gave him an ultimate test by wrenching his leg from the socket. Gasping with pain, Jacob imprisoned the angel in his grip and begged for forgiveness. He knew his life was pointless without God's blessing.

In one cunning last attempt at victory, the angel said, "Let me go for the day is breaking." But Jacob, still writhing in pain said, "I will not let you go unless you bless me." So the angel relented and blessed Jacob saying, "You have striven with God and with men and have prevailed." In that final hour Jacob reclaimed his life and his future.

Jacob knew that within the fold of God's grace he could face anything, even a rage-filled brother. Once more he had hope. He dreamed of reconciliation with his family, especially Esau, and of their future together. He sent a messenger on ahead to announce his arrival. Cautiously, the two brothers approached each other. In a final moment of faith, Jacob reached out to Esau and embraced him.

Do you ever lie awake, wrestling with a dilemma? You want to do the right thing but you fear there will be painful consequences: hurting someone, embarrassment or disrespect?

Past mistakes masquerade as demons, stealing our dreams and our futures. Like Jacob, we can achieve financial success and spend our lives chasing the gods of acquisition or philanthropy. We will seem to have chosen life, but have we?

Without atonement for our mistakes, we relinquish our birthright of forgiveness. All our relationships become tainted with guilt. We will never know ardent love and spirit-free intimacy. We settle instead for empty alliances and material exchanges. Until we make amends and clear our spiritual slate, we establish a barrier with God and all of our relationships. Part of growing up is recognizing the Rebekahs in our lives. They mean well, but they muddle our dreams with their own desires. We must separate the dreams of our parents from those we should choose for ourselves. We need to make amends to those we have hurt. We must make our own stars come back. In these ways we choose life.

Laying the Foundation for Dreaming

At age six, Ruth dreamed of becoming a mommy and a nurse. These seedling dreams were sown by her mother and nourished by stories and play. She received a Play Nurse kit for Christmas. Her dolls were her babies. She bathed them, fed them and rocked them to sleep.

Ruth's mother instilled two of her own beliefs into her daughter's future: 1) *women need children to fulfil their dreams* and 2) *nurses can always find work*. For Ruth there would be no other choices. She was a gentle and good-natured child who loved to please her mother.

At age sixteen, Ruth activated the first phase of her mother's dream: she chose her mate, the likeliest boy in her senior class. George was nice looking and hard working. He came from an educated church-going family who were pillars of the community. George's parents held strong civic opinions; in fact, they were opinionated about most things. He fit her picture of a mate. She liked him, and he liked her. What could be better?

What Ruth couldn't realize was that by choosing her future at this ill-informed age, she was making a terrible mistake. Enamored by Ruth's attention, George, of course, didn't stand a chance. Other than his hormone-driven fantasies about girls he had no particular dreams. He possessed a curiosity about life but had difficulty in school. His boyish visions of putting out forest fires and racing fast cars were met with hisses and clucks from both parents. His family held a strong belief for the future of their children, "Get a good education and you will have a good life." Architecture was their dream for George.

Ruth wanted an educated husband with a solid career. She and George's father formed an unspoken coalition to get George into college. He really didn't want to go just then. He would have preferred to get a job and spend his earnings on some life experience. Parental logic prevailed and so it was decided. Ruth, the nurse, would work to support them both while George attended university. Just like Jacob, George went sleepwalking into the trap set by Ruth and his father.

Ruth and George had too little time to build the foundation for their marriage. She worked in the evening and he attended class during the day. Because their income was well below poverty level, there were no small luxuries like a movie or a milkshake. Still, they were happy, as newlyweds are, and they had a goal. Or, they thought they did.

One evening while Ruth was working at the hospital, George opened the refrigerator expecting to find leftovers for supper. Instead a single lonely carrot greeted him. George might have asked himself, "What am I doing?" Instead he deepened his resolve to live out his father's dream. Tomorrow Ruth would be paid. They would go on.

George finally graduated and found a job in his field. He and Ruth began their family and moved to suburbia. The pseudo-dream had come true. Ruth was happy enough but something was missing. She could never understand George's irritability or the remoteness that would come over him. He didn't want to go to church with her. More children arrived. Increasing responsibilities added to George's frustration. He became verbally abusive. The two drifted farther and farther apart, trying to co-exist *for the good of the children.*

As the children grew into adolescents and formed their own friendships they began to withdraw. Family activities were stilted and forced. Ruth tried to get George to go with her for counseling. He refused. Everyone was miserable, and no one knew what to do. The illusion of love between Ruth and George had died. The resulting divorce rendered wrenching grief and shattered dreams. It also brought blessed relief from a pain-filled life.

Could this tragedy have been prevented? Would counseling have helped? Ruth and George thought they held shared dreams. However, they were each driven by the visions of their parents. They were never encouraged to dream their own dreams, experiment with vocations or investigate differing worldviews. They missed out on the most essential dream-building stage of our lives: adolescence and young adulthood. People usually make poor choices for career and relationships when this happens.

At what point do parents cross the fine line from guidance to coercion? Most parents dream of their children's lives being better than their own. They forget that the mind of a child absorbs influence like a sponge. Each child is a dreamer-in-the-making. Parental influence that is too tight leaves the child with too little room to dream. Parental influence that is too loose creates weak boundaries in the child; he or she doesn't learn where dreaming ends and reality begins. Life will eventually teach them through disappointments and broken dreams.

Parents who make their norms and values known with loving clarity offer a firm boundary against which their children are free to dream. It is one of the greatest gifts we give our children. It requires persistence, a sense of humor and consistency. Such parents choose life not only for themselves but also for their descendents. Family beliefs repeat themselves generation after generation. Only when we choose life do we interrupt inappropriate family patterning. Building dreamers is one pattern we want to continue.

Building the Dreamer Within You

There are three stages in the developing human that override the child's desire to please the parent. They are toddlerhood, adolescence and young adulthood. These natural phases of rebellion are where healthy young people should regale against family norms and values. Each stage affords some experience of individuality, a mock attempt to be separated emotionally from the authority of the parent. They are each a part of choosing life.

The three separation stages may be chronologically delayed. An adult at any age who is striving to mature will go through them. Seeing our parents or other authority figures as normal humans, warts and all, shatters the childish illusion we each share. With a painful jolt we realize that these authorities are not always right, nor do they unceasingly know what is best for us. With this knowledge comes the salient insight, "I am responsible for my choices."

Young children live in a magical kingdom of fantasy and imagination. They relate to toys and stories better than explanations. Steering them toward our own biases pre-empts their natural dreams and possibilities. They should hear, "You can become anything you set your heart and mind to, as long as it is for good." They need to observe adults learning new skills and tolerating differences. They need to hear dreaming done out loud, even the outrageous kind: "Some day we will take a trip far, far away and see many people who speak a different language. How would you like that?" Don't short-circuit the dreaming process out of fear. Children can learn the difference between dreams and promises. A dream is an aperture to possibility. Teach them this process, and they will exceed your grandest expectations.

Our beliefs guide our behaviors, our fears and prejudices control them. We can stay stuck on the shores of life, or like a jetty, project into unknown waters. Wishing and dreaming frees us from a lifestyle limited by the solid and the familiar. We choose. We wake up, and then we choose life.

Going Places

"If only I had a crystal ball." Have you ever wished for one? What would it do for you? Allow you to prepare for your future? Keep you on course? Simplify your choices? Tell you what to do so you won't get hurt? Let you know that you are not standing still but going places? The problem is, most of us don't know we are standing still. We're so busy being busy we fail to notice.

Life is full of occasions where we just don't know if we are making the right decision. We want reassurances. We don't trust our own judgment for fear of making a mistake. Indecision is fear based. Eliminate the cause of the fear and you open to the dreaming. Do you want a future shaped by dreams or by fear?

We can spend a great deal of time mired in minutia because we have not clearly charted our course. We wish for this and for that, aimless thoughts that remove us from the responsibility of making things happen.

Character building begins in the first five years of life and continues until we die. People who have a solid sense of themselves figure out how living works. They rise like cream to the top of their dreams. They have strong personalities. They are quick to rectify their mistakes. They are seldom careless with their choices. They rarely neglect the needs of others. They are healthy and awake. They can suffer deeply and heal completely. They have boundless energy. They nourish their bodies, minds, emotions and human spirits. They dream. They mentor. Life challenges them just as it challenges everyone but it doesn't hinder their growth.

There is evil in this world, and it impedes dreaming. It poses as human weakness, human cruelty and human neglect. We must differentiate these characteristics from mistakes: mis-calculations based on a lack of knowledge, poor judgment or both. Evil has intention. It can be grossly obvious or subtly sly.

Victim behavior is an evil. It says, "Please help me. You can do it so much better than I." The unconscious message is, "My comfort zone doesn't include this activity. I'm too afraid to try. You see, I'm only partially awake and I'd rather stay here than face the discomfort of change."

People go to great pains to maintain their unconscious state of mind. This presents a paradox; *the energy one expends to prevent waking up is considerably less than the energy of waking up and dealing with the challenge.* This is a basic principle for choosing life. We cannot believe it until we create an experiential foundation of being awake and dealing with challenges.

Learned fears can easily skew our ability to reason with logic. The nonreasoning intellect masquerades as a sage when it really is a saboteur. It tells such lies as: "This situation is fraught with danger so you'd best avoid it." Or, "You poor thing, how could they do that to you. It's not your fault."

When we believe these lies we behave like victims. Once we behave like one we become one, reordering our world from that perspective. We pay close attention to the oppressed or the oppressive. We exert influence on others to do the same. We have bad luck. There are people who have a series of automobile accidents, none of them their fault. On looking closely, one discovers they are miserable in their work or their primary relationship or both. They have a mediocre spiritual path. Their creative expression is a void. They live marginally. Their car becomes a metaphor for their life. They want to stop it, break it, shake it up, buy a new one, but they don't know how.

There are people who try to step on your dreams for a variety of reasons, all of them emotional. Jealousy wears the mask of control. "Don't go to Hawaii this year. I can't go. Wait till next year and we'll go together." Unconscious interpretation: "You shouldn't have that because I can't have it. After all, aren't we equals?"

People are like magnets. Emotional need triggers the projection of an electromagnetic field that draws people toward us. Emotional need is the sustaining force in sick relationships.

Random Wishing

Jennie and Marge spent most of their free time together. They enjoyed sharing trips and activities, but their favorite pastime was talking about the men they wished they could meet. Their common need was loneliness.

Quite by chance, Jennie met a suitable gentleman. She saw less and less of Marge, and when they did get together, Marge seemed different. Suddenly, she possessed annoying little habits Jennie had not noticed before. These became increasingly irritating until finally Jennie terminated the relationship. Marge was hurt and bewildered. Neither knew what had really happened. Marge was disposable and so was her need.

A relationship with more substance would have sustained the adjustment. Marge hadn't done anything new. The two could have met their challenge of loneliness with some serious dream building. Instead they employed a lot of random wishing. We can have what we want from life, but most of the time it doesn't just happen. If we desire a lifetime partner, we should dream about that person while building the kind of character that will attract him or her to us.

Sometimes we get our wishes, those rare something-for-nothing occurrences that surprise and delight us. Wishes are like amorphous thoughts floating in a vacuum. Dream building, on the other hand, intends a result and sets a course to obtain it. In Jennie and Marge's situation, their dreaming could have included some research and an action plan. Eventually each would have found her partner because a corporate effort surpasses an individual one.

Dreams Are Meant to Lead Us

This year Susan would graduate from high school. Since eighth grade she had dreamed of becoming a marine biologist. Teachers and parents described Susan as a "poor student," one who struggled to make "C's and D's." Because of her scholastic record they discouraged her dream. They wanted to spare her the pain and struggle of failure. Since Susan was a very determined young lady, this logic made no sense to her.

One evening, following a family dinner, Susan decided it was time to have a talk with Uncle Mike. He was her favorite relative. She loved his way of listening, as if every detail was a piece of critical data. He would stand with head slightly bowed, brow furrowed, nodding and saying, "Yah, yah," after every thought so you knew he was getting it. He was patient too, waiting until you had run out of ways to expound your dilemma before commenting. Then he would come up with some profound and positive statement that made you feel superior.

As they were doing the dishes together, they began to talk about her dream and the dilemma of the grades. After she had exhausted her argument, Uncle Mike paused, then said, "I know your grades aren't there, but it's good to have dreams. Not all dreams are meant to come true you know, but they are meant to lead us, and sometimes they lead us to something better than we can ever imagine." This opened a whole realm of possibilities for Susan. Rather than feeling defeated she was liberated by the words: **"Dreams are meant to lead us."**

Lining Up

Going places in life involves many levels of choice. First, there is the choice of lining up our big picture goals with universal good. In any situation we can ask, "What is the choice here that will bring the greatest good for all?" This question is better than the often stated, "Never mind, in ten years it won't make any difference." This infers that we can behave badly and time will wash it clean. Choices have long-lasting consequences. Integrity matters, even in the small things of life.

When our big picture dream is for the greatest good of all, and when we seek overall healthiness in body, mind, spirit and emotions, challenges become all the more compelling because of their seeming impossibility. Struggles and failure do not harm us when we have mentors like Uncle Mike. The human organism has the innate ability to reorganize itself as long as it has adequate support. We don't need a crystal ball to see into the future if we awaken to the present. When we dream we automatically open up possibilities for the future.

When dreams become realized, it is human nature to reach for another one. Humans have always explored, invented, created and imagined. In the 1940's a popular comic strip detective named Dick Tracy communicated through a two-way radio wristwatch. Today wristwatches can talk to computers. Anything that humankind can imagine is within reach. It is just a matter of time. Even while we are dying we can dream of moving into another dimension of living. We always have a choice.

Awakening to Wonder

Magical thinking is a natural aspect of childhood. Wise adults can reclaim their own capacity for it through the eyes of children. You might try observing a six-year-old discovering the wonder of making Jello, or a two year old mastering a light switch. Can you recall the amazement that comes with such openings of the mind?

Too often adults trade in their own dreams of adventure and romance for work and success. Do you give your best creativity to the job or the business instead of to your family and friends? If all your excitement is garnered from the workplace, home becomes a confinement instead of a castle. We can feel trapped by the ones we love if they don't stimulate us with intellectual challenge. We trade dreaming for being responsible.

Once we've become bystanders, locked into the *high* of intellectual challenge, we forget how to wake up and dream, but we must if we are to choose life. A decision to choose comes first. We release ourselves from sleepwalking, not by willful effort, but through music, touch and laughter, confession, forgiveness and faith. Our physical and emotional systems need to be gently rocked back into wakefulness.

Adults can rekindle exploration and discovery by revisiting a child's world: take a walk through a toy store, read a story book aloud, visit a kindergarten classroom, sit in the school library, do some third-grade homework or go back to school via CD ROMs and field trips. In the mind of a child no wish or dream is too outrageous. Exercising the brain in this fashion stimulates seeking, risking, adventuring and exploring. This is how children learn the how-to's of living. It is through play that they become inspired to be generous, considerate and truthful.

It is never too late to begin being the kind of adult who breathes life into other people's dreams. Society needs people with vision. The complexities of global economics and human weakness require it. We can choose to meet these challenges dismally or hopefully. Each person has infinite possibilities for creative endeavor. We can replace those infamous nine words, "But we've never done it that way before," with a different nine: "Let's just see what we can come up with."

Choosing to explore these questions is choosing to live. We can learn how to orchestrate our own destiny by first stretching our minds in some simple, playful ways. We want enough flexibility to adjust our course yet adequate focus to follow our dreams. The first step is awakening the child within us.

The second step is aligning with a system of belief that is bigger than our own. We must first ask ourselves a very simple question, "Do I want to be good?" It is obvious by the amount of crime in most of the world's societies that many people choose not to be good. For multiple reasons, they choose instead to get even, to have power, to have money, to have influence, to be somebody but not to be good. Without choosing to struggle toward a clear vision of what is right, we become like Jacob. There will always be within us emptiness born from separation from God and our families. Choosing life is an invitation to wrestle with the angels of truth, integrity, intimacy and mercy.

When we choose to be good we can also choose to have money, power, positive influence and success. We can choose plenty as well as scarcity. We can choose dreaming or surviving. We can settle for a modicum of pleasure each day or an abundance of joy. The greatest sufferings will come and go. It is during those times of vulnerability that we deepen our relationships. The connections we can make with other humans can astound us. Decide today to dream about the good you can do with money and influence. You do have a choice.

The Creative Process of Dreaming

Children dream of being pretty and cherished or powerful and strong. *All* of us dream of love and intimacy, home and happiness.

A child's brain is unhampered by reason and, from that perspective, anything seems possible. Too much reality strangles the wishing and dreaming process. We have to get away from logic for a while in order to free up the creative mind. If we focus only on daily minutia we will settle for life as a bystander. Mediocrity will start looking good to us. After all, it is relatively painless. Beware of this illusion! Mediocrity is at the top of a slide leading downward to despair. Despair breeds bitterness. Nothing stays the same. It either gets worse or it gets better. We have choice even though we may believe we do not.

We all have the innate ability to dream, to stretch our imaginations and reach for the stars. Children are often taught that dreaming is bad, a waste of time and a habit of the immature. Fortunately, some slip through and make it to adulthood with their abilities intact. They may become the dreamers who live by the belief that "If you follow your heart, trust your instincts, and develop your intuition, you will stay on the right path." Other dreamers clearly envision the results of their dreams. This motivates them to move toward their goals. Still others logically plan out their goals for one, five and ten years. When we neglect dreaming we dismiss a part of who we are. Choosing life allows us the flexibility to reflect on the past, live fully in the present, and dream about the future.

There is no one right way to dream. Each of us solves problems and processes information in a particular style. The important point is that we engage in the dreaming process. It is upon dreams that we build our future. When we know what we want we can set up a plan to get it. Keep in mind that needs preempt wants. If we need food, we are unlikely to dream of much else. However, even when our survival needs are paramount, we can still set aside time for dreaming. We must always hold the intention of change for the better.

Beliefs shape our dreams. They emanate from parental influence and personal experience. When they line up with universal laws and are destined for good, they ultimately cultivate attainable dreams. Why is this so? Because people who believe in God, who understand the universal laws of choosing life, will help you.

We cannot change our past but we can do something about our present. When we are riddled with guilt, shackled by shame or veiled in victim-hood our present appears stuck. What can we do?

Sometimes we are lucky enough, like Julie in chapter one, to have someone come along and say, "I can't find a dream in you anywhere!" A jolt like this will stir our emotions, often to anger. Once the anger subsides, a creative process begins. Its first phase is a questioning one. "Have I really given up? Have I 'settled'?" Questioning eventually yields to yet another emotion, one of sorrow.

This shock wave of despair passes through us when we realize we've become bystanders. "I have missed so much!" We must not despair over sadness. Tears are healing, and grieving makes room for even more creativity. The cells of the body begin to vibrate and shimmer as yearning for change creeps in. The body, mind, spirit and emotions click into the automatic reorganization process. Hope returns. We ask, "What can I do about this?"

Beyond My Wildest Dreams

Dreams are like gifts. They become liberated and expanded when shared with another in mutual love and respect. Corporate dreaming is the most fun because of the synergy it creates. When we love someone we want the best for him or her. We want their dreams to come true and we support them.

When we work for a company that builds a good product we share the corporate dream for success. This type of buy-in with resonant alignment offers the greatest degree of freedom and the greatest potential for success. Everyone wins because people help each other move toward the common dream.

There is an old story about two groups of people who died and were challenged about what they had learned while on earth. One group had believed in goodness, the other in selfishness. Each was locked into a separate room and told they would be there for three weeks. At the end of the three weeks the healthy group would be allowed to proceed, while the unhealthy group would not.

Each room held tables laden with delicious, fresh food that was replenished three times a day. The only limit placed upon the people was this: while they were eating, both of their hands would be tied behind their backs.

The group who had chosen life had no difficulty with the challenge. They were participants, choosers of life who thought not only of themselves, but of each other. In no time at all they established eating groups and simply fed each other. At the end of the three weeks they were happy, well-fed and ready to move on.

The other group had pushed, squabbled and devoured as much as they could by eating like pigs from a trough. They developed indigestion, paranoia, and violence was rampant. Needless to say, they had no future.

Corporate dreaming lifts the physical body and the human spirit beyond its self-imposed limits. It offers the possibility for an epiphany.

Where one person might have doubts and ask, "Do you really believe we can do this?" the members of a group will look at each other and say, "Sure we can."

Sacrifices can be willingly made when a larger dream is shared. A group of people who dream of wealth will work long hours in a start-up company. Dedicated missionaries often risk their lives spreading God's word, knowing they are supported by many faith communities back home. There is tremendous mutual satisfaction and pride in a group effort. Participants in life seek out these opportunities. It is a type of choosing life unlike any other. It allows us to thrive beyond our wildest dreams.

What are your wildest dreams? Do you desire to retire with enough money and health to travel, create something or just relax? Do you dream of having a close, intimate relationship with another person? Do you dream of working hard for some cause that is of benefit to society? Do you see yourself as having the resources to create a healing environment where children play safely and the doors are unlocked? Do you dream of being healed from a physical illness, a mental illness or emotional suffering? If your self-limiting brain is telling you, "But that's impossible!" it is an excellent place to begin. Dream for the impossible. Go ahead. It's free.

Dreaming is a process that leads us to a place where we either learn the skills to attain our desire or discover something better. It is a forward moving course, one that opens our minds to do more, be more and share more than we ever thought possible.

Dreams and Wishes

First, we must sort our wishes from our dreams. Wishes are wonderful. They are the yearnings of the child, even if the child is embodied in the adult. But wishes are void of a plan. They are mind wanderings. They lack belief and conviction.

Dreams, on the other hand, contain both faith and fervor. An only child who wishes for a baby brother may be implanting a dream that says, "When I am grown and have power, I'll never be lonely again." That childhood dream may manifest itself in a marriage with a large family.

When adults find themselves wishing for something, they should ask themselves, "Why am I wishing for this? What is the emotional need behind this wish?" A wish is a child's voice. A dream is the voice of an adult.

Dreams, even the wildest ones, start coming true the minute we realize that they can. Wake up and have faith in yourself. Accept your wholeness and your rightful place in the greater scheme of life.

How can you tell if you are waking up? Colors appear brighter. Your spirits lighten up. You will begin noticing serendipity creeping into your life: a parking place right in front of the restaurant, a radio talk show host who is discussing your problem, the person next to you in line who knows your uncle Harry. Suddenly life appears livelier, funnier and richer.

Choosing life evokes the dreamer. Why not try it? Give up the idea that dreaming is merely nocturnal. Active, wakeful dreaming is the stuff of living. It stretches the mind and the human spirit. It generates aliveness and hope, creativity and options.

Be willing to take a critical look at your beliefs. What do you believe about God, family, holism, faith, hope and health? Open to new ideas. Get to know people whose opinions differ from yours so you can hear other perspectives. Expand your world view by meeting people from other cultures. Cook with them. Attend their faith communities with them. Respect their differences and they will strengthen yours.

Study people whom you admire. How might they think, solve problems, choose life? Imagine being one of these role models. What aspects of their personalities might enhance yours? Quickly you will discover either that you like yourself just the way you are, or that you might change something.

Set a course of action that is inspired by good. Activate your creative process through faith, confession, forgiveness, touch, laughter, quiet presence, music and beauty. Devise a path to activate each of these qualities in your life. Align with the principle of good. Orchestrate your relationships so they involve other dreamers: life's visionaries who encourage and stimulate your thinking.

Care for your physical, mental, spiritual and emotional bodies. Nourish and honor them. Recognize that life is a process, not just a series of events. Let your dreams lead you. When you are ready to delight in them, even the wildest ones will come true.

Dave Severn, American entrepreneur, says of dreamers, "Successful people are dreamers who have found a dream too exciting, too important to remain in the realm of fantasy, and who day by day, hour by hour, toil in the service of their dream until they can touch it with their hands and see it with their eyes." [2]

Stars are patient. They are doing what stars do: waiting for you to bring them back into your life. Dream the biggest dreams you can imagine, and you will discover that the stars were there all along.[3]

Chapter Six
Faith

Flying into the unknown offers infinite possibilities.

W e do not arrive in this world equipped with the faculty of faith. We learn it. If we observe it in our families and communities, we arrive at the following conclusion: "Having faith is good." Faith allows us to surrender to the seemingly impossible. Some of the most endearing words we can ever hear are, "I have faith in you."

Faith and Community

When the world was sparsely populated, groups of people gathered into easily defined communities. This is still true wherever rural settings exist. However, urban sprawl is a reality for every nation and it is here that faith gets lost. Community boundaries offer a sense of security to the individuals who reside within them. When we are secure we are more inclined to be faith-filled.

Humankind is experiencing a paradigm shift in its notion of community. The idea of a global society is coming, but it has not yet arrived. When it does, and each person assumes ownership for it, our world will be a much healthier place.

During the transition, however, our faith is being rocked by the uncertainty of differences in language and philosophy, customs and beliefs. What has always seemed so "right" to some of us is unacceptable, even intolerable, to others.

Survival of humanity demands that we learn how to get along. Unfortunately this concept is still obscure to many. The exciting aspect is that once we are past the initial stage of change, we can begin thriving in unimaginable ways. Just think of the possibilities of global synergy. They are boundless!

Our task, in the meantime, is to strengthen the integrity of communities within communities so that faith in the goodness of life can be restored. Faith should be nurtured in all levels of community so that the world can be molded into a more healing place. It begins in the smallest community of all, the family.

Faith in the Family

Young families of today, more than ever before, must reinforce their children with faith in themselves and in the goodness of humankind. It takes effort because television, the Internet, and movies bring life's crudities into our homes as never before. Paradoxically, the opportunity for renewing our faith in humankind has never been greater. The computer can be a crayon, a pen, a library and a connection with a friend on the other side of the world. It assists people of all ages to put thoughts into words. Some learning disabilities vanish with the stroke of the keyboard. Students can learn at their own pace. Computers will never replace schools, but they will give lagging educational systems the boost they need to succeed. As we wake up and participate in the positive uses of this and other revolutionary tools, we will add a whole new dimension to world peace. What a way to choose life!

Each generation brings unique challenges to the world of parenting. The Western definition of what constitutes a family is changing. We have single parent families, blended families and same gender parents. These phenomena are being addressed in a haphazard fashion. The greater community responds with confusion, disdain, custody battles, foster homes and some tolerance. Adults struggle to find love and acceptance. Children do the same. Solutions are being created, but faith in the family remains dubious.

Children need a father and a mother to learn about the special qualities of their own masculinity and femininity. A culture is strengthened not by its sameness, but by its diversity. Single mothers can help balance this deficit by involving their children in youth organizations and faith communities that provide strong male role models. Single dads can do the same, making sure that the women in their children's lives are nurturing and strong. Programs such as Scouts, 4-H, Big Brothers and Sisters and Camp Fire are crucial to the future of society. As a community, we must make every attempt to provide competent mentors for our growing youth and young adults.

The power of the healthy partnered relationship must never be taken for granted. The strength of this connection is still the best model by which young children grow into faith-filled adults. Children not only need role modeling, they need a strong parental team to rebel against. It is all a part of growing up. The nest is the source of comfort and acceptance, love and forgiveness, learning and hope. When youth launch from an intact nest they learn to fly with the least amount of turbulence. If the nest breaks around the time of leave-taking, adjusting to young adulthood becomes much more difficult.

Strengthening the Nest

How then, do young couples reinforce their relationship with each other during the childbearing time? As a family expands, the coupleship is stretched by financial and emotional demands. Navigating the inevitable passage of any life stage is stressful, but the needs of young children require seemingly unlimited physical and emotional resources. A combination of faith, flexibility and support is necessary during this hectic and extraordinary time.

We learn our navigational skills by observing others. Young couples bring to their marriage competence or incompetence in this arena based largely on what went on in their own homes. How did Mom and Dad behave when Dad lost his job? Who had the faith that he would find another one? Did the nest fall apart because of this crisis or did it become stronger? Couples who believe in their abilities to cope with change do very well at creating sturdy, healthy nests. Choosing life at this stage involves working at the coupleship in a variety of ways.

Parenting classes teach partners how to understand the tasks they face with each new challenge. Children have so much to learn. Knowing how to teach these little ones, guide them, encourage them and set limits for them is a full time job. Couples who take classes together benefit themselves as well as the family. Knowledgeable parents have a more relaxed attitude toward each other.

Most young couples need some type of coaching to help them manage the internal and external pressures of their relationship. Professional counseling teaches the skills to handle situations that cannot even be imagined during the premarital stage. Who could project, let alone plan for, the whole family having the flu? One young father tells about such a time: "The only one who didn't have a temperature of 103 was the three year old and he answered all the incoming phone calls. People were confused for months."

Couple's counseling teaches several skills:

1. *negotiating while under duress*
2. *fighting fairly*
3. *getting support when there is nothing left to give each other*
4. *recapturing intimacy*

5. *listening and being heard*
6. *stopping the hurt*
7. *daily caring*

Successful parenting often needs more than faith. It needs help.

Caring does not come automatically when a young mother has walked the floor all night with a colicky baby. She will be irritable and tired. Partners now are learning the benefits of sharing the infant caregiving. Young fathers are assuming a more active role in parenting by changing diapers, giving baths and walking the floor. Couples with small children feel exhausted much of the time. There is little physical or emotional reserve left for each other. Sometimes little ones need to be carted off to Grandma's for a few hours just so Mom can get some rest. Until children reach the age of six years, fatigue is the major stress factor for young parents. Have faith. It gets easier.

Sexual intimacy often suffers during this busy stage. New mothers may encounter ambivalence in their own sexuality following the birthing process. New fathers often feel an added sense of anxiety and responsibility that can interfere with their sexual expression.

When couples realize that these are normal reactions they can begin to work at resolving them. The withdrawn partner needs careful wooing by the other. One young mother describes how her spouse did this for her after the birth of each child. "Sex was always important to us, but after giving birth I had no sexual desire for James whatsoever. I was so bonded with the baby that all my emotions were centered there. Rather than be offended by this, James set out to seduce me as if we were courting. He brought me flowers and arranged a special night of love for us, complete with champagne and caviar. He was a sensitive caring lover and without his gentle touch our marriage would have been in serious trouble." Sandra had lost her faith that this part of their relationship could be restored. James took charge of retrieving their future. This is choosing life.

Young couples often band together forming a close-knit community of shared social life and support. The quality of this life stage is so precious to the future of humanity that systems in society should do everything they can to protect and support it. If Moms must work outside the home they need adequate maternity leave. Bringing another life into the world requires a big adjustment. The definition of adequate means at least six weeks prior to the delivery and six months following it. Private and public industry can make this possible. Working mothers in Sweden have a one-year leave of absence following birthing. In order to have faith in the evolution of a strong society we must nurture our youngest members and their parents.

Unfortunately, much of Western society does little to nurture young families. Instead, there are strong negative forces at work that pressure couples to behave in certain ways. Media proclaims, "Be slim, be slick. Buy this, buy that." Government says, "Pay us and we will protect you from harm." Academia stresses "Get a higher education and you will be healthy, wealthy and wise." Health Care emphasizes "Your life depends on us because we cure people." Religion says "Do as I say, overlook what I do." The extended family says, "Raise the children our way." We turn to these systems for guidance. We lose faith in them when their leaders behave in ways that are contrary to our beliefs about integrity and growth. Parents must make discriminating choices for their families. They must participate in choosing life. No one will do it for them.

Couples need time for themselves away from the nest. They should have a weekly date night and engage in conversation concerning the things that interested them before the children arrived. They must continue to court each other throughout the years and have faith that their love will grow. They should support each other's dreams and set life goals. Strong marriages that are the most likely to succeed have partners who are participants rather than bystanders. They do not fear diversity, differences or difficulties.

The family is still the best crucible of protection against an unconscious world. It remains healthy when its members are steeped in a strong faith. Given adequate support and resources, young parents will maintain faith in themselves and in each other. They will believe in their ability to weather any of life's storms that threaten their solidarity. Young couples who choose life teach their young to have faith in God and the natural rhythms of life. When their children leave home they can move into their next stage with a sense of adventure and hope.

Faith Has Wings

Jane knew she was dying. Cancer had consumed her lungs so that she could barely breathe. Oxygen had earned its place as her best friend. She was riddled with fear and so was Joe, her spouse of thirty-eight years.

Jane had grown up in a struggling Armenian/American family with five children. The father was absent much of the time and died when the youngest was seven. Jane, age twelve, was left to shoulder much of the responsibility for her siblings' basic needs. She liked to work and took pride in her abilities to sew, cook, clean and parent. There was nothing she would not try. When little Jenny needed a coat Jane said, "I can do that," and so she did. Difficulties did not bother her because of her profound faith in herself.

Jane's faith stemmed from her ability to imagine solutions and get help. She was fear-less. It was as if her thoughts concealed a movie camera with endless film. When she realized there was no hand-me-down coat for Jenny, she envisioned herself cutting, sewing, measuring, adjusting, and finally, Jenny running off to school in her warm new garment. She could always make things happen. But that was long ago, and now she was dying. The pictures would not come. There was only a fear-filled blackness.

Jane departed this life one crisp wintry day when Joe stepped out for a cup of coffee. It was as if his fear of losing her was all that kept her there. For Joe, it was a time of tragic mourning. Tender nurses and clergy attempted to console him but their words rang hollow. Over and over he repeated, "I wish I had their faith, their belief in a soul that lives." His suffering remained intense for many years. He was a realist, a rational thinker, a good person who, in time, lost all his bitterness and much of his yearning. He never loved again. Faith requires wings, and wings are necessary for every passage.

Faith-fostered Beliefs

We have faith in what we believe to be true. There is a paradox in this because beliefs are not always truths. They represent a reference point based on prior learning. Our experiences and our rules for living color them. In order to choose life we must examine our beliefs about the aspects of life that are most important to us. Failing to do so will cause us to continue along the path of life having placed our faith in falsehoods. If we believe that work is good, we get a job. If we believe that work is stupid, we sabotage every job we take.

Societies both enhance and rebuke our individual beliefs. Western society has a strong work ethos. People who do not work are viewed as inferior by those who do. The work ethos is a learned behavior, which is passed down to us from our parents or other authority figures. It is supported by our culture for a number of healthy reasons.

Work is a vehicle for choosing life when it has monetary, intellectual and creative rewards. These meet our survival needs but the remuneration needn't end here. We nourish our human spirits when we give some of our working skills away. Because work is such an important part of choosing life, we should do everything we can to participate in good work. We must shape a working environment that is healthy for us and our co-workers. It is important to have faith in what we do and use work to further our hopes and dreams.

We have choice in the type and amount of work we do. Working too much is just as unhealthy as working too little. For some, the work ethos becomes a god, a pathway toward self-satisfaction and identity.

Believing that work is a panacea for gratification precludes choosing life. When we direct the bulk of our energies toward work there is little remaining for other creative endeavors such as relationships, artistic expression and spiritual growth. Healthy societies are made up of individuals with verve for life and a healthy verve for work. When we choose life we choose both. What are your beliefs about work, play, rest, family and money? Think about them and ask yourself, "Are these the kind of beliefs that deserve my faith?" Choose those that are and replace the rest. Be a participant! Choose life!

Faith and the Senses

We believe what our senses have told us in the past, and too often this is where we place our faith. We forget that we cycle our way through life and that we change. Binding to life primarily through our senses causes us to relinquish our full capability for experience. It doesn't allow us to choose life.

There is more to life than that which we can see, feel, smell, hear and taste. We cannot see wind but we see what it moves. We feel it on our bodies. Sensory memories stem from embodied experiences. They are true to the extent of those experiences.

What happens when we take a leap, or even a baby step, by faith? Let's say that since childhood you have hated the taste of liver. You go out on a date with a very likable person and what does she order? Liver! When the meal arrives she admires it, smells its aroma and offers you a bite. What do you do now? All your sensory memory recalls a dislike for liver. Your body recoils at the thought. Do you open to the possibility of a new experience, or do you remain locked in the old one? This is a choice. You can choose life here, having faith in the prospect of a pleasing new taste. When we anchor ourselves to sensory memory we miss much that life can offer. We are bystanders, not participants.

Activating Thoughts

Renee Descartes, a 19th century philosopher is renowned for his statement, "I think, therefore I am." "How absurd," we say, "how arrogant to elevate the intellect to the highest point of human capability. Does this mean that in order to choose life we have to be smart? And where does this leave faith in the scheme of things? Is faith an intelligent choice, or is it the choice of the weak and impractical?"

Try looking at it this way. Consider our thoughts to be energetic projectiles that launch an impulse toward action. Physical law demonstrates that an impulse once initiated strives to complete itself. Once we activate a thought we automatically create a goal. Our conscious and subconscious minds are programmed to complete that impulse. If you are thinking about having a new refrigerator, suddenly refrigerators appear to be everywhere. They leap at you from billboards. You hear them advertised on the car radio, and one is delivered next door while you are mowing your lawn.

There is a well-worn adage about this very subject that says: *Beware of what you ask for, you may get it.* All this means is that a natural process of awareness causes us to focus our attention. When we focus our attention, our intention is activated. Much of the time this is a haphazard process whereby our minds latch onto what is being thrust toward our senses.

Supposing you are stopped at a red light. You begin thinking about warm, sunny beaches. Suddenly you realize that you have been daydreaming while your eyes stare at a huge billboard strategically placed above the traffic light. It reads, "Sunnyvale straight ahead, Bermuda to the right." Our present intention had nothing to do with Bermuda. We were wondering how to deal with our increasingly difficult boss and wishing he would just go away. Before we know what has happened, the thought of a warm sandy beach enters our mind. Our intention shifts. A billboard has distracted us. Our problem with the boss fades as a vacationing scheme begins to unfold. "Let's see ... the Visa card still has some credit." Perhaps

Descartes was right. Our thoughts, be they random or intended, will lead us into action.

If we had really taken charge of our conscious mind that morning, would the outcome have been different? We all do a certain amount of daydreaming. However, many times we wander aimlessly through life making pathetic choices. Imagine what we could bring toward ourselves with conscious effort! When we get clear on our intention, or goal, our conscious and subconscious minds will focus in that direction. Even while we sleep the mind will wrestle with ways to bring this goal toward us. We can have faith in this phenomenon of our human psyche.

Good and Evil

Thought management plays a major role in our choices about living. We order our thoughts based on our beliefs. Two people who each believe in justice will conduct their thinking about it in very different ways. Both want the same outcome: that the wrong be somehow made right. One will believe in creating justice through punishment, removal from society and death. Undergirding this position is the belief that people should pay for their crimes and that many criminals cannot change. The other may believe that the whole of society is responsible for the actions of the few, and that moneys allocated for the cause of justice should be directed toward prevention. They have faith in humankind's ability for healing and rehabilitation. Each has faith in the system that fosters his or her particular belief.

When we have a basic belief in doing what is right, our thoughts, actions and influence will follow it. The struggle for change comes with our thinking. What if we are wrong? What if this belief that we have so much faith in, does more harm than good?

As conscious participants in life, it is our choice to wrestle with good and evil, with right and wrong. Answers do not always come easily. Sometimes, like Jacob and the angel, we struggle all night long, holding onto our belief because it is grounded in our relationship with God. At other times we gather with friends and debate an issue. Grappling with the not so obvious choices of right and wrong is part of choosing life. Decisions based on an intention for the greatest good of all can be painful in the moment. We must have faith in our beliefs, act on them with conviction, and examine them carefully from time to time. This is the conscious living of a participant, one who chooses life.

Faith in the Goodness of Humankind

Participants in living have a responsibility to maintain their faith in human goodness. This has never been more critical than in our present era of the information explosion. We learn about the crimes of the world every day. Our attention is drawn to the negative news-making headlines, whether we seek them or not. Choosing life requires a strong resolve to do what we can about these situations and focus on positive thoughts and actions.

If people are going to change, locating and calling out their goodness is key to initiating this process. Believing that each individual is intrinsically good bears out a faith in humanity. This faith gives us the power to refrain from retaliation when someone hurts us. This is not to say we should stand idly by and allow others to abuse us. We must never be abused. We also must not retaliate and become an abuser because of it.

I have observed police officers standing firm in the face of some of the most objectionable human behavior imaginable. You can see their jaws clench and their backs stiffen as they move in with direct resolve to restrain but not retaliate. They are consciously controlling their natural instincts to quash the behavior with an equally inhuman act. If there is any possibility of unearthing the goodness in this individual, it will begin right here, with the choice of the arresting officers.

Demonstrating our faith in the goodness and strength of another is one of the best choices we make. It is a participant's choice. It is never too late to master it. Initially we learn to have faith in ourselves when our parents and other authority figures respect this goodness in us, calling it out rather than squashing it every time we try their patience.

The next grand opportunity to learn about faith is in parenting our own very young children. Punishment is used as a consequence for undesirable behavior. Toddlers are often angry and frustrated and as a result they act out their feelings. The action message to give an angry toddler is "I understand you are mad. What you are doing is not a good thing. Our rule is 'No spitting!' You will have a time out for one minute. Take this piece of paper and spit on it until I tell you to stop. I know you can do it, and you'll never spit at anybody again."

We demonstrate four important concepts and experiences in this manner:

1. *our understanding of the child's feelings*
2. *our tolerance for the child's humanness*
3. *our conviction about the lesson to be learned*
4. *our faith in the child's ability to change a behavior.*

Children who grow up around adults who have faith in all four of these concepts have little difficulty learning how to choose life.

Faith and Negativity

Have you ever had an inner sense about a situation? You just knew something was amiss but you didn't know what it was? Such instinctual responses can help or hinder our ability to choose life. Let us consider one of humankind's strongest instinctual drives—FEAR.

Our earliest teachers in life profoundly influence our instinctual development. They amplify our sense for danger when they repeatedly send us the message, "Don't fall! Don't hurt yourself! Beware, life is dangerous." Such admonitions may render an unhealthy perspective that says, "Peril lurks around every corner."

How very different this is from the child who receives positive messages: "Life is good. Take precautions against the evils of the world and then forget about them." This child sees life filled with possibilities and knows that something good can happen at any moment.

Both responses are faith based. One puts faith in danger and the other in opportunity. Participants who choose to choose life need to develop their instincts and intuition, their sense of knowing. As adults we initiate this process by managing our secondary reaction to the instinct of fear. Life's bystanders are fraught with fear because they see no alternatives. They do not know they have a choice.

Much of what we fear is imagined. We can spend a substantial part of our lives fearing what might happen. In doing so we miss the very opportunities we need to resolve our problems. When we are fearful we are on guard, maintaining a constant state of readiness for self-preservation.

A fear-based state of arousal exists in our bodies when we believe that the world is an inherently bad place. We think that we will be ready when it happens, prepared to act quickly, always on guard. We hone our observational skills by paying close attention to negative possibilities. Just like the awareness for refrigerators, negative possibilities appear everywhere: in the glance of a stranger, in the mistake at the check-out stand, in the person walking toward us.

Just as the positive in life begets the positive, so does the negative beget the negative. Fear is a negative force. Others sense it in us but will not recognize it for what it is. Fear-based behavior masquerades as arrogance, intimidation and isolation. It says, "Stay away." This contrary mirroring of our self-image further reinforces our belief that the world is indeed an unsafe, unlivable place.

Skillful paranoia has its place in society. People who possess it make great prosecutors, detectives and troubleshooters. Each of us needs some sense of impending danger otherwise we relinquish a natural instinct that has helped preserve humankind. On a day-to-day basis, however, a suspicious nature raises havoc with interpersonal relationships.

It is never too late to re-order our attitudes by listening for the positive. We might as well acknowledge that there is good and evil in the world. We can also accept our abilities to choose between them. Once they are initiated in a consistent pattern, positive directives will eventually replace the original negative ones. When we seek the positive we develop an instinct for creative solutions. This allows us to see the good side of all situations, even the disappointing ones.

Faith and Intimacy

Faith fosters intimacy but fear forbids it. If we suspect that the dry cleaner is going to cheat us, she will probably miscount our change in her favor. Trust empowers faith. If we trust the dry cleaner's honesty, she will relax in our presence and have no difficulty counting the change correctly. Integrity empowers trust. If we do not know the dry cleaner, but assume her to be an honorable person, she will probably behave honorably toward us. What happens if we trust and believe in the other person's honor, and they cheat us anyway? We choose another dry cleaner.

To be trustworthy, and therefore faithworthy, we must be honest with ourselves and with each other. This is accomplished by touching our fear-filled beliefs, acknowledging them and then creating a process to release them. In so doing we open a place within ourselves for new beliefs that have a positive focus. With practice we then re-order our behavior toward faith-filled opportunities.

While we are practicing these behaviors, people respond to us differently, coming toward us with trust and positive regard. This reinforces in us that we are good, and so we become bathed in goodness. Now we see it everywhere. Our world becomes a gentler, more healing place. We know it. Our relationships improve, and we begin to enjoy life in an entirely expanded dimension.

Choosing life means experiencing a full range of life's good and evil opportunities while being able to discriminate between the two. We do not need to fear evil. We just need to recognize it and choose to set it aside.

Relinquishing fear-based attitudes and behaviors makes room in our personalities for the development of compassion. Compassion is the key ingredient for interpersonal relationships. When we can look beyond our own needs to the needs of another, we open the door for intimacy. Have faith in your ability to become a compassionate participant in life. Begin by confronting your fears, naming them, containing them and lastly, letting them go.

Faith and Sensitivity

Some people embrace a strongly developed instinct for knowing when others are suffering. We call this empathy. People who empathize do more than sympathize. They can actually perceive another's experience in their own body. Their autonomic nervous system responds to what is happening to the other person just as if it is happening to them. We name them "sensitive" and ask ourselves, "Why do they go through life like that? It's their own fault for feeling so much."

Participants in life feel a great deal. They have a high degree of awareness about everything around them. They live as if everything affects everything else. Highly sensitive people often find life difficult, but they also find it exceedingly rich. They have to work at strengthening their own boundaries so they don't get swept away by other people's troubles. They have faith in what they know, and what they know is what they feel. Acting on faith is easy for them because they place so much trust in their own instincts.

Sensitive people bring caring to us in great measure. Sometimes they annoy us for knowing better than we do what is good for us. Each of us is born with this capacity for sensitivity. Some, more than others, have the body composition and hormone structure to be highly developed in it. In addition to our given genetic inheritance, we develop our instinctual sensitivity in two ways.

Firstly, sensitive children, born of sensitive parents, will be raised in an environment that reveres and fosters this quality. These children are especially susceptible to the beauty and pain in all of their relationships. They have little tolerance for harshness, sarcasm, hostility or conflict, and they suffer a great deal because of it. They need consistent validation of their goodness and their gift of perception.

When they receive this, they navigate childhood and adolescence with a tremendous appreciation for many facets of life. If they can hold onto this empathic quality until adulthood, they make noteworthy contributions for the good of humankind. They frequently enter the types of professions that care for people.

Without strong and perceptive parenting, however, these children feel buffeted about by unkind words and other people's pain. They can become the abused victims of society, helpless to assert themselves. Without some powerful redirection they are destined to a life of shattered faith, devoid of dreams.

Secondly, children raised in damaging environments encounter so much pain they come to know its every characteristic. Rather than hardening themselves for protection, they can become extraordinarily soft and malleable. They learn to be chameleons, pleasing the adults in their lives in order to be acceptable. Their faith in adults is shattered, but their faith in manipulation is strong. They also assume the posture of life's victims. We say, "They wear their hearts on their sleeves."

Consistent mentoring and guidance heals victim behavior. Healed victims make excellent parents and caregivers. They dedicate their lives to service because they understand pain so clearly and can teach others how to overcome it without bitterness or victimization. Their life goal is to relieve suffering. It is as important to them as breathing. Their powerful faith in the recovery process is based on embodied experience.

Becoming a conscious participant requires faith. The sensitive, caregiving people, so often rejected as weak and impractical, are the glue that holds a society together. Choose to have them in your life. Choose to become one. Choose life.

Faith in the Body

The human body is wondrously made. It is an intricate, complex system, a collection of pulsating forms. Yet to most of us it remains a complete mystery. We treat it like a cheap car, giving it oil when it coughs and gasoline when it stops. We have high expectations for its performance, and when it disorganizes we label it *in-valid,* or *invalid.* We place the responsibility for its care on others while taking little time getting to know it, let alone meeting its needs.

This peculiar relationship of faithless disrespect and high demands robs us of our full vitality. In order to choose life, and be an active participant in it, we must establish a healthy association with our physical bodies, one of nurturance along with an interminable faith in its dynamic potential. We begin by acknowledging that it exists not in isolation but in exquisite partnership with the mental, spiritual and emotional aspects of our totality. This is the holistic view of ourselves, the one that leads to 'a full life, rich in experience and healthy relationships.

Understanding ourselves holistically leads to a faith-filled style of self-care and personal involvement. Health and illness are naturally occurring phenomenon within the human condition. When each is allowed, wholeness exists. Many of us take health for granted, blaming the body when it lets us down. By adjusting our thinking about each of these innate aspects of life we gain opportunities for a new relationship with ourselves, one filled with positive regard. We can eliminate the victim mentality of pagan times which suggested that we are as marionettes, managed by a god-puppeteer. We can abolish the mechanistic view of the human body introduced during the scientific revolution of the 19th century.

Each of these influences colors our thinking about health and illness. They propose a fatalistic attitude about healing that invalidates the spiritual and emotional aspects of the human system. We are not puppets, nor are we mechanical! The human mind and spirit can overcome any physical pain or disorganization. Each of us knows of people who, when faced with tremendous physical disability, discover ways to be vitally alive.

The more recent Systems Theory, when applied to living systems, helps us understand the relationships that exist within the human body. It also renders a holistic view of life in context with the external environment. Even though individuals have the same number of parts we are each unique. The distinct interplay of the parts results in a distinguishing personality and human spirit. Moreover, we both influence and are influenced by our environment.

The information explosion of the 1980s and 1990s has accelerated a global interchange of medical knowledge. The West is just beginning to see value in Eastern medical philosophy. Global health is possible when all aspects of all systems are embraced. Our faith in this concept will make us well.

Western thought surmises that when illness occurs, the body has made a mistake. It should then be taken to the body shop, fixed up, wound up and sent on its way. Why not stop and consider that the body might be wisely requesting a rest or an attitude adjustment? Western diagnosis targets the ailing part in isolation from the rest of the system. Why not examine how the individual is choosing life? Western treatment involves the eradication of physical symptoms with minimal attention paid to mental, emotional or spiritual needs. Why not determine if the person is ailing in these areas as well? Where is the faith in our natural ability to heal?

We must stop treating individuals like clocks. Even in the world of clocks we have advanced well beyond the wind-up variety. Surely humans deserve as fitting a promotion in issues of health and illness!

Illness is not a failed mechanism. Illness is disorganization. It requires reorganization of the whole system, not just the symptomatic body part. Placing all our faith in only the physical sets us up for personal failure. Why not seek healing as well as curing? What we gain spiritually and mentally from physical illness can be life-enriching. These disorganizing experiences can bring with them wonderful new relationships and acts of personal heroism. Even when the outcome is death, individuals can achieve personal and spiritual greatness.

Currently, most of our focus on the human body targets its external appearance. We eat and exercise in order to *look* a certain way rather than to *be* a certain way. If we are to appreciate and nurture our wholeness we must pay attention to our internal milieu, the pulsating systems within us.

From a purely physical standpoint, internal functioning requires that the dynamic nature of the cells be supported. Cells need to work, to ingest and to eliminate. Life sustaining nutrients and gases influence this pulsating function. Food nourishes the body chemically and the soul aesthetically. We can learn to heed the aliveness in food, developing our tastes and expanding our relationships around the eating experience. Food plays a vital role in health and well-being. It is also significant in the treatment of illness. It was Hippocrates who said, "Let thy food be thy medicine, and thy medicine be thy food." We lose faith in our body when it disappoints us, when it does not look or behave as we would like it to. Much of the time it is we who disappoint the body.

What goes on within the movement between the parts is every bit as important as the movement of the parts themselves. An example is the quality of tissue fluid that bathes each structure, creating a chemically suitable environment for pulsation and exchange. How do we support our tissue fluid? By replenishing it with liquid and essential nutrients.

We lose approximately sixty ounces of fluid each day through normal elimination by way of perspiration, exhalation, urine and feces. This fluid must be replaced with water, non-dehydrating beverages, fruit and raw vegetables. Many liquids that we ingest do not support the tissue fluid, they actually deplete it. These include caffeinated beverages, teas that contain bromine and sodium carbonated drinks. A person needs increased hydration to offset the effects of these dehydrating beverages. We have faith in our cars if we give them gasoline and oil. We can have faith in our bodies if we give them nourishing foods and fluids.

There is a high degree of nonequilibrium always working within the system so that the body can adapt to changes in its environment. Most people living in Los Angeles will, over time, adapt to air pollution. However, a newcomer invariably experiences burning eyes and constricted breathing.

Basic to life is the pumping action of the cells initiated by the rhythm of breathing. For an adult, normal breathing rhythm involves approximately eighteen inhalations and exhalations per minute. Cells that are grouped together for a specific function such as respiration will pulsate in their unique rhythm. The heart beats at approximately seventy-two contractions per minute. The cerebral spinal fluid pulses at fourteen beats per minute. The large intestine undulates past a given point at around twenty-three waves per minute. When any of these systems disorganizes and the rhythms are disrupted, disease can occur. Disease relates to multiple factors, not just one type of germ.

No organism as complex as the human organism can function indefinitely. When we support the body's cell integrity nutritionally and emotionally, we facilitate maximum cell regeneration. It is seemingly a miracle that pancreas cells die and replace themselves in twenty-four hours. White blood cells replace themselves in ten days and ninety-eight percent of the brain protein replaces itself every three to four weeks. Yet amidst all of this dying and rebirthing we each maintain our same physical identity. As the physical body ages, the spiritual, mental and emotional bodies grow wiser. When we have faith in ourselves we make sure this happens. We choose life.

An eighty-three year old woman, receiving chemotherapy for bone cancer, was confined to her home and her wheelchair. She had always been a social person and the constraints of her disease hampered her spirit more than her body. Adding to her confinement was her son's fear that she would fall and break one of her fragile bones. His well-meaning attention irritated her more than the chemotherapy's side effects.

One bright day she propelled herself out to the porch of her mobile home. She thought of her friends gathering at the clubhouse for a game of Bunko[1] and all the fun they would have. Undaunted by her son's admonitions, she straightened her wig, and standing precariously at the top of the steps, shoved her wheelchair over the edge. Then she sat down on the top step and painstakingly scooted down the rest. At the bottom, she retrieved her wheelchair and made off to the clubhouse. Her astonished but delighted friends asked how she did it. Her eyes twinkled as she replied, "I had faith in my behind not in my beware." Our bodies will do what we ask of them. When we choose life we choose to make healthy requests of these marvelous creations.

Learning to Fly

This is an ideal day for flying. Put on your helmet, adjust your radar, and feel the power of us cheering you on. Your thoughts have already taken off, so give wings to the rest of yourself and soar into the faith-filled unknown.

It is never too late to develop our faith. We must continually listen to our hunches, feelings, intuition and instincts, in other words, our consciousness that goes beyond the senses. We know about a gentle breeze even though we cannot see, smell, touch, taste or hear it. It moves us. Faith is like that. We are moved by it. This can be difficult for those of us who believe that the correct way to choose life is by moving and shaking it.

When we are bound to life by our senses we relinquish our full capacity for experience. Some of our greatest satisfactions emerge when we act from faith. If we believe in something, a cause, a purpose or a service, we instinctively create a path for its success.

There are times when we need to lean on another person's faith because ours is weak. We grow when we make a conscious choice to reach out rather than stubbornly insist that our way is the only way.

We strengthen our own faith when we validate another person's courage and capabilities. By speaking the words, "I have faith in you," we endorse the whole concept of faith. These words can be the first step to helping someone create his or her own path for choosing life.

Have faith in yourselves and in others. Adjust to the changes life brings. Absolutely expect the world to become a better place because of your personal integrity and hope. Believe in God and an orderly universe. Resist isolation. Most of what we learn about choosing life we learn through our relationships with others. Cherish all of yours.

Join a community of faith for support and for supporting. Know that you are as one pearl in a whole necklace and that you carry within you the plan for the entire necklace. Have faith in your holism. Choose it, and be it. In your brightest moments and darkest hours choose life so that you may soar with its infinite possibilities.

Chapter Seven
Confession

Always do what is right.

I n Judaism, each new year (Rosh HaShana) calls for Ten Days of Awe climaxing with the Day of Atonement. At the end of each day, Jews acknowledge sins they have committed against God and humankind. It is a reflective time when individuals pray for themselves and for each other. Their appeal seeks God's justice and God's mercy. Each person stands alone before God, but in community as well.

Avinu malkeinu, chatanu l'fanecha.

> *Our Father, Our King, we have sinned against You.*

Avinu Malkeinu, chamol aleinu v'al olaleinu v'tapenu.

> *Our Father, Our King, have pity for us and for our children.*

Avinu Malkeinu, kaleh dever v'cherev v'ra'av mealeinu.

> *Our Father, Our King, rid us of pestilence, sword, famine, captivity, sin, and destruction.*

Avinu malkeinu, kaley chl tsar unmastin mealeinu.

> *Our Father, Our King, rid us of tyrants.*

Avinu maleinu, kotvenu b'sefer chayin tovim, chadesh aleinu shanah tovah.

> *Our Father, Our King, inscribe us in the Book of Life, and grant us a blessed New Year.*[1]

As the Day of Atonement ends, Jews savor restoration into the Book of Life. Once more they have consciously chosen to examine their faults, confess them and ask not for punishment but for ablution. In this way they have chosen life.

Each great religion offers some formal method for contemplative contrition and soul cleansing. Eastern philosophy theorizes that the human soul births again and again as it seeks to create a state of benevolent human integrity. The goal is to get it right, living each day with full intention for physical, mental, spiritual and emotional wellness, the pathway to oneness with God. Christian belief also teaches the renunciation of evil and care for the soul. Christians are called to make peace with their brothers and sisters before communing with them. Throughout recorded history both religious and secular writings portray humans making mistakes and attempting to heal from them. Confession is part of this healing process. It precedes at-one-ment.

Burdens in the Body

So often it is during the course of physical pain when we attend to our mental, emotional and spiritual discomfort. It is tempting to avoid the warning signals of sadness, lethargy or conflict. We evade confessing our guilt or fears to ourselves and to others, especially to health professionals. We carry debts and grudges around as if they are meaningless. The mind may forget, but the body remembers.

Such costly delays create tremendous burdens in the body. Emotional symptoms are indicators of physical disorganization. Physical dis-ease involves emotional dis-order. The human spirit yearns to be free of such expensive baggage. In order to heal one aspect, we must bring healing to the others, for they are inseparable. Disorganization is multi-dimensional and so is healing. Confession is a necessary ingredient in the reorganizing equation. In order to bring the body, mind, spirit and emotions back into balance we utilize our thoughts, words and deeds.

The Healing Sequence

To choose life we must seek ways to unburden our bodies. Living does not have to be a struggle. Rather than wasting energy on obligations, why not create opportunities and possibilities? We can learn how to clear out the guilt surrounding our mistakes. We can transform our dislikes for other people to a neutral co-existence. We can abolish opinions that prevent us from enjoying life. There are times when we must remind ourselves of the importance of honesty: shunning the pretense of living out other people's expectations. People who choose life occasionally sit in a proverbial mud puddle. At first we may not enjoy it, but after a while we can learn to value being transparent. We all look the same when we're muddy.

Harboring a grudge against another person inflicts a burden upon the human system that slows its functioning. It is an internalized secret, a piece of information stored in the memory of both the intellect and the physical body. It takes up space. We can ignore it for a time, pushing it away from current consciousness. As with any unfinished business, it eventually resurfaces, flooding the system with harmful chemicals. These chemicals eat the lining of our stomachs and contract the muscles in our chests. They narrow our blood vessels and increase the motility of our intestines. Any memory shrouded in painful feelings yearns for healing. Only the person immersed in a state of unremitting denial can continue such suppression. Even so, the burden remains in the body, operating from the subconscious mind and reeking havoc at a cellular level.

We can heal the most grievous of burdens when we realize that healing is a process and not an event. This process has three stages. Each stage takes its own time. Change does not occur with a snap of the fingers.

1) First we embrace the information about the burden fully, acknowledging its every detail. This involves naming and describing the situation to ourselves a bit at a time until there is nothing secretive at large.

2) Next we talk about it with another person, a carefully selected confidant. As we speak aloud, nuances of truth will emerge to challenge us. Something may not feel right. The stomach may gurgle. The head may ache. The chest may tighten. The breath may quicken. A friend can help us, draw us out, and put words into our mouths that elude us. Sometimes we must retreat again into the first stage, taking even more time to search for deeper truth. We must embrace all options fully, exposing them to light. If we do not, small remnants will thrive in the darkness to emerge again, bigger than before. Complete healing requires complete cleansing.

3) The last stage involves action. Our burden begins to lift the moment we set our intention toward its release. It concludes with our making amends to ourselves and to others.

In the healing sequence, action has a twofold purpose: 1) to make a public statement, and, 2) to offer reconciliation. Making a public statement requires courage and humility, which is notably more difficult than confessing to ourselves. It can be made aloud, directly to the principals or in writing. The public statement contains a description of the issue as it is viewed at the time. It should be factual, blame-free, shame-free and guilt-free.

The offer of reconciliation proposes that because the relationship is valued, we wish to make amends. Ask the person what type of amends would help him or her to heal. Discuss the request and devise an action plan to bring this to fruition.

Robert and Sheila came to a miserable impasse in their marriage. Sheila had an affair. Robert knew they were having problems, but the betrayal caught him completely off guard. Healing seemed elusive but not impossible. Both Robert and Sheila wanted to save the marriage.

Through several months of separation and couple's counseling, Sheila arrived at the second action stage. When she asked Robert what would bring him healing, he said, "The thing that would help me the most would be to walk into church on Sunday morning, hand in hand, and renew our vows." Sheila was stunned. There were so many actions she was prepared to offer: a romantic weekend, taking a part-time job to help with bills and even having another child. She agreed to his request. It fulfilled both requirements of the public statement and the amends. It was what *he* needed. The burden of the affair lifted from them both after that act.

Once we have released a burden we need to create some new behaviors. For Sheila and Robert, the new behaviors involved much more than remaining faithful to each other. Their marriage lacked honesty and openness. Robert worked very long hours and had buried himself beneath pressures of time and money. With help they were able to find ways to manage both of these resources more effectively.

We can rejoice in new insights and the gifts that come from a joint healing process. Not only do we gain the release of the burden from the body, we strengthen our physical, mental, emotional and spiritual anatomy.

Reactive Burdens

There are times when a burden is ours alone. We do not like something another person says or does. It bothers us. Logically it sounds small and petty so we keep it to ourselves. It continues to gnaw at us, a festering emotional sore that slowly poisons our system.

Our action in such a situation becomes the challenge of creating a nonreactive state within ourselves. Again we follow the healing sequence. First we explore all aspects of the issue: our thoughts, our ideas, our perspectives and our feelings. Next we disclose every fragment of it to a friend. Together we search for insight and any fresh shred of understanding that can shift our perspective. Lastly we take action. This might involve talking through the issue with the person who irritates us. It may mean a daily prayer for healing. It can involve writing, laughing, good deeds, or creative expression. When our clear intention is for healing we will find a pathway to it.

Careless words and neglectful behaviors will hurt others. A bland "I am sorry" will not ease such a burden. A genuine "I am sorry" will assuage it for a time, but if we continue in our thoughtless ways, such apologetic words are useless. Speaking them becomes not an action but merely an utterance.

An action response demonstrates a genuine attempt to stop the onerous behaviors and replace them with ones that show caring. Relationships thrive when individuals help each other to understand and alter even the smallest irritants. Actions really do speak louder than words.

Once we gain insight into a situation we can no longer ignore it. Newton's First Law of Physics states that "Every body persists in its state of rest or of uniform motion in a straight line unless it is compelled to change that state by forces impressed upon it." The very moment we realize we are committing any kind of mistake we can head off in a new direction. Waiting for the right time or the right words is a myth. Delay merely results in a missed opportunity. Instead, we can follow the healing sequence: own it, confess it and act on it. This frees the body from the burden. This is choosing life.

Thoughts, the Acknowledgment Phase

Acknowledging that we have a problem is the first step to solving it. Most of us don't waste much time focusing on the things *we* do that annoy others. We go about our daily business until someone hurts us or we make a mistake and hurt someone else.

When conflict arises we, at first, have a feeling about it. If we are insecure, we feel angry or afraid. If we are empathic, we feel sad. We can over-react, believing the situation to be entirely *our* fault or entirely *their* fault. Once the feelings subside we can be more objective and begin sorting the facts. It is time to start taking the problem apart with a fearless disregard for whose fault it is.

Sorting facts begins with the question, "What do I know?" Answering this is simple enough. We merely make a list of every aspect of the situation we can truthfully say is factual. The second question to ask ourselves is, "What are my hunches?" This is a little more complicated but nonetheless relatively easy. We begin these sentences with words such as "probably, could, my gut sense tells me, or maybe." These probe our intuition and are tenets to be proved or disproved. This process leads us to the next question: "What do I *not* know?" Now we are ready to acknowledge that we need more information.

The first two questions can be asked in solitude. The third requires outside advice. Our emotional undercurrent will color whom we approach. If we are afraid, we may go to sources who will give us tea and sympathy but little insight. They fully support our illogical side of the story, thereby perpetuating our denial of the truth. If we are brave enough, we will seek the truth even though we may not want to hear it. We should test our theory on our toughest critic.

Shame, guilt, and fear keep us stuck in the thinking phase. It is much easier but far less productive to ruminate over an issue. We worry, second-guess, jump to conclusions and make assumptions when we ought to be asking direct questions.

Marguerite loved red wine. She enjoyed it publicly and privately. Intellectually, she knew she drank too much. Logic told her that the amount she consumed each week must be harmful to her body. A powerful co-conspiracy of body and mind told her something else: "You can't do without the self-soothing liquid." The craving won.

She drank moderately for many years and might have continued in this fashion had she not developed a thyroid condition. Her physician suspected the drinking but did not confront her about it. As he began running lab tests to diagnose her ailment he included blood alcohol levels. This revealed the fact that the woman was more than a social drinker, she was an alcohol abuser. When confronted with the test results she continued denying the degree of her drinking: the lab had made a mistake, the doctor was inept, the doctor was doing something illegal. Eventually the woman experienced an acute medical crisis that brought her to the brink of death. Her entire family now became involved. She was forced to confess. From that point, she began her healing actions of recovery.

There are times when withheld thoughts seem to take on a life of their own. They dominate the mind, won't be still, refuse repression and pop up inappropriately.

Graham's zest for living came to an abrupt halt the day Lilly said, "I don't love you any more, and I'm ending our relationship." He could not stop thinking about her. She ruled his nightly dreams and every waking moment. He felt so betrayed, so abandoned. He was terribly angry with her for leaving him. Lurking underneath his emotional turmoil was a sea of self-doubt. If only he was a stronger man. If only he was a more accomplished pianist. If only, if only....

His obsessive thinking persisted beyond the usual amount of time of normal grieving. In desperation he decided to seek professional help. During the painful process of disclosure he began confessing his own self-hatred and shame. This went on for several weeks. Suddenly, as if a switch had been tripped, he had said enough. He was ready for action. What could he do beyond words? With some gentle prodding he explored a full range of possibilities. Some outrageous ideas poured out of his mouth, and hearing them, his sense of humor returned.

Finally, he hit upon one that was harmful neither to himself nor his beloved. He would allow himself the indulgence of thinking about her while he was showering. When he shut off the faucet, he would shut off the thoughts. If they popped into his head at any other time he would summon his strong will and tell them they must wait.

As water poured over his anguished body, Graham gave his beloved undivided attention. He recalled the scent of her hair and the touch of her skin. He heard her laugh and he watched her cry. He relived their parting. He remembered his failures, his hurt and his anger. Eventually, the pain diminished and the thoughts faded. It became increasingly difficult to bring the memories back into focus. They seemed to lose their vitality, as if to say, "If we can't run freely through your mind whenever we wish, we just won't bother."

Later, Graham talked about this agonizing time in his life. "I was afraid I would die from the pain," he said. "Then there were times when my thoughts and feelings hurt so much I was afraid I *wouldn't* die. But suicide was never an option for me. I knew I could get beyond this, I just didn't know how. When I began to fully disclose, to confess my insecurities, I could begin to feel the healing. The idea about the showers was great and I was strong enough by then to access my will power. Interesting, how thoughts and feelings will fade. But for a while there, I had some really intense showers."

Spiritual Tuning

The human spirit needs dissecting and self-examination from time to time. Our primary relationship is the one we have with ourselves. In order to know ourselves better, and so heal ourselves, we must pay attention to thoughts and actions that choke the human spirit. Burdens in the body distort the anatomy of the human spirit. Confessing to ourselves is like taking a spiritual cathartic. Here are some self-confessions that put healing into motion:

- *I used poor judgment.*
- *I said biting, sarcastic words.*
- *I wished the person would fail.*
- *I wished the person would die or just go away.*
- *I inflicted physical pain on another.*
- *I inflicted verbal pain on another.*

· *I acted carelessly.*

· *I behaved badly.*

· *I looked away when I should have looked more closely.*

· *I judged another too quickly.*

· *I whined and complained without acting.*

· *I excused my part in it.*

· *I overestimated my tolerance and ability to listen.*

When we open up and objectively look at these undesirable behaviors, we have taken the first step toward change. We know that people who are afraid to speak up during the day grind their teeth at night. We know that those who avoid confrontation are prone to immune suppression diseases. We know that patients who accept defeat die from cancer sooner than those who fight for life. That which we deny, resist or reject will surely persist somewhere within our system. Once we accept realness we can begin making realistic choices. We choose life!

Words, the Verbal Phase

When thoughts interfere with living it is time to release them. This *letting out* is a key element in the healing process of confession. We express our thoughts through words and body expressions. This stage has several pitfalls.

Sometimes we selectively choose a confessor who will defend us without regard to reality. This, of course, validates our illogical position: "I have done no wrong." At other times we talk endlessly to anyone who will listen, with no intention of taking action. This is called *complaining*. Sometimes we confess to everyone except the person with whom we have disagreement. This we call *avoidance*.

Stanley wanted to surprise his wife, Helen, and prove to her, once and for all, that he was a "man of the world." Although he had never played the stock market, the lure of quick and easy money seduced him into investing. He envisioned doubling, perhaps quadrupling, their retirement fund in a matter of days. The speed of creating this additional income would surely please his wife and impress her with his bravado. After all, it had taken her years to accumulate the pitiful reserve. She was the salaried one in the partnership. Stanley could never hold onto money for very long, even though he had always worked.

Without her knowledge, Stanley borrowed from their meager savings and bought the stock. In a matter of days it plummeted, becoming totally worthless. When Helen learned of this, she responded with anger and pain. Stanley admitted his error. He felt ashamed. He acknowledged to himself his poor judgment, his foolish whim and his ill-advised action that erased years of her hard work. He sulked for days, refusing to talk. He wasn't sure what he felt, but it wasn't good.

It didn't occur to Stanley to hold Helen in his arms and grieve with her. Instead, he began talking to their neighbors about how angry she was. They could understand it, they said.

Stanley continued to whine and complain. What began as disclosure transitioned to dumping. The neighbors drifted away, unwilling to listen or challenge his attitude any longer. Eventually, Helen's emotions abated and their lives returned to their usual pace. She forgave his foolishness. After all, he'd done similar things in the past and would probably do them again. She accepted that he could not, would not, change his behavior.

Stanley carried the incident with him for years, like a tarnished coin. Later, as he recounted this event, the salient element he recalled was her anger. There was no choosing of life here. The choice was avoidance.

Verbal Disclosure

The verbal disclosure aspect of the healing sequence is often the most frightening. Shameful feelings stand in the way of confession. We don't want to admit our stupidity or errant judgment. We look around and compare ourselves to others, thinking, "She was able to handle it, why can't I?" Well, why didn't you? Would you have acted differently with greater knowledge and experience? Perhaps.

This crucial verbal stage plays a vital role in the healing sequence. By confessing our thought or impulse out loud to ourselves, and then to another, we acknowledge its existence. From this point of acknowledgment we have greater choice in our subsequent actions. There is a healing rhythm in acknowledging and accepting, confessing and releasing.

Confessor

Confession requires a confessor, someone who will listen to our silliest fears and gut-wrenching guilt. [2] We can admit anything to such a friend, knowing our own embarrassment will not be amplified. We will be neither shamed nor punished.

Everyone needs one such friend in order to choose life. This friend provides an emotionally free space for us to talk without fear of judgment. Sometimes this friend is a partner, spouse, relative, pastor, spiritual director or professional therapist. The category doesn't matter, it is our ability to freely connect with the other person that counts. This is the kind of friend who tells you when there is lettuce between your front teeth or your zipper is open. There is no shame, blame, guilt or fear of humiliation with this friend. We can be honest and vulnerable about our biggest mistakes. This person helps us choose life, not so much by giving advice, as by listening unconditionally when we feel stuck.

There are times when our lives seem confused and devoid of direction. Yet, as logical as it seems, reaching out to another can be difficult. Our internal dialogue goes something like this: "I'd really like some help with this. Who could I ask? Mary? No, she's too busy, I don't want to bother her. Joe? No, he's been through a similar situation, but I didn't see him asking anybody for help. Joan? No, she's worse off than I am; who am I to complain?" Don't listen to this stoic voice. It takes us away from that which we need most: a confessor.

Confessors like to listen. They feel honored to have that role. They choose it. Many times a confessor will simply stand beside us and help us to choose life, to take a risk and do what is right.

Friends and Acquaintances

Choosing life involves choosing our friends. It is up to us to seek out and create many friendships in order to meet our many needs. This sounds self-centered, and it is, but not in a self-serving way. The goal is to learn about ourselves through these relationships and to enjoy the mutual process of understanding and caring.

Much of what we learn about choosing life we learn through relationships. Our primary job is to continuously seek our highest hopes, our deepest integrity and our greatest capacity to give and receive love. In learning how to relate to others, we are forced to stretch and grow into greater dimensions of compassion, understanding, and tolerance. In doing so we can become the biggest, the fullest and the richest. We are fully choosing life.

Friends and acquaintances help us to grow because they reflect who we are and who we are not. In our formative years we mimic the behavior of others as we attempt to define ourselves. This natural phenomenon reaches peak intensity during the teen years when our eyes open to the frailties of our parents. In the midst of great pain, we reject our parents as role models and their definition of who we should be. Then with one last great surge of growing up, we take on the behaviors of peers and idols. Alas, these do not quite fit either, and we are hurled from the nest, a featherless fledgling of dubious self-identity.

As a young adult we begin to settle into that self-definition. We resent others who try to tell us what to do or how we should act. We can, however, pay attention to the way people respond to us. It really is very simple. When people avoid us it is because we are toxic. When people surround us, we know we are lovable. Even the choice to be toxic or lovable is our own.

It is from this pool of friendships that we draw our mentors, confidants and confessors. People raised in families with close relationships count on their friends, even their most casual associates, to listen to their troubles at the drop of a hat. In close families there is always someone to listen, to read our body language and ask, "What's the matter?"

On the other hand, people raised in rigid families are cautious with disclosure. It is an unfamiliar behavior to them. They have difficulty sharing fears and feelings because it seems an imposition.

Regardless of how we were raised, we all belong to the same human species and, as such, are not perfect in our physical, mental or spiritual anatomy. We make errors in judgment every day. Our mistakes range from the merest slip of the tongue to the most skillfully calculated crime. It is mythical to believe we will perfect ourselves. A realistic goal is to perfect our skills at dealing with our mistakes: thoughtfully examining each one, consciously confessing it to ourselves and another person, then moving on to take appropriate remedial action. When we have faith in this healing sequence, we choose life.

Words Can Interrupt Action

There are many occasions when we know better, and still we act mistakenly. When these occasions become habitual, we call them *addictions*. Habits and addictions meet a need for self-soothing that is stronger than knowledge.

Knowledge is a combination of concepts stored in the intellect and physical experiences stored in the body. The physical body tries to overpower the spiritual and mental bodies in moments of duress. It craves comforting. The drive for self-soothing is an impulse well on its way to completion. Once the thought, "I need a chocolate bar," initiates, we automatically proceed along the familiar path toward satisfaction. We buy the chocolate bar and immediately devour it. The thought quickly progressed to an action: an unhealthy action!

What happens when we insert a middle step into this process? In an attempt to interrupt the impulse, we call on our confidant. "Mary, I need a chocolate bar." Now we have created a verbal expression of our need. Not only have we opened ourselves for feedback from Mary, we actually hear our own words spoken aloud.

Words become much too powerful when they are allowed to run around inside our heads with nothing but the strong will to control them. However, when they come out of our mouths, and travel into our ears, they reach a different part of the brain. The auditory interpretation process has its own unique sensors. We don't believe everything we hear, let alone leap to act on it. The same thought, "I need a chocolate bar," confessed to another person can now be followed by a healthy action.

Deeds, the Action Phase

Healing from our mistakes nurtures the whole organism. It frees us up to become participants in life rather than bystanders. Each phase of the healing sequence has its possibilities, its rewards and its perils. After scrutinizing a problem and talking about it to another person we are ready to take action. The action phase requires just as much care as the thinking and confessing phases.

Danger lies in rushing to re-cover from our mistakes. We might try to smother them with activities, gifts or apologies. We want to cover the deed with other deeds, quickly, so it can be forgotten. Sometimes we say a little prayer: "Forgive me Father for I have sinned. Tell me what to do right now so I don't have to feel this uneasiness. Let me get on with my life. I'll hurry and make things up to her so she will know I'm really a good person. I'll meet her for coffee and say, 'I'm sorry.' That will do it."

We are cure-seekers, not that there is anything wrong with cure. Everyone desires it. What we don't realize is that we fail to stretch our human potential by limiting ourselves only to cure. We err when we believe that re-covery is an end result. It layers our pain and we can get just as stuck in the covering as the curing. Healing, on the other hand, can occur without cure. It will even transcend death. The physical body may die, but the richness of mending a relationship is eternal.

Healing in a relationship is more than an independent act of confession and contrition. It involves patience and a genuine attempt to have our apology received. What do we do when it is not? How can we give our gift of closure when the wound remains open? We assuredly cannot continue the layering.

There are times when we must begin the entire healing sequence again, and sometimes, again. Each time we uncover a layer of shameful thoughts or mistaken beliefs, we get closer to truth. With truth comes healing. With healing there is release from pain, be it physical, mental or spiritual. Once the thoughts are formed and our words confessed, the action will logically follow.

In order for actions to be accepted, they must be given with no recompense in mind. They should be agreeable to the one we have harmed. It does no good to buy someone a fur coat if she needs shoes. Much of the healing aspect of any action comes with the conversation that goes with it. "Is there anything at all that I can do to help you feel better? Is there anything you need?" In itself, this is an act of healing, for it requires attentive listening.

Taking the time to really hear someone express their need is a humbling gesture. Get down on your knees if you have to. There is nothing more healing than a genuine offer of submission. When we have harmed another, choosing meekness demonstrates strength. It demonstrates choosing life.

Obstacles

There are several reasons why healing may not occur. Perhaps we have not spent enough time in reflective thinking and verbal disclosure. True healing is, after all, holistic. It means embracing our mistake in all of its gore: acknowledging it, thinking about it, ruminating over it, stepping back from it and sorting out its logical and illogical parts. It means talking about it with others, and in particular with our confidant. Again, we reflect on it: think out loud about it, inviting critique and comments, including the most direct and difficult to hear.

When this process is done thoroughly it leads us to the root of the issue. We suddenly acquire a clarity that is impossible to miss. We are filled with an excitement that arises out of learning something new. It might be that we want to talk about the whole experience with the one we have harmed, trusting that she will accept it. We then may want to ask for her understanding and forgiveness. We can let her see what we have come to learn and how we will be able to behave differently in the future. The only way our amends can be wholly received is if we have first expended the effort to heal ourselves.

We are choosing life in this moment. We are ready to move on. We must be patient and empathic with the person we have harmed. She requires time to receive our apology. We may need to have more than one conversation with her. We also must recognize when we have said and done enough. In relationship we strive for a two-dimensional deliverance, theirs and ours. Once we have touched the root of the issue, accepted it and processed it, we go forward whether our apology is received or not.

Fear Inter-feres

Why are we so afraid of truth? Perhaps it stems from early childhood. The human brain is not fully developed until age twelve or thirteen. When our brain tissue is younger than this age it does not have the functional ability to fully anticipate consequences. Young children sometime behave as if they understand more than they do, when in fact they are mimicking the adults around them.

Children develop their own internal parenting as their brain grows. Telling a three-month-old baby "No" when he drops his rattle doesn't work. His brain does not yet make the connection between clutching something and letting it go. He is not even aware he is holding a rattle. Closing the fist around an object is a reflex, not a conscious action.

A six-month-old baby will drop a handful of food over the edge of the highchair and watch it miraculously land on the floor. Telling this baby "No" doesn't work either. Baby is busy discovering how to open his hand and let go of the food. It's a natural progression in his brain and muscular coordination.

Telling an eighteen-month-old "No" when she throws her peas at you may work. Her act is deliberate and includes more than learning how to throw an object. She is either bored with eating or wants attention. At this age children are old enough to understand the meaning of "No" and the body language that comes with it. Toddlers generally like to please adults and may respond to a "No" if it is couched with a firm touch and some affection. If they continue throwing peas after saying "No" a second time it is better to address the boredom by switching from peas to cereal or moving the child to another activity.

Eventually children stop throwing their food. With parental guidance they develop an internal censoring device that prevents it. They use this important tool throughout their lives to control impulses. This parenting of the self is qualified by early authority figures and modified by succeeding ones. If the parent slaps the child and threatens future slaps for throwing peas, the child will indeed learn to stop the behavior. He will learn other things too: that he is a bad child, he is not understood, and there are times when he is not loved. His world makes no sense to him. More importantly, he learns to fear rather than trust his teachers.

If the parent says a firm, "No," and removes either the peas or the child, the inner parenting device does not become infused with the element of fear. From the same situation, he can be learning that throwing peas is not a good idea, that his parent understands his need to move onto a different activity, and that he is lovable. As the teachers, parents make these important choices.

Fear aborts logic. We just do not reason things out when our mind skips forward to the potential punishment for something we have done. What happens instead is that we divert our energies into avoiding the penalty. This is a learned response to making mistakes. Our entire legal and justice systems are the result of humans resisting the truth about their inappropriate behaviors. They have never learned how to confess. When children are punished for telling the truth, why, as adults, would they see the value in it?

Truth and Confession

Confession allows us to move toward the truth. Sometimes a truth is so painful we shove it away. This is not a bad thing but a human thing. We can only experience so much of our learning at one time. Learning is both conceptual and experiential. Past victories and humiliations influence our interpretation of current situations. We build files of reference in our entire system based upon such experiences. These files contain truth, as we know it. We believe it, and we behave based on these beliefs. Determining what is really true often requires that we check our reality with another person.

Truth and confession are building blocks of an integrated human being and a healthy society. They are the stuff from which integrity is made. Is Western society allowing them to be forgotten elements in human behavior? Are we fooling ourselves into believing we teach justice only through punishment?

What we need are people who can tell the difference between right and wrong. We place more emphasis on the consequences of bad behavior than we do on the teaching of desirable behavior. This emphasis begins early in life in a myriad of ways: hitting, shaming and withholding love. Adolescents and young adults are educated to believe, "I can do anything I want as long as I don't get caught. If I do get caught, I just lie consistently. I never admit to anything. If I'm incarcerated, I just wait it out and then I continue as before." When we don't develop an inner parent with an integrated sense of justice, we don't have any need to practice confession. We don't know right from wrong.

Confession without remorse and a behavior change is a hollow exercise. Being able to admit one's mistakes and confess to them is a learned behavior. It takes a teacher that can impart a message saying, "Yes indeed, you didn't do what is right, but I have faith in you. I know you are a good person, and you can do better. That one behavior of yours has got to go. Now, let's talk about ways to eliminate it."

In the above example, the focus is not on the punishment but on the teaching of what is right. Nor is shaming involved: "You embarrass me with your behavior. You know better too." A better way to say it would be, "A lot of people will lose respect for you when you do that. Your friends may think it's cool, but where will they be when you are sitting in Juvenile Hall?"

Words that blame might be, "I've told you over and over again, but you just don't get it!" A better way to say it would be, "We've talked about this before haven't we? What part of it don't you understand?"

Words that withhold love are perhaps the cruelest of all because they attack the human spirit. "You disgust me. Why did you turn out to be such a loser?" When we teach our youngsters right from wrong as best we can, we don't have to say much to them. Most of the time, "Always do what is right" will suffice.

Confessing our mistakes in a truthful manner requires a healthy degree of self-esteem. We gain self-esteem from our teachers and mentors who point out our successes as well as our failures. When both are acknowledged in a matter-of-fact manner, they become the building blocks of a good foundation.

Walls

Walls separate us from ourselves, from each other and from God. Confession allows us to melt our walls even though others may maintain theirs. When we make a mistake, an automatic wall surrounds the most vulnerable part of ourselves: the human spirit. We know that words spoken cannot be retracted. We know that deeds done cannot be undone. We know other things too—that we make mistakes and that we inflict pain.

If we don't pursue healing, each of these become burdens that will harm our body, mind and spirit. Where walls separate and diminish, confession empowers and expands. It clears a path to healing and shows us that we have a future after all.

In the aftermath of horrific pain there can still be opportunities for choice. There is the choice of being honest with ourselves. There is the choice of processing the pain with another person. There is also the choice of confessing our insights, feelings and longings to the person we have wronged or who has wronged us. Another choice is reaching for a higher purpose as the result of a painful event.

When Worlds Collide

There are rare occasions when worlds collide that test our human resources to the limit. When two masked men forced their way into Sophia's apartment, the foremost thought she had was for six-month-old Michael in the adjacent room. "All I ask is that he be safe," she prayed. And he was.

The burglars came and went as the child slept. Sophia was so relieved that her first inclination was to tell no one. But then another thought entered her mind. Would they stop here? Of course not. They were experts. In less than ten minutes they had bound and gagged her, then deftly removed her money, jewelry and small appliances. They were gone as silently as they had come. She could hardly believe it had happened. But here she sat, with hands tied behind her, looking at the front door where she had planned to install a deadbolt next week.

As she wrestled her wrists to freedom, she wrestled with decision. "What should I do?" She glanced at the bedroom door. "They know what I look like. Will they come back? They said they would. Maybe they'll hurt Michael and me next time. And who else might they hurt?" The thought of old Mrs. Ryan living alone downstairs rushed into her mind.

She called the police. The burglars were picked up and booked into jail. They were wanted for a number of crimes, including aggravated assault. Sophia identified them in the line-up. Her baby was safe and justice was done. Two higher purposes were achieved within the context of this frightening event.

Healthy Choices

When we choose life we choose confession as a healthy and respected practice. It fosters integrity in the confessee and tolerance in the confessor. Being able to confess goes hand in hand with over-riding our fear of external consequences and internal shame. It is also an act of courage. It shapes integrated individuals who in turn will shape an integrated society.

Each painful life experience holds unlimited opportunities for intimacy and growth. Even when the person we have wronged cannot accept our genuine remorse, we can still recover. When we acknowledge our mistake, confess it to the one we have harmed, and take an appropriate action, the burden will leave our body. We will heal.

When we embrace that which we dislike, get to know it and accept its realness, we can sometimes achieve greatness. We can confess our fears and frailties to ourselves but we don't rest there. We go on to confess them to others, and then take action. In Sophia's situation, her motherly instincts were powerful. Protecting her baby and others gave her a higher purpose. It helped her to conserve integrity and transcend fear.

Confession allows us to touch the sacred in others and ourselves in the following ways:

- *Dislodging walls and interjecting intimacy*
- *Bridging thoughts and actions*
- *Fostering understanding and forgiveness*

· *Restoring us to wholeness and to the Book of Life*
· *Guiding us to do what's right.*

You can begin today by creating some quiet presence. Begin thinking of the people who have hurt you and those whom you have hurt. Sift through your friends and acquaintances until you find the right person who will act as your confessor. Talk over each situation with care. Decide on an action to take for each one. Feel the burdens lift and your wholeness return. You have just chosen life. Good for you!

An eye for an eye makes both of us blind.

F orgiveness is one of the most misunderstood and difficult aspects of choosing life. In our list of human miseries, being hurt by another person is probably near the top. It seems so unfair! Isn't life difficult enough without someone else coming along and messing it up? We make our own mistakes, so why should we have to suffer at the hands of another? But suffer we do, each in our own way. Paradoxically, learning to forgive is not about suffering. It is about healing.

The human system is a remarkable one, capable of healing from some of the most heinous crimes. Even the sharpest edges of emotional pain will soften with time and intention. Healing on a spiritual level is greater than forgetting. It requires a willingness to go the distance, with forgiveness as the goal.

Spiritual healing is multifaceted. Perhaps this is why the word forgiveness has several meanings. Derived from the Old English word, *forgifan*, it means:

· *Give pardon for insult committed toward or directed toward.*

· *Give up resentment against the offender.*

· *Give up any claim for restitution in behalf of the insult.*

· *Make room for human error, be it either lenient or harsh.*

· *Make peace.*

Forgiveness is a process and not an event. It is a journey as well as a destination. If we forgive before we have leaned into our pain, felt it, questioned it, raged at it and learned from it, then we violate our soul which is the deepest part of ourselves. Anything less is an empty exercise deprived of embodied experience.

Healing comes through feeling our emotions so much that our joints ache. The body cries. It retches and vomits. Old physical injuries resurrect themselves, driving us to the chiropractor or the massage therapist. Gentle hands relax the mind, soothe the body and help to heal the spirit.

After the body rights itself, tears of angry hurt can begin to flow. It takes a river of them to cleanse the toxic waste created by emotional pain. For some, tears gush like water from a broken pipe. For others, they trickle out over time. There is no right or wrong way to cry. Tears cleanse the present, making room for a hope-filled future. The event is in the past.

Eventually, the emotional body empties, leaving the reasoning mind to search for meaning. Anger and sorrow persist within the system. As long as they are permitted to be there, the grieving process continues. Eventually, they will decrease and subside. Channeling anger through revenge stops the healing process. Attempting to inflict punishment sidetracks the grieving. Seeking restitution through the justice system merely bandages the wound for a time. There are no short cuts when it comes to spiritual healing.

Justice

There is a grave misconception that justice heals. When justice is done, it brings some sense of relief to the victim. Blame has been appropriately placed. There is public witness to the deed and to the perpetrator. However, this is not the end of the story. Justice doesn't lead us to forgiveness, and it is forgiving that allows us to heal.

In many situations there is no justice. Crimes go unsolved. Medical practitioners err in judgement and people die. Offenders deny wrong-doing and are set free. In certain circumstances we are left to *swallow* reality without as much as an "I'm sorry." These times stretch us to the extreme. Intentional acts, where one human assails another, are some of the most difficult to comprehend. Our belief in the goodness of humankind is jolted by the realization that there is, indeed, evil within the human condition, and now it is on our doorstep.

Paradoxically, for those who believe in God, there is a factor that balances human injustice. It is called *grace.* Grace is a gift from God that is always available to us. It is an encompassing love that gives us the opportunity to relinquish any burden when it becomes too heavy. Grace is not an excuse for inactivity on our part. It allows us to surrender our grip on an issue, knowing that God will render justice but not vengeance.

The opposite of forgiving is condemning. Condemnation and punishment are both judicial matters. They will not erase the scars created by an intentional assault on our property or us. However, forgiveness will. Acceptance, healing, and forgiving ultimately lead to peace within ourselves.

Whole Person Healing

From a physical perspective, we know that retaining a grudge poisons the body. Thoughts of revenge and hatred throw the human autonomic system into a state of pugilistic readiness. Our countenance wears a scowl. We are curt and short-tempered. Few escape our rancor. An aroused metabolism robs precious nutrients from the rest of our cells. As long as we remain in this mode we are bystanders to life. Our physical, mental, emotional and spiritual self is compromised. This is not choosing life. It is choosing death.

In the early days of civilization, village shamans and medicine women enacted the combined role of healer and peacemaker. An attitude of revenge would not be tolerated for long. The culprit would be promptly rebuked for disrupting the good of the village.

A residue from unresolved emotional conflict sits in the cells of the body. Debts, crimes, and other inhumane infractions stress the system, often to the point of disorganization or illness. When a member of the village became ill, the shaman would visit and ask many questions: "Who angers you?" "To whom are you indebted?" or "What law have you broken?" The shaman would mediate the dispute before treating any chronic physical symptoms. At the close of mediation, each party would participate in a spiritual cleansing through music, dance and prayer.

Sound reasoning dictated this practice. Much of the time, the physical symptoms disappeared right along with the dispute. Punishment was swiftly dispensed so that the community could get on with living. This no-nonsense judiciary approach addressed a basic human need: to forgive and be forgiven. This is choosing life.

Forgiveness is a state of being, not a deed. We have within us the capacity to fully heal from the most bestial atrocities. It is always difficult to imagine how severe emotional pain can fade into a mere memory. This fact is one of the great miracles of the human system. We are designed to heal. It requires time, an intention to do so, a certain degree of spiritual strength and adequate support.

Healing Variables

Sometimes we want to forgive another who has hurt us, but we just can't. The hurt won't go away. The human organism is a complex one, influenced by many variables in body composition, social influence and the ability to use what we learn. Understanding some of them can help us accept our unique healing needs.

Distinctive behaviors accompany our constitutionality. People with linear, ectomorphic bodies have a large skin surface per overall volume.

They are acutely sensitive to their environment, and healing for them takes on some particular characteristics. Their heightened sensitivity causes them to pull back from pain. They need quiet and withdrawal in order to re-group. They like to analyze a situation and will scrutinize every aspect of it. They must come to peace intellectually before they can move on.

People with endomorphic, rounded bodies, feel their emotional pain in a physical way. Their bodies have large visceral organs in relation to their overall physical volume. Emotional pain is gut wrenching for them, and they spend a long time feeling hurt and angry. Unlike the Ectomorph, they do not like to be alone with their suffering. Expressing their feelings helps them to heal.

Those who have a mesomorphic, or muscular body, cope with emotional pain through vigorous physical activity. You will find them scrubbing the ceilings, cleaning out closets or rototilling the garden. They use externalized work to exorcise the grief from their system. Often they exhaust themselves in the process.

Another aspect of healing has to do with our ego strength or sense of ourselves. When we suffer childhood trauma, either through the repeated insults of abuse, neglect or over-indulgence, we have a weakened ability to heal. Unresolved emotional pain lurks in the system waiting for an opportunity to strike. The victim in us rises up, begging to be noticed. We react inappropriately, becoming depressed, enraged or anxious over a trivial offense.

When this happens, there is no restitution great enough to satisfy us. Old wounds continue to fester. In order to forgive someone in the present, we first must forgive our offenders from the past. This can be a long and difficult journey, one traveled beside trusted friends and compassionate professionals.

Childhood trauma does not always leave emotional scars. There are variables within the types of stress that assault the system. A young child may have a tantrum when refused a piece of candy. This will not leave an emotional scar. If the same young child is rigidly forced to eat everything at every meal, a pattern of weakness forms. It is one of yearning. It says, "Please stop force-feeding me. Just love me and accept me as I am." The child is an adult-in-the-making. She will carry this yearning in her body, mind and spirit until it can be erased and replaced with healthy acceptance.

The variables of trauma include severity, duration, repetition and frequency. In addition, humans are more susceptible to scarring early in the phase of any developmental stage. Fresh surges of growth occur in the neonate, infant, toddler, young child, pre-adolescent, adolescent, young adult, middle adult and older adult. Trauma permanently wounds the system when it occurs often enough, is severe enough, lasts long enough and occurs in the beginning of a growth stage.

Once the learning for each stage is well under way, the system can withstand more insult. However, even in the latter half of a stage, if pain or neglect is inflicted often enough, long enough, and with sufficient intensity, it will leave scars. It becomes ingrained within the very cells of the system.

Children believe that the conflict surrounding them is their fault. They feel it in their bodies. Their stomachs ache, their heads hurt, and their appetites go out of control. Small children, usually have no difficulty forgiving their perpetrators. But, once they are old enough to be capable of abstract thought, resentment infuses their systems. It is carried forward into adult life where it pollutes every relationship.

Choosing life involves confronting these traumas and healing their scars. The emotional wounds must be opened and cleansed. Spiritual healing and inner peace comes later. They include some degree of understanding and compassion for the offender. This is forgiveness.

If we cannot seem to heal, we may direct our wrath toward others, as if they are to blame. We rage and demand, never slowing our battle with life. We are harsh and driven, perfectionistic and unrealistic. Holding onto the pain becomes a way of life. This is slavery, an addiction to pain, unforgiving pain. How does one begin to reorganize from such a tortured bias?

Forgiveness is not a single act, but a complex process of growth. It is not something we do **to** or **for** someone else. There are several stages to forgiveness, none of which can be omitted. Eventually, when we no longer feel our pain, we are at peace. When we are at peace we are able to give up any claim for restitution in behalf of the insult. The first stage of healing is one of grief.

Grief

We have the right to hurt when people do or say things against us. The degree of pain we experience varies from person to person and crime to crime. It is important that we not compare ourselves with others when we are hurting. Each of us has our own embodied experience of pain. We react to it uniquely. There are no rules, only our own realities. If someone says to you, "You shouldn't feel like that," ignore it. You are you, and you feel this way! Period!

Our first response to being hurt is one of shock. We can hardly take it in. One moment we are fine and then WHAM, our whole life changes. Once reality begins to take over, we react instinctively. Sometimes we stay frozen, paralyzed and unable to do anything at all. At other times we attack the attacker. This may be totally unrealistic. I've seen a small child throw himself at a bully, twice his size, who teased his little sister. We may turn and run the other way as fast as we can. We do each of these acts without thinking. Danger is at hand, and our automated response devices take over.

When we are no longer in peril, our physical body begins discharging tension. We shake. We cry. Our teeth rattle with cold. Our noses run and turn blue. Sometimes the bowel or bladder may spontaneously empty. These are self-correcting measures that follow shock. Blood begins to shunt from the extremities and heart to the rest of the system. Our core has preserved our safety. Now it relaxes, and the entire system begins to reorganize.

Denial

One way of dealing with hurt inflicted by another is to avoid dealing with it at all. Some people say, "I won't go there. I refuse to even think about it. If I do, they win and I will not let that happen." This example engages a very strong will power and it is extremely effective. (It is also rarely done well.) In cases of physical illness, people with the highest rates of remission are those who absolutely refuse to believe they are ill.

Others reject the situation out of fear. Many of us will fall into this category. It is nothing to be ashamed of, but it needs redemption. When we are afraid to experience the feelings, we expend huge amounts of energy keeping them at bay. We get very busy, or bury ourselves in a work project. Sometimes we cover the feelings with drugs. Healing eludes the fearful. Failing to confront the pain and the reality of what happened suppresses the human spirit. Right or wrong, justified or not, feelings are feelings, and we have them. When left unexpressed, they have a way of slinking back into our behavior when we least expect it. Sneak attacks of anger spoil our ability to have friends and other healthy relationships. In the same way, sneak attacks of sadness will cause us to feel victimized by ordinary events.

Confrontation

We need to let people know when they have hurt us. It empowers us to do so. Learning how to confront someone without arousing his or her defensiveness is simply learning a skill. There are two popular methods. One is the *Paradox*, the other is the *I Message*.

The Paradox is especially effective in business or professional settings. It leaves emotion entirely out of the equation. Preparation includes a careful sifting of the facts. This is perhaps the most difficult aspect of the process.

In order to employ the Paradox you must identify two pieces of information: the other person's unwanted action and the desired action. This paradox is the crux of the confrontation. You should hone each piece into simple, factual language. When the time is right, present them directly to the person responsible for creating change. "Mr. Anderson, when you hired me, you said that I would have every other weekend off. (The desired action.) I've worked every weekend for the past six weeks." (The unwanted action.) You have presented the paradoxical information in simple, factual language. Now, you wait for Mr. Anderson to respond.

Mr. Anderson is now responsible for figuring out the discrepancy and making a statement. If he is vague, you simply repeat the Paradox again. Keep going until you have come to a resolution you can live with. Mr. Anderson may deny saying any such thing. He may say he was in error. He may admit the discrepancy. Remember that the goal of this confrontation is to reconcile your time off. The contract can be re-negotiated. It is strictly business.

The *I* Message is an excellent way to confront within personal relationships. It requires more preparation than the Paradox, but is well worth the effort. Maintaining relationships requires work. Taking the time and making the effort to resolve differences is a necessary part of every relationship.

If you think of the I Message as a recipe, you will easily be able to remember its ingredients. There are three components. You fill in the blanks.

I feel _____
Because _____
I want _____

Identifying what we are feeling is the first component. Often we have many conflicting feelings: confused and sad, hurt and angry, scared and frustrated. We can feel manipulated and betrayed, hopeless and rejected. Keep in mind that these are your feelings. You are the expert here. Don't let anyone minimize your experience.

Other people may try to tell you that you shouldn't feel this way. What they are really saying is, "I wouldn't feel like that in this situation, so why should you?" You have to stop at this point and calmly say, "I just do, and that is why I'm talking with you about it. Can we go on?"

The second component of the I Message is a brief, factual statement of what it is the other person has said or done that brought your feelings into play. "Because you didn't call me last night when you were going to be late." Or, "Because you didn't tell me you had invited four people to dinner." These are factual statements. There is no legitimate cause for argument about either your feelings or the facts. So far, the walls of defensiveness are kept in check.

The last component is the most important and the least used. We must ask for what we want. Again, this takes some preparation. What we want emotionally may include some inappropriate actions. When we are hurt, all manner of retaliatory images pulse through our brain; from hiring a *hit* man to locking someone out of the house.

Once we've settled down emotionally, we can decide how to direct our own healing. We must assume that the other person also wants healing for the relationship. Asking for what we want gives that person something to focus on. If we leave the individual to guess what we want, he or she is sure to miss.

We also take into consideration what the other person is capable of giving us. We may ask for an apology. Perhaps we need a change in behavior. We are much more likely to get what we ask for if we follow the steps of the I Message. Venomous insults, resurrecting past issues and breaking objects are precursors to guaranteed failure. Asking for what we want should be reasonable and clearly stated. "I want you to call me if you are going to be later than midnight."

A specific request is much easier to answer than a personal attack. It calls for a *yes* or a *no*. Assume that if you get a *maybe* as a response, it is really a *no*. When you get a *no*, you can go back to the beginning with your new feeling and state the reason for it. Once again you can ask for what you want. You may not get it, but you may gain new insight into the situation and be able to see that your request is unreasonable.

The beauty of the I Message is that it allows an honest conversation to take place. If both parties hold the intention of reaching compromise and healing, it will occur. If healing is not a mutual goal, then the person who has been harmed can get on with life having stated his or her case well. This gives a tremendous boost to the human spirit.

Lifelong experience teaches us that confrontation and attack are one and the same. They are not. Employing the Paradox and the I Message helps curb the automatic wall of resistance that emerges with any confrontation. Healing and reconciliation come quickly when we don't have to tear the wall down in order to begin.

Learning to manage differences and hurts must be built into every relationship. People cannot possibly second-guess each other's needs one hundred percent of the time. Friends, partners and parents do not get up in the morning, saying, "Well, I guess I'll hurt Mary today," or, "I think I'll screw up my kid today." Most hurts are unintended.

We can work at healing our relationships by helping each other return to a state of peaceful balance. Settling our differences in a healthy way accomplishes this task. Such caring is the glue that keeps alliances strong. It makes honesty possible. We will hurt each other. No healthy relationship is exempt from human frailty. Practicing healthy confrontation is a lot more fun than asking for forgiveness. Conscious participants in living learn it well.

Asking for Forgiveness

Asking for forgiveness should never be a trivial petition. When handled with care, it can lead to complete healing for both parties. Whenever we create pain in another person, intentionally or not, we must go the distance and ask for forgiveness.

The first phase of asking is not a request at all. It is an acknowledgment. We may believe that the other person's reaction to our behavior is unjustified, but that is beside the point. He feels what he feels, and it is real for him. If we care about him, we accept his emotional state with sympathy and without judgment. Acknowledgment is necessary so that trust can be restored. It always precedes change. These words become a peace offering: "I can see how much this hurts you."

The next declaration should be "I'm sorry. I wouldn't hurt you for anything." After saying these words, you will probably have to endure an angry response. "Well, you did!" This is good. Healthy anger directed at the appropriate target (you) clears the air. Your offers of genuine remorse may now stand a chance of being heard and accepted. Say it again, this time asking for forgiveness: "I'm sorry. I don't want you to hurt. Please forgive me."

Asking for forgiveness too quickly is dishonest. It is an attempt to gloss over the pain and assuage our own guilt. Acknowledgment, sympathy, remorse, and understanding are the precursors to the question, "Can you forgive me?" When we take time to use them, we offer healing to the one we've hurt, to ourselves, and to the relationship.

Making Amends

Offers of reparation can be made at any stage of the healing process. Sometimes this is difficult to calculate. We can replace a broken window or a bent fender, but how do we make amends for another person's time and inconvenience?

Each of us has an idea of something that will make us feel better when we are suffering. Sometimes we just need to vent our frustration. In other situations we demand a huge price for our pain. When someone asks, "Is there anything at all that I can do?" it is natural to give an answer commensurate with our hurt: "You can buy me a whole new car, that's what you can do!" Such a response releases the intensity making a path for a more realistic request: "You can call the insurance company for me and help me borrow a car so I can go to work."

As time passes, and the pain lessens, it serves our healing process to facilitate closure of the discord. There is no better way to do this than by accepting an offer of making amends: "Thanks. I appreciate your offering to get me the rental car. It really helped out."

Accepting a gift of reparation signals forgiveness. The gift can be proffered at any time, but it must not be received too soon. Sincere forgiveness follows sufficient healing.

Gifts intended to repair brokenness can come in various packaging. They can be acts of kindness. They can be material in nature. When accompanied by genuine remorse they lead to forgiveness. Demonstrating an improved behavior is an absolutely potent gift. It may be the most difficult, but it guarantees restoring trust to the relationship.

Changing Our Behavior

We might as well accept the following fact: Relationships cause us to change and grow. Behaviors that annoy, and behaviors that hurt, need to be replaced with ones that show kindness and respect.

We get so much from our relationships: love, companionship, compassion and intimacy. These are priceless treasures of the heart.

They are well worth any effort we can put forth to let go of careless words and reckless deeds.

When we set our intention to change a habit, we activate a healing process. Sometimes all we have to do is make up our minds and the behavior disappears. In some situations we have to employ all our skills to help us.

There are a variety of methods we can use to trick ourselves into breaking a habit. One is repeating positive, present tense statements several times a day. "I **will** call Judy whenever I'll be home after mid-night." Another technique involves asking others to tag us when we slip. Some people find rewards and consequences to be helpful. These little disciplines are the work we do to change. Practicing them con-sciously and consistently always reaps positive rewards.

Identifying our habit, and setting our intention on releasing it, is the first phase of change. Catching ourselves after we've slipped is the second. Catching ourselves while slipping is the third. Catching our-selves before we slip is the fourth. We are almost home free at this point. Soon we will forget we even had that habit.

When we cause pain in another person, asking for forgiveness is not enough. We need to make a genuine attempt to stop our noxious behavior. Since humans usually resist change, recalling the benefits can help us:

1. *savings in time expended in doing this behavior*

2. *savings in energy expended in carrying out this behavior*

3.*savings in resources expended for this behavior*

4. *improved health and well-being for not acting this way*

5. *improved relationships that are tarnished by this behavior*

Changing builds character. It is another opportunity to choose life, and it opens the door to forgiveness.

Why Am I Always the One Who is Wrong?

We all have people in our lives who react more than others. They have unpredictable outbursts of tears or rage that catch us off guard. If this occurs within a close relationship, it bears attention and some working toward change.

Over-reactions tend to follow a pattern. John would fly into a rage whenever Susan failed to put the top on the toothpaste. After several of these explosions, she approached him about it. Wisely, she chose a time of relative calm. John couldn't explain why that little act made him so angry. Talking it through helped him curb his anger. Their compromise was an investment in two tubes of toothpaste.

Often we can trace these reactions to prior scolding by parents or teasing by siblings. Talking about it with a compassionate confident will help to erase the original pain. Once we know the root of the injury, it is just a matter of time until it heals. First comes an awareness that we are behaving inappropriately. This may be difficult to accept, for the feelings are real and profound.

It is our responsibility to do whatever we can about our unresolved past. It is not our parents' job, even though they may have been instrumental in creating our pain in the first place. It is not the work of our spouse or children. We have to do it. If we don't, others begin to tiptoe around us, never knowing when we might erupt. Our reactive behavior unfairly stresses the relationship.

If we set our intention to let go of past hurts, healing will come. We can repeat to ourselves, "This pain comes from the past. I am here now. I am adult enough to let this go." But, sometimes it is not that simple. If so, find a suitable professional and enter a therapeutic relationship to heal your unresolved emotional conflict. Asking others to tolerate our reactivity is a way of avoiding life. Choose the honest direction: choose life!

Healing Our Inhumanity

Some say, "Only God can forgive." If we think about forgiveness as an act of grace and pardon, it does seem too grandiose for mere humans. Forgiveness is difficult for us, sometimes too difficult. Unusual cruelty can break the mind as well as the human spirit. Fortunately, this is not the usual case. As humans, we have a tremendous capacity for healing. We can transcend brutality. It takes prayerful resolve and others to help us.

Willful hurt thrusts the whole system into a state of disbelief and despair. Healing comes through an intentional process that eventually leads to peace. In time, when the pain subsides, the need for restitution passes. It is also possible for feelings of compassion to replace those of hatred.

When we choose life, we want to participate with positive wholeness. Once we've been deliberately violated, we often feel less than whole. One goal of healing is to restore our belief that we are untarnished. We want to move from a violated state to one of mercy.

Mary Jo's Story

Mary Jo was a thirty-four-year-old single mother. She and her ten-year-old son, Adam, lived in a small suburban home. One frosty November morning, around 6:00 A.M., she heard a knock at the front door. Half asleep, she opened it. There was something strangely familiar about the tall, heavyset man who stood on the doorstep. The back of her neck prickled, but before she could heed the intuitive warning, he shoved her backwards into the room. She gasped and covered her mouth, not wanting to awaken Adam.

This man, where had she seen him before? Then she remembered. He was the homeless person she had given money to last week. In that moment, the freezing morning air could not compare with the chill that clutched her heart.

"What do you want?" she whispered. "I'll give you money. Let me get my purse. I know I have almost $50.⁰⁰." He grabbed her long blonde hair, jerking her five-foot tall body around. "It's not money I want," he snarled, as he grabbed her forearms, holding them with one hand. Using his teeth and free hand, he tore off a piece of tape and deftly bound her wrists. He forced her to sit as he ripped more tape and began covering her face.

"Oh, dear God," thought Mary Jo, "if only Adam doesn't wake up." "I won't resist you," she said in desperation, "if you'll promise not to hurt my son. Please, be quiet. There won't be any trouble for you. My bedroom is right in there. I'll do what you want." As he continued to tape her face she had another thought: "I have to keep my mouth open or else I won't be able to breathe, or scream if I have to. Concentrate! Concentrate!"

He grasped her once more by the hair and pushed her ahead of him into the bedroom. "God help me to be calm. Help me to stay in control so I won't be damaged. Please, don't let Adam wake up. Spare him this nightmare. Help me!" Tears welled up in her bandaged eyes as her assailant proceeded to rape her.

For a few moments after his climax he was still. "Say something, anything," screamed a voice from inside her head. What does a rapist do after his crime? He could easily kill her now. Aloud, she whispered, "Why did you tape up my face?"

"Because I hate the way women look at me, as if I'm the ugliest person on earth." His face was ugly. Acne had rendered pockmarked scars over the distorted features.

"You're not ugly," she said. "Untie me and I'll make coffee. If my son wakes up, he'll just think it's my husband who's here and he won't get up." He rolled off her and zipped up his jeans.

With trembling hands she put on a robe and got out the orange juice, pouring two glasses. "Please God, help me to act normal here." Facing him, she said, "While I make the coffee, why don't you have a shower. You can trust me. I just don't want anything to happen to my little boy."

He went into the shower, leaving the bathroom and bedroom doors open. Mary Jo made the coffee, then went to the closet, removing a Chicago Bulls football jacket. "Wear this," she said. "The neighbors will think it's my husband who's leaving. There won't be any trouble."

They sat and had coffee. She talked with him about ugliness and told him he mustn't think of himself that way. He left as abruptly as he had come. She dialed 911. The police picked him up within four blocks wearing the easily identifiable football jacket. His fingerprints were all over the orange juice glass and the coffee mug. He was wanted for murder and for raping three others, all teenage girls. Adam continued to sleep.

The District Attorney's office handled it all for her. How could she pardon her assailant for this outrage? How could she give up her anger and resentment for this offense? How could she make any allowances for his behavior, his judgement of himself or others? How could she forgive him?

Mary Jo didn't pardon his action. Could she pardon the person? She was grateful he hadn't harmed Adam. "It could have been so much worse," she argued with herself. "I'm strong. I know I will heal."

She felt some restitution when the justice system stepped in and removed him from society. The trial was grueling, but by that time she had allowed him some leniency because of his warped emotional development. "I guess a lifetime of rejection can do that to a person," she rationalized. All the while, a slow-burning ember of torment smoldered deeply within her spirit. She would wait.

In time her body repaired itself. She believed that God had answered her prayers and was with her throughout the ordeal, telling her what to say and what to do. She experienced extreme anxiety for two years. To help with her healing she engaged an experienced psychotherapist and massage therapist. The nurturing touch did much to replace the violent physical memory. Mary Jo went on with her life. After four years she arrived at a state of peace. She eventually saw her assailant as a pathetic hulk of humanity. "How can someone get like that? Surely there was no love in his life." It was this thought that made the most sense to her. It brought her comfort and, finally, forgiveness.

Finding the Positive

Within any healing process there will be a lesson, a blessing or a positive element. Once we have gone through the stages of shock, anger and sorrow, we begin to shift our focus away from the trauma. Now is the time to look for the positive. With the gentle support of another we will find it.

Healing from an ordeal such as a rape seems impossible. Yet, we are designed to reorganize and be whole. For Mary Jo, the fact that her child had been spared played a significant role in her healing. She claimed a conscious path for full recovery. Nothing less would do. She was already one of life's participants.

Mary Jo surrounded herself with healers and helpers who continually reminded her of the one positive part of her story. Daily, she offered prayers of thanksgiving to God who, she believed, had sheltered her child. This helped her resist the seduction of victimization. She let herself be angry, really angry, as long as it propelled her forward. Anger became a compelling force, allowing her to go through the trial and speak out to the world.

Finally, Mary Jo stopped being angry. Looking back over these troubled years she said, "Those two positives, Adam's safety and the lifetime jail sentence, gave me the freedom to be angry. I knew that as long as I was angry, I wouldn't get depressed. So I focused on them every day. It was worth it."

I Would Bear It for You, If I Could

Mistaken judgment, inappropriate words or actions, major and minor crimes, all come and go in a lifetime. If we are lucky, we are spared such violent offenses. Walking the healing journey with a traumatized friend can be almost as devastating as being the victim. It can take a very long time. There are no *shoulds* when it comes to letting go of emotional pain. This type of genuine support may be the best choice. Healing has no timetable.

When we hurt other people, we must offer them whatever we can with authenticity. We can accept their level of pain, refraining from minimizing it in any way. We can create a safe emotional space for them to vent their anger and hurt. We can show genuine remorse and ask for forgiveness. If they are not able to forgive us, we wait and ask again. We can make amends by inviting restitution. When all of this is done, we then stand by with respect, as they find their own path to forgiveness.

Choosing life is sometimes complicated and difficult. Whether we are seeking our own path to forgiveness, or helping another find theirs, we are doing what is right.

Attitudinal Weeding

Without a doubt, the world would be a better place with more love and forgiveness. If we learn to be more tolerant of other people's misguided actions, we will have less to forgive. Most of us waste too much time on negative words, thoughts, ideas and images. These are spiritual pollutants. While standing firm on our own integrity, we must avoid letting life's crudities weasel their way into our thinking. They keep us from choosing life.

Mike had the greenest thumb in the neighborhood. Gardening was therapy for him, and he spent several hours each weekend immersed in its soothing activities. His corporate job kept him indoors for long hours. Thankfully, his office had a huge window overlooking the treetops of a nearby park. Job stress was something he could cope with. Gwen's illness was another story.

Six months ago, Mike's wife of twenty-three years had been diagnosed with stomach cancer. It was a horrible disease. They had done everything they could think of: chemotherapy, radiation, surgery and complementary therapies. Some of the treatments seemed worse than the disease. Her strong spirit kept moving her beyond the terminal four-month sentence. Even so, the ravages of illness were taking their toll, and she grew a little weaker every day.

With sadness weighing heavily on his heart, Mike wondered how much time they had left. He looked around at the dead flowers and weeds staring back at him from the watering end of the hose. His yard was a mess. It seemed to reflect the chaotic feeling he had inside that he couldn't shake. It was taking over his life, and he didn't like it.

Just as tears of despair began stinging his eyes, he noticed something pink. The big floribunda rose bush, fading now in the shadows of late summer, had tiny emerging buds. His eyes moved around the yard noticing a bit of yellow here, a dash of purple there. The grass was full of rich, green clover. If he'd been keeping up with it, the clover would have been sprayed into oblivion by now. After all, it was a *weed*. But, weed or not, here it was, lush and green. A sudden realization exploded in his mind: "I've only been looking at the weeds. What a fool! Even the weeds and dying flowers are part of life's natural rhythm. I can make a conscious choice to see them as beautiful. I'm free!"

Tears of happiness rolled down his cheeks. A great weight lifted from his chest. "You're beautiful," he said to the yard, as he quickly rolled up the hose and rushed into the house.

Gwen sat in the big chair beside the living room window. Her pale face and frail body were bathed in sunlight. He pressed his cheek to hers. "You are so beautiful, Gwen. I've only been looking at the weeds. When I look at you now, all I see is how much we love each other. Thank you for that incredible gift. I love you so much." It was the most intimate moment they had shared in months. Rather than mourning an ending, they embraced a spiritual beginning.

Don't let dying foliage and unwanted plants shroud your vision. One tiny blossom can make up for a whole yard filled with them if we can only see it. We must not blame the weeds or the natural rhythms of life for existing. After all they are here too and they play an active role in choosing life.

Co-existing with weeds is not an impossible task. It requires tolerance. Don't be judgmental and critical of another person's weaknesses. Forgive her mistakes and imperfections. Confront her if it will help the relationship, but forgive first. Be grateful that you don't have that one particular habit to overcome. Don't you hope that others will overlook your garden variety of noxious behaviors? Choose life, and demonstrate how it is done. Grab hold of those pesky negative thoughts and replace them with something positive. In doing so you release one more aspect of bystander behavior. You are choosing life.

Forgiveness is a lens through which we see an invisible pathway waiting patiently on the other side of blinding pain. We must remember that suffering is a temporary condition, if we choose it to be. When we choose life, we obtain the help we need to transcend it! Learn how to forgive. Choose life!

Chapter Nine
Hope

Arriving is only temporary.

Hope is a chance for something better. Whether we're thinking about our next coffee break or a Christmas bonus, having something to look forward to gives us a lift. In that moment, we have a future.

Hope and optimism are accompanied by feelings of well-being, improved coping skills and attaining goals. Some of the most recent wellness research bears this out. Dr. Rick Snyder, professor and director of the Graduate Training Program in Clinical Psychology at the University of Kansas has been researching and developing *hope theory* for many years. In a six-year longitudinal study of 200 students (100 each of male and female), his research team came up with some striking results. Reliably more hope-filled students graduated than their low-hope counterparts. The high-hope students reached higher grade point averages and fewer of them dropped out of school.[1] In other studies, Snyder draws correlated conclusions for health and social challenges of children and adults.[2-5] Hope is fundamental to choosing life.

Immunilogical studies show that depression compromises the disease-fighting cells of the immune system. Cynicism, pessimism and despair are attitudes of depression. On the other hand, nerve receptors on the T-helper lymphocyte cells eagerly respond to happy, hopeful feelings. Not only do these white cells reproduce faster, their numbers increase, as do the macrophages that sweep up the debris of dead cells.

A loss of hope will often lead to unhealthy anger, although it may not be recognizable. Irritability or rage is obvious enough, but there are other angry assertions that mask hopelessness: complaining, whining and grumbling. These can become habitual. Their negativity invades our belief systems that, in turn, influence our immunity. When we believe that the world is a hopeless place, we engage in self-defeating behaviors. We feel angry and believe we are unloved. In truth, it is we who have become unlovable.

A downward spiral of self-hatred is reversible. We are designed for healing. It takes an intention to change and adequate support. That's all. Each one of us can get our futures back. We must pursue as many healthy paths as we can. Hopefulness is certainly one of them.

Control

For some, the path to a secure and hopeful future lies in controlling situations and people. This is confused with being in charge, a truly hope-filled facility. This need for control can often be traced back to inconsistencies in social development. Children are incapable of controlling their environments. They rely on adults for physical and emotional safety. Hope for their future depends on it.

When a home environment is fraught with change, laxity, rigidity or erratic emotional outbursts, children may grow up with an exaggerated need for order and predictability. They can become compulsive cleaners and organizers who have difficulty thinking if their desks are messy. They find internal comfort from external activities. Children who develop in a home where love and firm limits prevail will learn how to prioritize tasks. Straightening the desk would be low on their list of things to do.

The older we get, the more difficult it is to recognize and change our controlling behaviors. Fear drives it: fear of failure, fear of making a mistake, fear of shame or fear of embarrassment. Clinging to rules and regulations offers an external form of security. Each of us has encountered bureaucrats who make decisions based solely on policies and procedures. If a request falls outside of the rulebook, they are stumped. Envision also a father saying, "Do as I say, not as I do." The correlation between these two examples is a nonreasoning, inflexible style of figuring things out. When we are rigidly raised, we tend to follow this path into adulthood. We may choose careers with military or governmental organizational styles. Controlling works well for the head master of a boarding school, but fails miserably for the pastor of a faith community. In order to maintain an external appearance of control, the controller takes on a physical as well as attitudinal stance of assuredness.

Adopting an arrogant demeanor makes the controller appear tall and wise. The physical body reflects this false superiority by becoming rigid and stiff. Its stance says, "Don't test me," which disguises the insecurity lurking beneath the surface. It is really saying, "I can't let you know the true me. You might find out that I have weaknesses. I cannot tolerate my own imperfections. You would reject me if you found out. I would fail."

There is a sad fallacy in this line of reasoning. The controlling behavior that is created to make relationships safe is the one that destroys them. As mature adults we come to understand that attempting to control situations and people is unreasonable. If hope for our future depends on control, we are in for a very rough ride, and so are those who love us. It is not choosing life.

Taking Charge

Hope enables us to take charge. It allows us to interact with others who think and behave differently than we do. Hope-filled relationships are those where the participants learn how to agree to disagree. This can only happen if they both give up the need for control. Each can have strong opinions and beliefs. What they relinquish is the drive to convert the other person's point of view. This creates a safe environment for vigorous discussion and debate. It is choosing life.

Real take-charge power comes through listening and responding, then listening and responding some more. We don't have to know it all. In fact, we don't have to know very much. All we need is a willingness to find out and to learn from our mistakes.

When challenges arise, and we are taken aback by them, the participant in life says, "I have arrived at an impasse. I don't see the pathway through to the other side as yet. I am afraid because I am wandering around in the unfamiliar. It is temporary. I hold onto the hope that someone will rescue me because I will extend my hand. I have faith. In the meantime, what can I do about this? I'll begin by taking an inventory of my assets." Hope allows us to ride the waves of challenge and despair, knowing they are temporary. Each will yield to a new opportunity. Riding these waves lets us know we are alive and choosing life.

Hope is an Attitude

There is an old folk story about the elders of a rural parish who were struggling with the concept of *grace through suffering*. "Certainly," one argued, "the idea of grace fills us with hope if we can believe it. Can it be possible that God loves us so much, we are forgiven before we fail?"

"How can this be?" said another. "Isn't bad luck a punishment for wrong-doing?"

A third elder sat bolt upright, "Do you mean, the only way to achieve God's grace is through suffering?"

As the discussion moved into its third week, the oldest of the elders came up with a suggestion: "Let's talk with Brother Jones and his wife.

They always seem so calm, but tragedy has surely been their lot."

"Yes," said one, "didn't they lose their crop two years ago because of the flood?"

"And" said another, "didn't their boy break his leg trying to rescue the lambs in that flood?"

"And," said a third, "didn't their barn burn last spring?"

All agreed that the Jones family claimed more than their share of suffering. At the same time, they came to church each Sunday and seemed so filled with grace.

So, the elders traveled the dirt road to the Jones farm where they were warmly received and invited to sit by the fire. After enjoying their fill of strong tea and hot muffins, they settled into a contented silence. Seizing the moment, the senior elder cleared his throat while assuming a pose of respectful deference. "Brother Jones," he began, "we've come to ask you a rather personal but very important question." The other elders nodded in encouraging agreement. Mr. and Mrs. Jones looked attentive. "What we want to know is, since you've all suffered so much, how is it that you have no anger towards God? How can you be so calm, so filled with grace?" Brother Jones looked at his wife. She looked back at him. Then they smiled at the elders and said in unison, "But we're not suffering!"

People who live hopeful lives learn to grieve fully, then pick up the broken pieces of the present and mold them into a future. What the elders learned that day sent them back to pursue God's word in search of hope. They realized that they had been looking for truth through a veil of despair. The Jones family had clearly discovered grace by looking at their misfortunes through a window of hope. They had chosen life.

Bolts From the Blue

Life will present us with inevitable *bolts from the blue.* At first, we are stunned. This is normal. Assuming we will never experience such a blow is irrational. Believing we cannot heal from it is also unsound. With adequate support, we can heal from any situation.

This is not a perfect world. Circumstances collide, and there are times when we are caught in them. Often we can assume some responsibility for the collision. Then what do we do? Can we learn from the experience? Possibly, and if so, we are better off than before. However, there is more than cause and effect in our imperfect world. Happenstance and nonsense are just as prevalent. Perhaps we can't connect ourselves to the current misfortune. We can learn to develop hopefulness from it, even so.

Troubles test our patience. They make us pause, and many times they demand that we give up our plans. We have to stretch, accommodate to change, and alter our familiar path. Troubles force us to have a new experience.

Learning to flow through a crisis builds character. Whenever we have to give up something, the ghost of hopelessness hovers in the wings, waiting to sink our spirits. It says, "You poor thing. How shocking! You must feel terrible. Now is a good time to feel sorry for yourself. Everyone will understand. Go ahead. Take the day off. You deserve it."

Now we have choice. If we are badly in need of a day off, we will probably take it, using our jolt as the reason. This may be a sound choice. But we need to make a clear distinction between choice and excuse.

If we succumb to hopelessness logic, we will use it as an excuse. It is bystander bait. This voice would like us to believe that we are incapable of yielding to the circumstances. It tells us we are weak, and that we cannot cope. It says, "You can't possibly go in to work today." The voice lies.

When a crisis strikes, we must create a new set of present circumstances. Sometimes we do need time away from our routine duties. We may need the help of friends, family or experts. Setting aside our plans and grieving the disappointment is part of the reorganization. It is possible.

If we view this unwanted emergency as a task to be accomplished, it needn't rob us of hope. Instead, it teaches us that we can cope. It builds a fresh set of experience from which to draw strength in the future. It restores hope, because we can reflect on the learning with pride. We may even be able to say, "It was awful at the time, but looking back, I can see where it re-directed my life for the better."

There is another aspect of crisis-related hopelessness that warrants choosing life. In shocking situations, we naturally recall similar occasions and we may be tempted to feel victimized. They pop into our minds like weeds. If something is stolen from our home, we suddenly recall the time Aunt Betty's house was burglarized. We must be alert to the seduction of despair. Refuse to base your current attitude on historical happenstance. It is as meaningless now as it was then. Shrug your shoulders and say, "So what!" Do whatever you can to remedy the present situation, and move on. A thump to the human spirit is just that. It does not mean we are being victimized. Bad things happen to cool people. We must believe that.

Hopeless Victim

Assuming a victim stance is a terrible habit. Our medical language if full of it: "Victim of AIDS," "Came down with the flu," "Under the weather," "Fallen ill," (or "Terminally ill"). Do you recognize the futility in these phrases? There is an implicit message of hopelessness in each one.

When we are feeling hopeless, we must learn to recognize victimizing thoughts and get rid of them. These thoughts can be felt in the pit of the stomach. They propose that we are unlovable by saying: "What's the use?" "Nobody cares," or "Why bother?" They tell us we will fail and that we are inadequate: "Don't make waves," "It's not worth it," or "Better not risk it." Another common scenario implies that we are somehow bad: "I deserve what I get," "My number is up," or "What can I expect?" Then, there is the voice that says we are too stupid to be tolerated: "I told you so," "You'll never learn," or "Use your head." Of course, these are all lies. We've heard them before and believed them. They poison the mind, deflate the spirit and weaken the body.

The hopeless voice is as sneaky as it is nasty. It compares us to others. "Jerry broke his leg last year and he didn't have any complications. What's wrong with you?" It sets impossible standards for us. "Sally has five children and she bakes all her own bread. She's on the school board and is a Girl Scout leader. You don't have any children. Are you lazy or just plain disorganized?"

This same voice relives our failures while ignoring our strengths. "You never could cook. Let's go out to eat." It calls us names and uses *put-downs* to attack our person. "You're a fool. If only you would pay attention, this never would have happened." Messages such as these steal our hopes. They keep us from loving and respecting ourselves, and they interfere in our close relationships. Once we learn to recognize them we can mount a counter-attack that will erase them for good. Victim messages speak with authority. We can create auto-authority messages that will neutralize them: "That's just not true ninety-five percent of the time. Five percent is not an *F*." This cleans the slate and allows hope to return.

Becoming a Hope-filled Optimist

Nobody wants to feel hopeless. There are some who attach themselves to it because they know nothing else. They are the Eyores of life, behaving like the fabled donkey in the Winnie the Pooh series. Even people who are suicidal don't want death as much as they want the pain to stop. Their pain is that of hopelessness, for they see no way to choose life. We all have times when we need to hear, "Lift up your eyes and look outward from this place." [6]

Being hopeful is a natural state. Our body, mind, spirit and emotions will always seek ways to reclaim it. Healing from hopelessness is the gift of getting our futures back. We can learn how to adjust our present perspective and, in so doing, we gift others as well.

Basic Beliefs

There are three basic beliefs that exude hope. They tell us that we are lovable, good and sufficient. We begin learning them in our earliest experiences, and they direct our behavior throughout our lives. They are the cornerstones of choosing life.

Humans need love. It is in the giving and receiving of love that we choose life. Participating in this fundamental exchange lies in our ability to trust others. This is where hope enters.

Too often, we limit our trust because of past betrayal. Hope is a special quality that lifts us from this pit of despair. Hope doesn't depend on the past. In fact, it requires that we disregard all previous experience, good and bad. When we hope for that which we do not have, we anticipate that something good will happen. It allows us to wait patiently and confidently. While we wait, we can open our hearts to give and receive the love that we need.

Hope-filled people know that they are good most of the time. They direct their intention toward being good citizens, good children, good parents and good in any other roles they adopt. What does it mean to be good? Goodness includes patience, tolerance, accountability, integrity, kindness and honesty. It looks beyond the self to the greatest good of all. It is able to set aside gratification in the present in order to strive toward something better. It is grounded in the confidence that good prevails.

To know that you are enough, blemishes and all, fills you with hope.

You have special gifts, and if you don't know what they are, you need to discover them. Each one of us is an expert in something. It may be swatting flies or climbing mountains. Refrain from comparing your expertise to that of another. Accept that you are sufficient right now. It is from a point of acceptance that you can choose to be more. Say to yourself, "I am good. I am lovable. I am sufficient, and from this day onward I can be even more if I so choose. I am a gift to the world."

The Body Wants to Help

If you bend forward in a crouched position with your head near the floor, and say, "I feel hopeful," chances are, you won't sound hopeful at all. If you sit up straight, push your shoulders back, open your chest, look up and say, "I'm hopeless," nobody will believe it. Our words may say one thing while our body says another. We can use our body to help us restore hopeful feelings.

Posture is just one way the body helps us shift our attitude. When we expand the chest, we expand our lungs. By taking a full cleansing breath, in through the nose, and out through the mouth, we automatically release tension. If the chest muscles are contracted, we have too little oxygen coming into the lungs and too little carbon dioxide going out. Shallow breathing and holding the breath are unconscious acts. They are a response to hopelessness. It is as if we fear opening up to anything, even the positive. As a result, we collapse into ourselves, becoming victims of our posture. Conscious awareness allows us to reshape our bodies through stretching and breathing deeply.

Vigorous physical exercise of a pleasing nature helps to restore hopefulness. The body's natural hormones go into production when we run, walk, dance, bounce on a trampoline or ride a bicycle. Twenty minutes of aerobic exercise, done six days a week, provides enough good-feeling hormones for most of us. The body does want to help. When we listen to its responses, it guides us. A healthy amount of physical exercise is as good as a tune up. In some ways, people's bodies are like cars. If they sit in the driveway they get stiff and rusty. If you drive them only in high gear they wear out. When we care for them and use them well, they last for a very long time.

We are not designed for continuous work. Humans are cyclical creatures. In each twenty-four hours there needs to be a rhythm of activity and rest. Sedentary jobs must be balanced with physical action. Work must be balanced with play, and activity with rest. It is the balance that allows us to sleep secure in the knowing that this day, we have chosen life. Tomorrow forecasts hope.

The Mind Wants to Help

Our thoughts are powerful messengers. We can program our minds to tell us hope-filled words. Saying them aloud makes them even more believable.

Hope-filled thoughts should be positive, personal, and spoken in the present tense. Hope begins now, not later. "I am confident that the person I will marry is coming toward me now."

Hope is lively, not fearful and guarded. It grants us freedom from the shackles of doubt. Hope-filled thoughts should reflect excitement, enthusiasm and a positive attitude. "I am delighted by the notion that the love of my life is preparing to meet me now. I can feel it and I am confident that all my preparation is being rewarded."

When there seems to be a traffic jam inside of our minds, we can use relaxation and centering techniques to achieve quiet presence and restore hope. The cleansing breath is one such practice, a good stretch is another. Taking a full-body shake is wonderful (dogs do it all the time), and so is letting out a loud sigh. Go ahead. Try one of these now.

There are many forms of meditation. If you are a physically active person, choose a moving meditation such as Hatha Yoga, or T'ai Chi. Seated meditation is suited to people who enjoy physical stillness. Self-distraction can be achieved with anything that rests the intellect such as a good book, a crossword puzzle, creative writing or a computer game.

The mind readily opens to suggestions once you teach it to be still. It doesn't need to be empty, just uncluttered.

The Emotions Want to Help

When feelings and emotions are undermining hopefulness, we have to pay attention to them. Sometimes we just need to give them an opportunity to vent. If you are feeling sad but unable to have a good cry, rent a sad movie. If you are angry, take a big breath and open your mouth as wide as you can. Then, bend forward and let out a low growl. You will be amazed by the sound of rage releasing from your body.

Emotions can also release through outlets of creative expression. If you play a musical instrument, choose a selection that matches your mood and play it as passionately as you can. Then change to something lighter and more hopeful.

Working with art materials heals emotional conflict. You don't have to be good at any of it. Just splash powdered tempera paint all over a large piece of newspaper. Dip a brush in water and swirl it around. You might try ready-to-use finger-paints. Smear them on waxed paper till your heart is content. Squeezing and releasing two blobs of clay works wonders. If you like to cut and paste, gather up last month's magazines and make a collage. You will be surprised at how your choices tell a story. Any time you take time to play *artist*, you will heap a bounty of emotional healing on your soul. Try it. This is really choosing life.

Hope and Health

There are ways to think about calamities and illnesses that maintain hope. First we must separate the situation or the diagnosis from our wholeness. The human organism is a complex one and given adequate support will always seek to regenerate itself. Within the basic human blueprint is the innate drive to adjust to environmental stress, either internal or external. *Support* comes in many forms.

Internal and External Support

External support can come from the various medical systems, Western, Chinese, Ayurvedic and combinations thereof. Other sources for caring come from family, friends, groups, counselors and faith communities. For some, prayer is a profound source of hope and encouragement.

Internal support manifests itself in many modes. First, we can grasp the idea that only part of our physical body has become disorganized. The remainder is intact. It is time to call on the mind, the organized parts of our body, the spirit and the emotions to rally around and help out.

Many medical professionals believe it is their duty to offer the worst case scenario as part of a diagnosis. This gives an imbalanced picture to the patient. Realism is one thing. A death sentence is another. Sad news can be couched in optimism: "It is time for you to get your finances and personal affairs in order. Use this time as the precious treasure that it is. Tell others how much you love and appreciate them. Share the hopes and dreams you cherish for their lives. Work at your emotional and spiritual healing. You can do it. Who might help you with this?"

When professionals fail to offer hope, it is your job to get it elsewhere. When someone says, "Based on what we know, you have about three months to live." Your response is, "We'll see about that!" A stronger expletive is even better. Say it over and over to yourself. Write it on the bathroom mirror. Believe it. Live it. Choose life.

You can adopt an attitude of humorous observation about all your tests and procedures. John had leukemia. One side effect of his chemotherapy was thrush. The mucous membrane of his mouth and rectum were covered with tender white patches. Every time the doctors and nurses came into his room to examine him, he would announce, "Here comes the sphinctre committee." The ensuing laughter broke up the despair. In that moment, John was in charge.

Coping with physical limitations requires not only a sense of humor, but also a hopeful attitude. Doctors wait patiently (at times not so patiently) for new drugs and procedures to be approved by the Food and Drug Administration. Treatment methods from other cultures provide cures and offer hope. Each year, millions of dollars find their way into research. The Van Andel Institute in Grand Rapids, Michigan, is a rare example of research that targets nutrition. Blessed by private funding, this exciting living legacy brings together a star-studded cast of researchers lead by Luis Tomatis, MD and several Nobel prize winners and laureates. Their studies focus on advanced molecular biology and genetics. Their goal is to unearth the riddles of nutrients and cellular function. When the body cannot use the food it ingests, it disorganizes into a variety of diseases. This group is determined to uncover these links.

Each of us can consider the above examples as personal systems of external support. Our job is to maintain hope until answers are found for our questions. We can learn all we need to know so we can make intelligent treatment and self-care choices. We can surround ourselves with people who will help us stay positive. This is how we choose life. We live each day in hope-filled anticipation of a miracle.

How Do I Cope When I Can't Find the File?

Fact-finding is an ongoing process. The more we learn, the more we need to know. This is natural because of the way we absorb information. If you can imagine your brain as a compact computer, it will help you understand how humans receive, store, access and use knowledge.

Consider a new piece of data coming toward the brain. It enters through our senses and begins searching for a folder of similar data. It looks along this pathway and that, trying to identify anything familiar. If it finds nothing, it creates a new folder. This new piece of information is then tucked away for future reference. Every time a related piece comes along, it goes into that folder.

Our lifetime of experience is stored in these folders. Since bolts from the blue are new and unusual occurrences, we have no folder of reference for dealing with them. The fact that we have a sudden trauma is shocking enough, but to have no prior experience from which to draw reassurance makes it doubly difficult to cope. In these moments we may feel helpless and out of control. Gathering information to fill up this new file is a strategy of coping. Once the file has enough data we can sift through it and choose what is useful.

Adapting to new information clears a pathway to our future. It allows us to explore options, weigh them and make choices. Often, new information, like another type of treatment, comes at us while we are just beginning the process of adapting to an old set. This creates even greater stress to the system. External support is critical in times like this because our internal system goes into shock. We need others to take over some of our daily tasks so we can experience the feelings that arrive with the new data. Choices we make during periods of emotional upheaval are usually unsound. This is not the right time to remodel the kitchen.

Healing is a process of shocks, feelings, options and choices. These experiences occur simultaneously and at differing levels within the system. Sometimes it is the body that reacts. At other times the mind recoils or the emotions explode. The human spirit can waiver just out of confusion.

One way to gain self-control is to share feelings with a good listener, one who will not give advice unless asked for it. Choose a person who is forward thinking and anchored in hope. It is difficult to relinquish control of our lives to others. We can feel incompetent or blame our bodies for failing us. Share these feelings with a friend. Conserve your energy for healing. Allow others to help you. Do what you can and be gracious about receiving assistance.

But, What If I Make the Wrong Choice?

Decisions about treatment methods are not always obvious. They are educated guesses based on other people's experiences. They are risks. Your best choices come from gathering as many options as you can and discussing them with positive people.

Professionals do not have all the answers. Many physicians keep a list of patients who are willing to share their experiences with you. These conversations can be of tremendous benefit. Ordinary people come up with ingenious methods for coping during the daily challenges of illness.

Choosing a health professional you can trust relaxes the mind and helps you feel hopeful about their recommendations. If you make a wrong choice you will soon know it. Speak up. State what you are feeling, what the health professional said or did that made you feel this way, and what it is you want. Resist the urge (old pattern) to feel a victim of this new circumstance. You must accept that professionals work for you. You pay them. You can't return the goods once they are delivered. You can, however, pick up the pieces of inadequate results and move on.

Choose health care with care, and ask questions. Allow your internal support system to take over. Hear it saying, "You made a choice that does not benefit you. You made it with the best of intentions and knowledge at the time. Now make a different choice based on what you've learned."

We have many more choices than we think we have. We can choose not to be insulted. We can choose not to be indignant. We can choose to commit ourselves to self-care and health. When we view illness as a threat, we get sicker. When we view illness as a challenge, our human spirit sings, "Way to go!" It allows us to reach deeply into a resevoir of strength we didn't know we had.

Hope Is an Anchor for the Soul

When someone feels hopeless, the first thing we should say to him or her is, "But I believe in you." In a less-than-hopeful state, who can remember their gifts and goodness? A hopeful reminder offers them a hook to hang their futures on.

Hope anchors our belief in ourselves. When we think about people who seem to have their lives together we notice some commonalties. They have a way of laughing at themselves and laughing at life. Troubles befall them, but somehow they land on their feet. They don't feel victimized by circumstances. They are constantly learning how to access both internal and external support. They plant seeds of hope in others, reminding them of the positive aspects of their lives.

A young man who had one of the longest periods of remission from AIDS was asked to what he attributed his ongoing health. "A lot of things," was his reply. "I relish every moment of every day. I invest in my relationships. I work. I spend time with my music. I pray and read works of the great philosophers and healers, Aristotle, Hippocrates, Holmes, Galen, Frankl, Bernard. When I can no longer read, I will have others read to me. When I can no longer play the piano I will listen to recordings of the music I love. When I can no longer walk, I will learn to use a wheelchair. When I am confined to my bed, I'll think of something."

Believe in the Mystery

Perhaps the biggest damper on hope is too much realism. Believe in the mystery of life. Don't try to figure it all out. You can't. A great deal of life is nonsense. It makes no sense at all.

Of course, it is fine to ask "why," because we all do. As humans, we love exploring. Just beware of scientific explanations, patterns and formulas for choosing life. Each discovery leads to more questions. Know that arriving at any answer is only temporary.

Your anchor of hope will remain steadfast if you don't take life too seriously. The next time someone asks you, "What's the use of it all," simply shrug your shoulders and respond by saying, "Please pass the brownies."

Know that the most trying of times are really the most hope-filled. Difficulty is the precursor to change. Rest in the knowledge that something is about to shift and things will be different. With the newness will come solutions you hadn't dreamed possible. Believe in the positive surprise that is just around the corner. Have hope. I believe in you.

Chapter Ten
Laughter

If there's no fun in it, don't do it.

People who choose life laugh a lot. They poke fun at themselves and love a good story. Researchers tell us that very young children laugh five hundred times a day. We adults might laugh more if we knew that frowning needlessly engages thirty-six facial muscles. Nobody likes to prematurely wear out his or her face. After all, we only have one.

In the Navajo culture a baby's first smile is recognized as such a significant event that the whole community celebrates. In Western culture, this first smile is acknowledged as the infant's first cognitive response, an act of recognition and reply. It is a rather boring twist to something that deserves a party.

Many things can happen to us between that first smile and adulthood, some of them not at all funny. Instead of receiving love and caring, we may receive blow after blow to our bodies, minds or our spirits. Repetitious insults will repress the sense of humor, but they can never delete it. The ability to laugh remains encoded in the original blueprint of our human nature, waiting for revival.

Life Is Ludicrous

Life is ludicrous. We keep trying to make it orderly with rules and regulations but when it comes right down to it, things rarely turn out as planned. Have you ever noticed how frequently people talk about the weather? It is because we have no control over it. Now, that's delightful. Weather is unpredictable and the human spirit loves the unpredictable.

People who go through life bent on controlling its every aspect tend to fall into a cistern of misery. Much of life is beyond our control. The minute we can accept this we begin to shift from being rigid to being flexible. We move from being tense to becoming relaxed. The next thing we know, we are chuckling at little oddities around us. If we don't watch out we will soon be rolling around, holding our stomachs and laughing uncontrollably. This is just another aspect of choosing life.

Anti-anxiety Medication

Excitement and anxiety share some common symptoms. The heart pounds, breathing becomes rapid and shallow and the muscles tense. These are the body's readiness responses. They prepare us to deal with the unfamiliar. However, there are differences. Excited people smile. Anxious people do not.

Anxiety speaks with phrases that begin with "what if?" Our fear of impending doom can take on overwhelming proportions. Oxygen floods the brain, causing it to leap from one unrealistic scenario to another: "What if I get lost? What if I'm attacked? What if the house burns down while I'm gone?"

Nothing reverses the anxiety response like laughter. Some people exude nervous little laughs over nothing in order to reduce their tension. Big belly laughs cause the dome of the thoracic diaphragm to rub against the heart and lower lobes of the lungs. The body's natural oxygen/carbon dioxide ratio come into balance and the anxious symptoms fade. Laughter truly is good medicine.

Paradox

Laughing at things paradoxical brings relief to the mind. It relaxes the body and lifts the spirits. Life is full of paradoxes.

One Sunday afternoon, the San Francisco Symphony delayed the opening of its performance when a person in the audience developed severe chest pain. The paramedics arrived and a concerned murmur was heard throughout Davies Hall. As the person was wheeled out on a gurney the crowd began a gentle applause of encouragement.

Their well-wishes were cut short, however, by a distinguished looking gentleman who stood up and shouted, "Quiet, this is serious. Be Quiet!" A shocked silence ensued. Before long, little giggles could be heard. The fact that the gentleman was noisily ordering silence was funny enough, but if you were the person in distress, which would you prefer, applause or silence? [1]

In the above situation, would the cheery applause have aggravated the person's physical condition? Probably not. The body's immune system is intricately involved with the health of the human spirit. Lift the spirit and you support it. Crush the spirit and you suppress it.

Spiritual Tissue

People in the Western societies fear emotional outbursts, especially in times of crisis. We shut down our feelings, hold our breath and wait in silence for something to shift. We expect everyone around us to do the same.

When someone has a medical emergency, he or she needs more than scientific, technological expertise. Compassion and encouragement acknowledge the human being inside of a disorganizing body. These qualities come, not with silence and withdrawal, but with audible, visible expressions. Well-trained professionals take the pulse of the whole person. They are assessing spiritual tissue, a body that houses a living spirit.

Sometimes we confuse *serious* with *somber.* When the word *serious* means *important,* it requires that we pay attention, albeit with skill and compassion. If someone shares a disappointment with us, she needs an attentive listener. She will want to be heard and understood. By then she will be ready for a little levity. A somber attitude will just make her feel worse.

Barbara called her husband, Max, to tell him that she just opened her letter from the Bar Association Examiners, and she had failed, again. Max felt for her. It had taken him four tries to finally pass. He listened. He didn't mention himself. Instead, he murmured, "Oh, honey, I'm sorry." He waited for the tears that didn't come. Then, he heard a long sign. It was time to say something. Platitude after platitude raced through his head, but none sounded reasonable. Finally, in steady tones he said, "I guess this means I get to support you for the next six months, and here I am planning to retire." She threw an insult at him, and he knew she was beyond the sharp edge of disappointment.

Why So Serious?

Taking life too seriously is why drinkers drink, snorters snort, and pot smokers get high. When these substances enter the bloodstream, a rush of well-being floods the system. Worries disappear and a relaxed, carefree feeling prevails. People will risk all manner of havoc in their lives to buy these feelings. What they don't know is that the human body has its own pharmacy filled with them. One good guffaw, and away goes despair.

Why then do we have such trouble accepting the lighter side of life? The body's natural chemistry can kill pain, manage depression and make us giggle. Endorphins flood us with loving, happy feelings whenever we have a good laugh, a good cry, make love, cuddle a baby, recall a happy experience or make plans for the future. Here is a simple prescription: laugh more, cry more, make love more often, cuddle more babies, recall happy experiences and put hope back into your future. This is how you choose life.

The Myth

Perhaps we mistakenly believe we must have security, safety and love all in place before we can enjoy living. Yet, we each know of people who remain good-natured despite hardship. Think of the Mom with seven children who always volunteers to help in the classroom. Or, those good-hearted foster parents who share their homes with forgotten children and anguish when they run out of bedrooms. As part of the human race we are equipped with the capacity to convert life's frustrations into spiritual riches. It is all a part of choosing life.

Coping with Pain

Laughter is the best medicine for pain. It stimulates the brain to secrete specialized substances that interrupt pain perception. Seratonin and dopamine help to alleviate the feelings associated with emotional pain. Encephalins are morphine-like substances that minimize physical pain. Through guided imagery and biofeedback we can learn to maximize their effectiveness. When we support our own physiology with positive thoughts and positive people, pain can often be managed without drugs.

People in the Western world fear pain of any kind. Fear actually heightens the perception of pain and will even create it where none exists. Pain is a warning. It lets us know that we are alive and something needs tending. We learn from our pain. It is a wake-up call. When we heed it we can say, "Aha! I'd better take a closer look at this situation and make some changes."

Bystanders, who are locked into a rigid state of denial, don't feel much of anything. They may have an exceedingly high pain tolerance just to prove it. They also believe that there isn't much in life worth laughing at. Their personal humor centers on sarcasm and hostility. Making fun of other people's pain may be the closest they come to experiencing it.

Chronic physical pain is debilitating to the mind and the human spirit, especially when it involves the face, head and neck. Our earliest living experiences include being nursed by our mothers. The touch of their warm skin stamps love and caring on our impressionable bodies. This is why trauma to the tissues of the mouth, cheeks, and jaw strikes at the very core of our beginnings.

There is an emotional component to ongoing jaw and facial pain that is unlike any other. It carries an opposing message, one of rejection that says, "See, you are not lovable, nor do you deserve tenderness and care." Opening our mouths and jaws with laughter helps to erase such negative messages. Smiling, softening and kissing will add to the healing. When we soften we open. When we open we relax. When we relax, our natural medicinals go to work.

Pain of any kind requires a certain amount of time to work its way through the human system. First, we must heed its warning. Next, we must examine all areas of our life to determine where conflicts may be lurking. They usually lie within our relationships or our work. Physical, mental, emotional or spiritual disorganization will produce enough symptoms to say, "Stop!"

We must listen carefully and hear the entire message. The answers are as much internal as external: "I haven't had a full day to relax for two years (internal). The work day is getting longer but I'm more behind than ever (external)." The messages can be as much emotional as they are physical: "When I really stop and think about it, I'm tired!"

How quickly we will believe what others tell us, rather than trusting our own instincts and intuition. With a reassuring smile, our boss might say, "Just a few more months and the project will be over. I can bring a cot in here for you." Who's best interest is being served here? Not ours! *If there's no fun in it, don't do it.*

Whether we are disorganized with physical pain, mental exhaustion or emotional grief, there is no short cut to the healing process. However, the presence of laughter will soften the cruel edge of any type of pain. We need it as much for treatment as we do for prevention. What then, can we do to foster humor in our lives: Can we buy it? Yes, through entertainment. Can we read funny books? Yes. Can we watch funny movies? Yes. There are numerous ways to lighten up. The following suggestions help us choose life more fully and revive our humor sense.

Tickling the Human Spirit

Look for Humor in Everyday Situations

Truth is funnier than fiction. Mistakes are merely bloopers. None of us gets up in the morning and says, "I'm going to accidentally delete my software today." Bloopers don't seem funny at first, and they deserve a full range of emotional experience: anger, frustration, sadness and disappointment. Once these have been given their due, we can look for humor in the situation. It is always there. The secret is in uncovering it. Once we do, we can have a good laugh with ourselves. "You know, it took me twenty minutes to load that program and two seconds to unload it. If I got paid as an unloading expert I could make a lot of money."

One word of caution about bloopers. If you find yourself saying, "I fail to see the humor in it," you may need a sympathetic listener who will encourage you to vent your disgust. Then, let him tell you why it is funny. Some day you will appreciate it. When we make a mistake we are usually much harder on ourselves than others would be. In most situations, it is our own skewed perception that clouds the lighter view.

Hanging Out on the Lighter Side

We don't benefit as much from the wisdom of others as we do from our own experiences. When things don't turn out as planned, and we feel the brunt of those *bolts from the blue,* we can choose a coping attitude. Participants in life will take optimism over pessimism every time. If we were raised in a pessimistic family we will most likely carry on that tradition, but we don't have to. We can change and it is important that we do.

Scientists at the University of Georgia have been studying centenarians since 1988. The research group headed by Leonard W. Poon, PhD, Director of the University of Georgia Gerontological Center, has drawn some interesting conclusions about reaching age one hundred. In one of the longest studies, the subjects were required to still live independently and possess the ability to think clearly. Their longevity appears related to a combination of advantages including a strong constitution, a positive attitude toward life and an ability to cope with stress in a positive way. [2]

It is never too late to discover that it is much easier to be positive than negative. Positive people are full of good humor. They love puns and word games. They delight in the paradoxical occurrences of everyday life. Their eyes twinkle. They are given to fits of laughter and urinary incontinence, but they don't care. People who live on the lighter side know how to have a good laugh at their own expense and they don't hesitate including others in the joke.

When George developed cancer, his family was devastated. He was such an outrageous, extroverted and beloved person that they couldn't imagine life without him. George had lived on the lighter side for sixty-nine years, and he wasn't going to change now.

George's voice sounded much like one of his son's over the telephone. In fact, people couldn't tell who was on the other end of the line. When concerned friends began calling about his health, George would answer the phone and say, "George can't come to the phone. He's dead." Then he would hang up. It would send him into gales of laughter. George knew how to choose life.

Look for Funny Typos and Word Combinations

Newspapers, newsletters, periodicals and church bulletins often contain odd word arrangements that make for very funny reading. The medical profession has for years poked fun at the charting done by well-intentioned nurses and doctors. The following note was found in a chart on a psychiatric unit: "Patient is responding to internal stimuli (voice hallucination) and having liquid stools." These are two completely different sets of symptoms that would never be related. However, when presented in this manner they paradoxically suggest that one followed the other.

Listen to Children During Make-believe Play

Children mimic adults in some rare and delightful ways. We are at once charmed and amused by their innocence. Four-year-old Michael was afraid to leave his mother's side. He screamed when she said good-bye to him at the day care center and stayed miserable for much of the day. His mother worked to support them both and those screams echoed in her mind to the point of distraction. Fearing she might lose her job, she decided to take Michael to counseling.

After a few weeks Michael was better. Through his child-language of play he was able to sadly, but reasonably, let his mother go off to work. He kept a battered toy telephone nearby where he made routine pretend calls to his mom. During one such conversation he said, "I can't come home right now, but I'll call you later on my Beep, OK?" After the session, Mom said, "Michael, shall we buy you a toy beeper?" A radiant smile covered Michael's face. Therapy was over. From then on, his pocket-sized connection to Mother gave him the security he needed.

Through the simple play of children we learn the secrets in their hearts. We adults each have a laughing, playful child inside of us. When we enter the make-believe world of little children it helps us unwrap that guarded child. In doing so, we may uncover some of our own secrets that wait for healing. Children will often lead us to deeper understanding. They already know how to choose life. They laugh at almost anything.

Tune in and Laugh

Garrison Keeler's *down home* stories, Laurel and Hardy's slapstick comedy, and Joan Rivers' sarcasm are each styles of humor. They appeal to some and not to others. Puns, jokes, irony and paradox all add humor to our lives. Within every funny story, there is an element of surprise. Perhaps it is a word or intention with two meanings. The story leads us along one path and suddenly switches us to another: "Some prankster made off with three toilet seats at the police station last night. Police report they have nothing to go on."

Laughter is contagious. Even if we don't understand the punch line, we can share some of the enjoyment with those who do. When we laugh we get an internal body massage and tears release toxins that are the metabolic residue from stress. Funny movies and television shows feed humor to us but we need to choose our nourishment carefully. Garbage humor is selective because we are each unique. Turn the knob to *off* if the humor offends you. There is no right humor, nor is there a wrong one. Don't let the humor police tell you what to laugh at. Humor that finds a path to your spirit is what is good for you.

Practical Jokes

Corporate America spawns row after row of gray cubicles bathed in fluorescent light. This is hardly an atmosphere conducive to creativity. Laughter and creativity are in partnership. Practical jokes will add some playfulness to such boring offices as these.

If you inhabit a mundane workplace, every so often, you might try a little balloon levitating or bubble blowing. How about putting on a pair of Groucho Marx glasses for your trek to the copy machine? Remember Whoopee Cushions? They look innocent enough, but when you sit on one it makes an obscene noise. They haven't been around for a while and are due for a popular comeback. Ignore the naysayers who sneer at your childishness. Someone will appreciate you. A good laugh refreshes the human spirit giving us renewed energy for the task at hand.

A young attorney, after winning a hard-fought local election, was asked to what he attributed his popularity. "Well, I've tried to figure out the funniest way to deal with adversity all my life," he said. "For example, I was so small for my age, I had to outsmart the classroom bullies. One trick I used worked very well. During recess, I would stay inside and break all of their pencils. Then I would carefully glue them together again. When they went to use them, of course they broke. Pretty soon the other kids caught on and everyone had a good laugh. Since the bullies couldn't beat up the whole class, they just had to be meek for a while."

A society of people, living high in the Ural Mountains, has an average life span of one-hundred and fifteen years. To them, middle age occurs roughly between the age of sixty and eighty-five years. Their diet is goat's milk, vegetables and grains. They smoke dried leaves, drink a vile-tasting brew, dance vigorously, and play practical jokes on each other.

Laughing uproariously is as common to these people as eating and sleeping. When a research team came to live with them, this group of strangers became the object of much revelry. A simple question such as "How old are you?" would send the local people into gales of laughter.

Some of them would fall on the ground, rolling around and holding their stomachs. They just couldn't get over how concerned these foreigners were with age. Sometimes the answer would be: "Who cares?" At other times they would pretend serious contemplation then add ten years to their previous answer. This, of course, brought more unbridled mirth.

Nevertheless, the researchers agreed, this wonderful laughter had to be a key ingredient to the longevity and health of these delightful people.

What Is Fun?

We can expand our view of fun to include many aspects of choosing life. For you, it may be learning something new. Learning is accelerated when the student is relaxed and in good spirits. Perhaps you are on the inside of a delicious surprise. You giggle whenever you think about it. Teaming up on a special project can be fun. When we reach the goal, we pat each other on the back, saying, "That was hard work, but it sure was fun."

Fun often lies in the intimacy of sharing humor with another person. It even waits to be discovered within tragedy. When we allow laughter to permeate our stressful lives we boost our immune systems. We reduce our rigidity and live more fully. We choose life.

Why not give your spirit a lift by investing in a Whoopee Cushion, a squirt gun, or a four-year-old? You may just live to be a hundred and fifteen, and even if you don't, you will have more fun, more intimacy and more flexibility than you ever dreamed possible.

We must keep reminding ourselves that life is a process. The rewards come not at the end of each stage, but during each and every day. Laughter is one of those rewards.

Help yourself to as much as you can. You choose life when you do.

Chapter Eleven
Hospitality

Open the door, open your heart.

A seminary student, completing his senior field placement at an urban church, considered his last assignment with a mixture of excitement and dread. This would be his **first** Sunday as a cantor. It would be his **last** Sunday as a student. Soon he would seek his own call to be the pastor of a faith community. "I may never find a friendly bunch like this one," he mused. But that was next week's problem. "God, please get me through this service without losing it. And please, please, help me to stay on key."

He was extremely nervous about singing in front of the congregation. The choir had been generous with rehearsal time, and he focused on breathing deeply while chanting the refrain inside his head. The senior pastor looked his way. It was time. He stood up, said a brief prayer and walked to his place. He opened his arms in an encompassing gesture. Then closing his eyes, he opened his heart and his voice. It was perfect. As the last note began to fade, he looked up at the choir loft. Beneath a row of grinning faces, were three signs. They read, "10," "10" and "10."

A Timeless Art

Hospitality is a timeless art of giving and receiving. It includes all the words, gestures and rituals that make people feel welcome. The appreciative responses to these gracious offerings are equally significant. It is not better to give than to receive. Both lie on the same spectrum.

The gift of hospitality is one of human kindness. People who choose life learn to weave it into every day: greeting others, smiling, shedding a little light wherever we can. We don't depend on it for survival, but we need it. Humanity prospers from all forms of conscious humanism. Hospitality is one of them. It nourishes and warms the human spirit.

When the world was sparsely populated, travelers depended on the hospitality of each local group for food and shelter. In exchange, the visitors brought news from afar and items to trade. Often they were able to introduce new tools and remedies. These visiting strangers brought an exciting diversion to the community. It was usually a welcome event, but members of each settlement were equally ready to defend or to share their belongings. One Old English interpretation of the word *hospitality* is to *bring in angels* or *enemies.*

As each culture developed, so did each one's ideas of hospitality. Some continued the custom of offering food and lodging to strangers. One general rule prevailed. When a stranger approached, people stopped what they were doing and extended the hand of welcome. They eagerly listened to the visitor's words, just as they openly ministered to his needs. As hospitality became less of a necessity and more of a social concept, its definition began to change.

Hospitality evolved into two meanings. In the ancient French language it referred to what was called the *Noble Affection,* an extensive love of humankind. This exceeded the traditional meaning of offering relief to strangers. As towns and cities grew, their inhabitants didn't want strangers in their homes. The first shelters that were created for weary travelers were called *hospices*. The modern term, hotel, is derived from the Old French word, *hospitalite*.

The concept of housing the sickly poor, which also originated in France, was an expression of modified noble affection. These early hospitals were crude and inhospitable places. They served the purpose of segregating the ill from the well, and hardly reflected the *extensive love of humankind*. However, they were a beginning, and as the field of medicine gained credibility, so did the prestigious role of the hospital.

Today, economic pressures have once again relegated many hospitals to a less than hospitable status. Individuals working inside these systems struggle to maintain their warmth and humanitarian temperaments. They have little time to stop and listen to the stranger. Most of us have come to accept this change, even if we don't like it. Hospitality is, however, alive and well in other areas of our lives.

Food and Libations

Much of hospitality, as we know it today, evolves around food and beverages. Worldwide customs of welcoming friends into the home have a distinctly local flavor. A visit to an English home is sure to elicit a cup of tea, probably with clotted cream and a fluffy scone. In Brazil you will be served tiny cups of very strong coffee that will be refilled many times. The gesture of refilling is a hospitality ritual, as is the pouring of the tea.

In Middle Eastern countries, hospitality includes meals with many courses and vigorous conversation. It is hospitable to arrive with a huge appetite, for eating heartily is a sign of genuine appreciation. However, if you admire a piece of art you may be asked to accept it. Any refusal would be offensive.

"Can I get you something to drink?" It is the ritual of eating and drinking that causes us to stop what were doing and interact with our guests. This act of stopping is the richest aspect of hospitality and the one most difficult to do. Hospitality, as we've come to know it, is evolving into something new. We are replacing spontaneous hospitable gestures with scheduled events.

Changing Times

Fast paced Western societies are undergoing a transition in hospitable customs. People are so busy earning a living they have little energy for anything else. Women in the workplace don't want to come home and spend precious time preparing for guests. Eating establishments thrive because they offer a place for us to relax without the work of cooking and clean-up.

Entertaining in the home often demands a call to the caterer or the delicatessen. Children of today will know little else. The most popular vacations are forms of organized hospitality: Club Med, cruises, bed and breakfast lodging, tours, retreat centers, dude ranches and rail cruises. They allow us to rest, play, meet new people and above all, eat. Professionals combine continuing education with any number of planned vacations. The availability of these programs increases with each season. Are we really choosing life in these plastic opportunities?

Entertaining

Many of us succumb to some highly inhospitable actions while preparing to entertain. We view our home with the magnifying-glass-eyes of our guests, then without missing a beat, embark on a cleaning frenzy. We set up a working command post and bark orders to everyone within earshot. This has one clear advantage. In short order, we have accomplished the intended spring-cleaning of a year ago. A more sensible approach would be to wait until our guests leave, then clean up once instead of twice.

When we have enough help, we can create physical expressions of hospitality that say, "Be comfortable, feel luxurious, enjoy the fresh flowers and sparkling crystal. This is a feast for the senses." A beautiful environment enhances hospitality, but it is not an absolute prerequisite for it.[1]

All the hospitable embellishments that money can buy mean nothing if we fail to appreciate our guests for themselves. What is the good in providing so much food and drink that people become too sleepy to converse? Where is the wisdom in being so worn out from the preparations, that we are too tired to have fun?

If you were asked to choose between the conversation and the cuisine, wouldn't you choose the conversation? Genuine hospitality means paying attention to people by discovering who they are, what they like and what they believe in. We can acknowledge their struggles and their triumphs. We can embrace their differences. It doesn't take anything away from us if they are at opposite ends of the political, religious or artistic spectrum. We don't have to convince them they are wrong or we are right. It's enough to say, "Wow, we're a long way apart on that one, aren't we?"

The next time you entertain, try making genuine hospitality your goal. Do as much physical preparation as you want to. Let it nourish rather than deplete your body and your spirit. Throw out all the *shoulds*, such as the spring-cleaning and the yard work. Be rested and refreshed when your guests arrive. They want to spend time with you, not your house.

All the Lonely People

There are many lonely people inside our crowded, modern societies. They are bystanders to life, relegated to four walls, the Internet, crossword puzzles and television. For some, the workplace offers a modicum of hospitality. For those who do not work, human exchange is fast becoming a lost art.

If we are to choose life, we must take the high road of compassion and open ourselves to hospitable opportunities. Lonely people come out of isolation to buy food, visit the doctor and cash checks. They go to church, sit in the park and feed the pigeons. They ride buses and sub-ways. They stand in the same lines we do. We come in contact with them every day. It is up to us to stop what we are doing, turn, and say, "Hello. My name is Gerry. What's yours?"

True hospitality is colorblind. It implies freedom from pride and arrogance: two inhospitable characteristics. We have no need to distin-guish between infirmed and healthy, rich and poor, deformed and beautiful. It costs us nothing to share a smile.

The German language contains a wonderful word, *gemuetlichkeit*. It means *giving a friend free space.* In the literal sense, we interpret it as pro-viding a night's free lodging. However, the real meaning far exceeds such a limited view. Pronounced *gee-mut-li-kite* the word conveys a warm, cordial, peaceful atmosphere.

If you can imagine yourself on a brisk Sunday afternoon, sunshine pouring into your living room where you are curled up with your cat and a good book, that is *gemuetlichkeit*. If you walk into a cellar restau-rant in central Canada when it is 20 degrees below zero, and you are greeted with laughter and steaming bowls of French onion soup, that is *gemuetlichkeit*. You immediately feel uplifted, cozy and at one with the place. The implied message says, "You are as safe here. You belong here. Well? Come! Stay and rest. Sit and talk."

We need to become experts at creating gemuetlichkeit wherever we are. First we stop what we are doing and extend ourselves outward. All it takes is sharing a bit of ourselves with others: a smile that shows, "I like you already," some delicious food or libation that beckons, "Try this, it's marvelous," and a comfortable place to sit that says, "Your place is right here, beside me."

Practicing Hospitality

If we want to choose life, and be active participants in it, we must learn the art of hospitality. We can begin by being more hospitable within our existing relationships, more patient, tolerant and generous of mind and disposition. It is so easy to take others for granted. The people closest to us are the ones we need to treat with the greatest consideration. How often do we stop and really listen to those we love? How hospitable are we to our children, our partners and our dearest friends?

One of the foremost aspects of hospitality is listening, trying to appreciate and understand another person's viewpoint. When we really want to hear each other's stories we stop what we are doing. This is the first step of hospitality. When we try to learn the thinking that goes into another person's logic, we must pay attention with an absolutely open mind. Judgment is reserved until later. It's like putting on someone else's glasses and struggling to bring our world into their line of focus. Only through this investment of time and effort can we really understand why this makes sense to him and not to us. We don't need to agree with him, but we must try to understand him.

The place where people interact is termed a boundary. It is an imaginary line that surrounds each of us. This boundary shrinks and expands in a circumferential dimension. When we are cautious or frightened, it shrinks. When we welcome others warmly and treat them with respect, it expands.

A shrinking boundary sends a clear message that says, "Stay away." It will be accompanied by nonverbal physical expressions such as stiffening and turning slightly away. The eyelids will narrow and the eyes begin scanning back and forth. These are natural reactions to danger, real or perceived. It's as if the person grabs all his or her energies, wrenching them inward, saying, "I am deliberately creating distance between us. Don't come any closer." A safe gesture on our part would be a brief nod and a smile.

An expanding boundary is just the opposite. It reaches out in greeting, radiating warmth, attention and openness. We immediately respond by moving toward it. Hospitality simply means stopping what we are doing, smiling warmly, softening and opening our eyes and reaching out with some form of physical touch. In our rushed world, the most difficult part is the stopping. However, even one moment of undivided attention is an offering of pure hospitality.

Difficult People

It is easy to be hospitable to cordial people. It is much more of a challenge to reach out when we are given the *cold shoulder.* If we are in line at the bank, we can turn and greet the person waiting behind us. The conversation may end there, or we may sense that the person is not antagonistic just introverted. People who believe they are not worth very much feel invisible. We show them they are worthy when we speak first. "Hi. Do you bank here often?"

People who believe they are not lovable will never speak first. We can show them they are just fine by saying, "Hi. You look like a nice person. What kind of work do you do?" People who believe they are *no good* just need to hear that they **are** good. "Hi. What sort of a day are you having? Here. Trade places with me. You look like someone who does a lot of kind things for people." Others will overhear these little conversations. You will influence many with these few words and your attitude of gemuetlichkeit.

How can we extend ourselves to someone we don't like? Can we be genuine and still be hospitable? Let us consider the idea of *free emotional space.* What do we have to do with our own attitudes and beliefs to create such a space?

Suspending pre-judgement and dislike is not an easy task. The first thing we must do is set our intention to that goal. "Until now, I have not liked this person. As of this moment I am open to liking her. I am wide open for a pleasant surprise." When we do this our demeanor changes. Our face softens and relaxes. We relinquish the narrowed eyes and set jaw. Our expression says, "I am being hospitable, and I anticipate that you will be too."

There is an old mystical saying that goes something like this, "Be careful who you name as your enemies, they may turn out to be friends." Often, we decide we don't like someone before we really get to know him or her. People who are at all insecure will live up to our expectation of them. If we act as though we expect the positive, we will usually get it. Participants in living who choose life avoid labeling others because it leaves no room for improvement or options for change. The opportunity for discussion is closed before it begins. We all belong to each other. Enemy activity is temporary.

When someone says something we don't like, or acts disrespectfully toward us, we ought to speak up. The trick is to avoid judging the person, while confronting the negative behavior. Keeping the emotional space free between us is important. For example, "I'm finding it difficult to concentrate on the problem because you're making such derogatory remarks about my judgment. Let's stick to the issue, shall we? We both will benefit from a solution."

In dealing with those other difficult people, we have to stop and examine what we might be doing to aggravate the situation. Are we pre-judging, or are we open to something new? Do we anticipate the same behavior as in the past, or do we expect positive behavior? Are we afraid we'll be hurt, or do we have the skills to deflect insults?

In choosing life we become less difficult and so do the people we encounter. Hospitality brings the benefit of feeling good about ourselves. What other people do doesn't deplete us.

There is an old folk tale about a sparrow in the jungle. It is universally known that this particular species of jungle sparrow builds a unique home. Structural engineers come from afar to study this tiny domicile. It is three stories high and built so well it can withstand the annual monsoons.

As the story goes, one morning after a particularly heavy rain, Sparrow hopped out of her nest, fluffed her dry little feathers and looked up. Through the glistening leaves she noticed something brown. On closer inspection it appeared to be trembling. "It must be Monkey," she thought. "Good morning Monkey," she chirped. Monkey responded with an irritable grunt. Sparrow flew up higher so she could see him. He was a soggy, shivering mess. "Oh, Monkey," she exclaimed, "how cold and wet you are. Why don't you build a house for yourself? You are large and strong. Come down here and see my house. I will show you how to make one." With that, Monkey broke off a branch, swung down, and smashed Sparrow's nest to bits.

What is the moral of this story? Never extend hospitality to an angry monkey? No, the offer was fine. The response, of course, was not. When someone rejects our extending hand, we have a choice to make. We can retaliate or reorganize.

Sometimes humans behave like angry monkeys. They lash out from inside their trembling coats of misery. It takes many kindly offers before they can shed pessimism and reorganize their beliefs. Hospitality is a new concept to them. They are takers, not givers. When they reject us we should overlook it and consider: "I've given them one more positive experience. Perhaps this will be the one to sway their belief scale from the negative to the positive." Hospitality must be learned. The good news is that it can be, and when we do, we have chosen life.

Quality Time

It's easy to share things. But what good are things without the emotional, mental and spiritual aspects that are the true measures of hospitality? Gifts fall into this same category. One mother of four remarked, "It took our family thirty-seven years to accept the fact that what we really wanted at Christmas was just to be together. When we stopped running up the charge cards and took time to talk with each other rather than open a bunch of gifts, we really began to be a family."

If we spend short periods of quality time with the people we love and admire, an amazing thing happens: we become emotionally rich. This is an essential part of choosing life. If we sit on the sidelines, being bystanders and spectators, we will not enjoy the wealth of hospitality.

Here is another of life's paradoxes: the first step to becoming one of life's hospitable participants is taken by reaching out to others. It doesn't matter whether you believe you are emotionally rich, or not. Don't hesitate. Simply stop, wake up, look around and say, "How about going for a walk?"

Ritual of Compassion

Hospitality is, indeed, a noble type of affection, one that is an expression of the love of humankind. It demonstrates compassion. It considers the other person, whether stranger or friend. It presents an opportunity to share with dignity, from our bounty or our poverty.

Perhaps a current definition of hospitality might be: *Staying open in the presence of another with the hope of discovering something more.* May you be filled with such discoveries, for within them you will be blessed to bless others. You will have chosen life.

Chapter Twelve
Touch

To touch is to be touched.

T ouch is a basic human need. We inherently desire to touch others
and be touched by them. But touch is more than a desire; it is the
very essence of health and happiness. After birth, it is the first
sense that develops. Throughout our lifetime it brings us pleasure, security and communion. To touch is to be touched.

Unlike our other senses of hearing, smelling, tasting, seeing and
moving, touch presents us with a uniquely shared experience. Physical
contact with other living creatures is felt and perceived by both. When
this happens, a communication, often wordless, is immediately established. Even the most casual touch creates some form of exchange.

From conception to birth, the sturdy walls of our mother's uterus
embrace our developing life. There is significance to our being bathed in
warm liquid for these first nine months. As we gently rock in a friendly
sea, silky softness imprints our skin and membranes. When we are born
we bring this tissue memory into the awaiting world.

French obstetrician, Frederick LeBoyer developed underwater
birthing to smooth the newborn's transition from a wet to a dry state.
Newborns love to be bathed and massaged. The added enjoyment of
soap and lotion applied with a tender hand enhances the pleasure of
our earliest tactile experiences.

The way we are touched as newborns sets the stage for our ability to trust and relate as adults. At every age and stage, touch imprints our bodies, minds, spirits and emotions. Feelings and memories accompany every touch we receive and every one we give. In order to choose life we learn to create as many positive touch experiences as we can. They flood us with love and goodwill, helping us to withstand much of the adversity in life. Having someone to hold is one of life's greatest blessings. It helps us to heal and it helps us to live.[1]

Touch in Health Care

Nonsexual touch in the Western world has traditionally been associated with the healing professions. Before the technological revolution in health care, nursing was considered an art as well as a science. The *arts* aspect meant bringing physical and emotional comfort to patients. Bedside manner was taught to nursing students in a course called *Nursing Arts*. Procedures were to be administered with compassionate touch and accompanied by reassuring words. Students received instruction in massage and their patients received back rubs at bedtime.

Times have changed. Recently a nurse was asked, "What is your specialty?" She replied, "I like ICU. I never have to touch a patient; just nice, clean monitors." Of course, touching, caring nurses still do exist. Even so, technology has replaced much of the humanitarian contact in health care.

In ancient times, healers were chosen for their gift of touch for it played a major role in treatment. Salves and oils were applied with the experienced hand of an apprentice or master. Poultices and compresses were lovingly prepared from the earth's bounty of healing plants and just as lovingly applied. Dressings were changed regularly, requiring more touch. Soaks, baths, and steams offered yet another type of touch. Each of these tactile practices allowed for a relationship between patient and healer. The combination of touch, remedy and relationship inspired the patient, calling on his or her strong will to fight disease and expect recovery.

During the Golden Age of Greece, medicine came into its own as a special field of endeavor. Hippocrates, who became known as *the father of Western medicine,* urged other physicians to be knowledgeable in massage and use it routinely.

Decades later, in the United States, a division within the field of medicine arose concerning this very subject. Osteopathic physicians held fast to the tenets of touch and natural therapies. Others believed that the future of medicine lay in surgeries and chemicals. A split in the education and standards of practice developed. Today, osteopathic doctors (O.D.s) and medical doctors (M.D.s) differ in their focus, but their length of schooling and licensing requirements are similar. Osteopathic physicians often incorporate touch therapies into their treatment plans, as do doctors of naturopathy and chiropractic.

Massage as a treatment therapy is widely practiced in the Far East, Middle East and Europe. There are some American hospitals that currently offer a program of massage therapy to their patients. They are finding that in many instances the patients who receive massage use less pain medication and have fewer complications after surgery. This is a welcome turn of events for health consumers. The escalating costs of delivering in-patient care leaves little room for amenities, and massage has long been considered an indulgence. Now the stressful hospital environment can once again become people-centered through the touch of a compassionate massage therapist.

Touch Research

For the first time in American history, a program has been created for the sole purpose of conducting clinical and physiological research on the sense of touch. Dr. Tiffany Field, founding director of the Touch Research Institute at the Miami School of Medicine, began her studies with premature babies.[2] She was interested in the effects of touch on their ability to thrive. To her astonishment, the massaged babies showed a weight gain of forty-seven percent greater than the nonmassaged babies. They also scored higher on socialization and response skills. They were discharged earlier at a saving of $3,000.00 per infant, and at age eight months they still maintained greater weight than their counterparts.

This striking discovery led to both private and governmental funding for further study. Other research has demonstrated that babies born with cocaine addiction have a greater weight gain when given massage. Studies currently underway are showing positive effects on HIV-exposed neonates, infants with sleep disorders, colicky babies, depressed infants and some with cancer. Babies receive daily massage for a defined period and their responses are compared with a group of nonmassaged babies.

Research at the institute is not confined to newborns. At any given time there are over thirty studies in progress for children, adolescents, adults and older adults. Other important subjects include child abuse, asthma, skin disorders, eating disorders, migraine headaches and chronic fatigue syndrome.[3-5]

One interesting application demonstrated that foster grandparents who provided daily massage rather than just rocking to young children, lowered their own stress levels. The seniors used less medication, made fewer trips to the doctor and developed improved appetites. To touch is to be touched, and our elderly population is among the most touch deprived in our nation. If you are a grandparent, why not choose life? Find a grandchild to rock and massage. You will both live and be well.

Touch as Communicator

The sense of touch conveys information to us from our surrounding world. It warns us of extremes in temperature. Warmth is comforting and it invites us to relax. Painful touch teaches us avoidance.

Pleasing sensations stimulate our sense of well-being. All of these transmissions are gathered by the central nervous system and sent to the brain where they are interpreted and stored. They become a reference library of experience that serves as a foundation for all of our relationships. The tissues that received the touch also store a type of memory.

Touch-memories are embodied lessons. Each imparts a specific message. There is the hug of compassion when our favorite pet dies, or the hand on our shoulder when we don't make the team. The *kiss it and make it better* touch by mother guarantees instant healing. A friendly handshake implies, "I'm really glad to see you." Just think how dull life would be without the excitement of sexual touch! It declares, "You are desirable. Come close." The cooling hand on a fevered brow says, "I understand, I'm here. Live and be well."

Each affirming communiqué helps shape our self-understanding. It says, "You are a lovable person, worthy of care and consideration." People who choose life are generous dispensers of touch messages. It comes naturally to them. Others have to seek out healthy touch and learn how to receive it.

Touch is so important to us that its meaning permeates our expressive language. When we hear a beautiful melody we say, "I am deeply touched." We can feel touched by the gaze of an admirer. If someone is irritable, we say, "Wow! Is she ever touchy." We can live without hearing. We will survive without sight. Life without taste and smell would be dull, but we would manage. Without caring touch, babies fail to thrive and will eventually die. Adults become bitter and angry. Without loving touch, we too, shrivel and die.

Growth and Development

The skin is the largest organ of the human body. It develops from the ectoderm tissue layer, as does the brain, spinal cord, nerves and eyes. Its purpose is external and internal communication.

Newborns and Infants

In most cultures, infant oiling and massage is part of the daily routine. These bonds of caring touch build trust that babies will carry with them into their adult lives. It is an exceptional way for fathers to begin building a tender and playful relationship with their offspring. [6]

Most parents resort to walking and rocking when their little ones fuss. Babies with a variety of health problems, such as colic, can usually be comforted with specific touch techniques. Parents who invest a little time and effort in learning about infant massage will reap countless rewards, among them, fewer sleepless nights.

Thankfully we have learned that holding babies does not spoil them. Mesomorphic babies, who have more muscle tissue cells than others, love to be snugly bundled and tightly held. Ectomorphic babies, with their larger skin surfaces per overall volume, prefer light, loose swaddling and holding. Endomorphic babies with their larger visceral organs respond to all types of physical affection. They want their tummies rubbed and their cheeks kissed. Cuddling is high on their agenda.

Children who are not touched with care and respect grow up with a skewed sense of life. They don't internalize the message, "You are a lovable person, worthy of care and consideration." Those who are physically abused are often marked to become abusers. Parental discord becomes internalized in the child's personality. Fortunately, loving touch and verbal reassurance erase it. Among the gifts of choosing life is the knowledge that physical affirmation can bring healing to the most devastating emotional traumas.

Young Children

For young children, early touch experiences graduate from nursing and cuddling to exploration. A child's world expands each day. When children are given an object to look at, but not to touch, it doesn't register as being important. As their eye-hand coordination develops, pushing buttons and pulling the cat's tail become much more interesting than snuggling with Mom.

A child's need to pull, bang and slap can be channeled toward appropriate objects. They delight in the vibration that vigorous touch sends through their soft little bodies. One tiny girl sat in her little chair helping her daddy *fix* the deck. With every pound of the hammer she squealed with laughter.

Engaging in touch-based play contributes to a child's social development. It can bring Daddy into the picture as the primary playmate. Being on the floor and rolling around, riding piggyback and playing *horsy* will advance the child's sense of touch and trust.

Pets provide a tutorial for many lessons, including touch and empathy. Even very young children can learn to appreciate the differences between a smooth nose and rough paws, or a soft coat and hard toenails. Some children are naturally gentle and sensitive. Others need demonstrations of how to touch a pet.

A child's hands should never be slapped in punishment. This instills negative touch into their memory. These associations last a lifetime and hinder our capacity for enjoying a tactile world. But beyond that, negative touch delivered to any part of the body, and especially to the hands or face, hinders our emotional growth. We grow up believing we are ugly and unlovable. Every human needs large quantities of caring touch.

Some children require more cuddling than others, but universally, they all want to be touched when they are hurt or sad. Natural development allows them to internalize these soothing experiences and later use them on themselves. When an older child stubs her toe, she doesn't just sit there, crying, waiting for someone to relieve the pain. She takes off her shoe and rubs her toe until it feels better. It is important to allow children to develop their self-soothing independence.

The advent of mothers working outside the home has affected the touch needs of many children. Cramped schedules rarely allow for the early morning touch children need to get their day off to a positive start. Much of the dawdling that goes on, with lost shoes and last-minute demands are really appeals for some focused touch and attention. Wise parents will find a way to squeeze a hug or a kiss good-bye into their busiest morning.

Parents can also set an example for their children by hugging and kissing each other *hello* and *goodbye*. Longevity studies have shown that adults who kiss before going off to work increase their earning power and add to their lifespan. Establishing healthy patterns of touch in the home is wise for several reasons.

As children master the skills of dressing and grooming they relinquish much of their parental contact. Parents need to invent touch time to make up for it. Dad can create a before bedtime ritual of brushing his young daughter's hair. Leg massages are wonderful for children who are physically active. Soothing back rubs are a great way to say good-night. As parents teach loving touch to their children they infuse them with an enhanced gift of life. They are stocking their libraries with positive touch experiences and showing them how to choose life.

Pre-teens and Adolescents

When children reach pre-adolescence they enter a stage of touch avoidance. Hugs are suddenly *uncool* as are other once cherished pats and caresses. One mother told how her fourteen-year-old daughter suddenly became clumsy, often bumping into her while they were preparing the evening meal. She finally realized that this clumsiness was her daughter's way of being in physical contact with her.

Rather than becoming annoyed, the mother relaxed. She realized that her daughter was growing up and ready for a fresh type of attention. "How would you like to go out for lunch and then do some shopping? I thought you might like a new dress for the school dance." The daughter smiled. She reached out to touch her mother's arm and quickly withdrew her hand as if from a hot coal. "Thanks Mom," she said, skipping away.

There is sadness in a mother's heart as she watches her children grow up. This growing away is a temporary necessity. When it happens, the wise mother takes a deep breath, chooses life, and respects the process. Touch returns later if it was instilled at an early age.

Another mother told how her eleven-year-old son had developed a peculiar habit during mealtime. "He would be busily talking and eating, completely unaware that his foot was on top of the foot next to him. This was annoying to all of us, but I knew it was just his way of making physical contact." Years later she mentioned it to him. He had no recollection of the behavior although his brothers and sisters each did. To him it was an entirely unconscious act of touch.

Parents who are comfortable with touch and display affection for each other in front of their children, teach the wordless example that "touch is good." It is an invaluable lesson in the school of choosing life. Once they are beyond the touch avoidance stage, young people resume the behaviors that were common in the home. Parents are living examples. Their choices are immortalized for generations to come.

Sexual Touch

The manner in which our bodies and genitals are bathed and lotioned during infancy become tactile memories stored for future reference. When we later choose a sexual partner, we will yearn for a similar type of touch because it is familiar.

Very young children begin tactile exploring of their own bodies around the age of two or three years. They soon discover that touching their genitals produces pleasing feelings. Children use touch as a self-soothing device. They love the sensation of a favorite blanket or soft toy. They suck on their fingers or thumbs because it makes them feel safe. Excessive touching in any area is usually associated with instability in the home or school environment. "My body is always here when I need it," makes sense to a child when much of their world may make no sense at all.

As puberty approaches, children begin learning that bodily changes relate to shifting feelings and moods. With adolescence comes the drive for sexual experimentation and expression. This drive is uniquely related to our need for creative expression. Teens who are guided into physical activity and the expressive arts find that they have a healthy outlet for some of this exploding energy.

Sexual touch, without the spiritual or heart connection, embraces passion and pleasure but falls short of our human potential. Giving and receiving sexual touch is instinctive to us. When this natural capacity is denied or damaged, we will inevitably seek alternatives in an attempt to satisfy our deeper needs.

Sex desire should not be confused with sexual desire, a deeply impassioned state of spiritual connection. Love and respect for oneself and one's partner are the keys to a successful sexual relationship. It takes a growing level of commitment and intimacy for any couple to weather the many cyclical storms of life. When the sexual relationship is strong, external pressures just have to wait their turn.

The sexual aspect of the partnership is energy-producing while at the same time deeply relaxing. It is sometimes playful and at other times romantically moving. Couples who choose life want to work at their sexual relationship so it stays healthy and alive. It is never too late to revive it. You begin by acknowledging its value, then set your intention to getting whatever type of professional help you need. Override any thoughts of shame or fear. Choose life. Choose all of it!

Cultural Considerations

The United States and Canada are uniquely touch-deprived societies. A combination of puritanical belief and inappropriate sexual touch has resulted in this phenomenon. It influences all aspects of our culture.

Violent touch parades across our movie and television screens, masquerading as entertainment. Touch-starved viewers vicariously exploit their deepest yearnings for personal contact through these media. Physical addictions to pornography are rampant. The Internet has brought it into our homes for twenty dollars a month. Great is the need for healthy touch in our society, both sexual and nonsexual. The yearning for intimacy is innate to all of us. If we lack the self-esteem and social skills to get it, we turn to the alternatives available. We will be touched.

Most Western child-birthing practices are unnatural. After a convulsing birth experience, the newborn is thrust into a cold, brilliant, dry and unsupported environment. The only way a newborn can easily adjust to this harsh world is to be kept close to its mother's skin. It should be allowed to root for nourishment and drink colostrum as desired.

Colostrum is a substance produced by the mammary glands for approximately three days following birthing. It replaces amniotic fluid and clears the newborn's gastrointestinal tract, preparing it for breast milk. Bundling the newborn close to its mother, with colostrum available on demand simulates the uterine environment. Instead, we take the newborn away from the mother, leave it naked in a warm bassinette while ignoring its tactile needs. Touch deprivation begins.

In many cultures, the newborn is carried next to the mother's skin for many months. Later it is strapped to the mother's hip. This gives the baby several advantages. When it is hungry it need not cry. It merely begins rooting for food, thereby announcing to mother, "It's mealtime!"

Indian mothers massage their babies daily with warm oil. Eskimo mothers carry their infants on their backs until they can walk. Ugandan babies spend most of their waking hours being held by someone. In each of these cultures, babies are surrounded with affection. They are fed, cleaned and cuddled on demand. They are never far from their mothers and other family members. They thrive in complete security within a world that offers social stimulation, prompt gratification of basic needs and freedom to explore.

The basic difference between Western mothers and those of other cultures is characterized by the degree of skin to skin contact with their infants. Bottle-feeding renders caretaking and nurturing. Breast-feeding and skin-to-skin cuddling provide a deeper form of love and affection. As Western humans develop their sexual expression, they may have to learn the delight of skin stroking. Sensate experiences such as applying lotion with a tender touch will help to reprogram the body and mind.

In any Latin, European or Asian country persons of both sexes stroll down the street, arm in arm. Both men and women will throw their arms around each other in greeting, often kissing both cheeks. In heavily populated countries, personal space is at a premium, so body contact in public is a common fact of life. In Hong Kong, for instance, the Chinese compress themselves into an already crowded elevator. In Canada or the U.S., people will hold their breath for fourteen floors lest they accidentally touch someone.

We interpret cultural directives about touching as being right or wrong. In order to choose life we must look beyond what we have learned. Only then can we discover the treasures that touch brings to all levels of our being: physical, mental, emotional and spiritual. The measure of the touching we give yields the measure of the touching we receive. It is good to choose life by filling your touch cup to overflowing.

Corporal Punishment

Corporal punishment, although a long accepted practice in the best of Western homes, is unhealthy for several reasons. It teaches that violence solves problems. It can never truthfully be separated from the anger of the parent. It gives a mixed message, "I love you; therefore, I am hurting you." The brain of a child is not sufficiently developed to be capable of abstract thought. He or she cannot comprehend the paradox: "My daddy loves me. My daddy hit me."

Strong-willed and hyperactive children challenge even the most placid parents.[7] They need help. Books, counselors and parenting groups can provide the support and guidance that parents need to master healthy disciplining and limit-setting.

Physical punishment is especially detrimental to these challenging children. They need structure and discipline mixed with understanding and opportunities for self-expression. Often they are highly intelligent but have no easy way to make themselves understood. They may be able to do many tasks at once for short periods of time. Homework should be set up so they can work on one project for ten minutes, then move to another one. These children are often artistic and should be encouraged in those directions. They may be naturally skilled in mechanical logic so that tinkering with cars or woodworking may help them achieve.

Children who act out are sometimes depressed. Instability in the home can cause them to divert attention to themselves in an immature attempt to unite the parents. Physical punishment teaches obedience through fear rather than respect. It relieves tension in the parent but does nothing for the child.

Love cannot erase the indelible print of a blow to the body from someone who is supposed to be trustworthy. Parents delude themselves when they believe that striking a child of any gender or age will teach them how to behave. Instead, it imparts a message of distrust and leaves a remnant of anger that will one day emerge inappropriately.

Parents who choose life strive for the higher road of discipline. When the children are very small, each parent must develop an authoritarian look and a no-nonsense voice. They shouldn't try to reason with small children. Parents need to agree on the rules and the consequences for breaking them. High-spirited children will always test the limits. It is part of their growth and development to do so. A firm touch that says, "I am in charge here, and you will do as I say," gets their attention every bit as much as the threat of a spanking. If you are a parent, choose life. Don't hit your children.

We Will Be Touched

Our need for touch is a given aspect of our constitution. Children learn to substitute pets, blankets, toys, siblings and television for parental touch and companionship. Sometimes these self-soothing techniques get carried into young adulthood. It is not uncommon for a sexually traumatized female in her twenties to drink from a baby bottle and carry a special blanket to bed.

At times, teenagers who have not been touched become isolated and withdrawn. Teenage suicide is an attempt to end the pain of living one more day. It is also an angry statement: "I'll show you! Now who feels bad?" Teens need contact sports, dancing, dating and pets to provide them with healthy touch.

A youngster's unmet needs for touch can also lead him to gangs, drugs or alcohol. Sexual promiscuity can often be traced back to early sexual encounters. These usually take place in the home or the residence of a trusted relative or friend. If the child has not been taught to resist such advances, he can easily be victimized with bribes, threats and promises.

Both boys and girls become easy prey to sexual social vultures. Violating a child's innocence stamps him or her with a confusing physical imprint: one of pleasing sensual sensations and a yearning for acceptance. This blurs their personal boundaries. Promiscuity evolves because they do not value their sexual anatomy. They have experienced it as a common commodity to be traded. It may take years of therapy to reintegrate head, heart and pelvis.

Children who are severely neglected or beaten may grow up to be sexually aggressive. Their need for personal power overrides common sense and restraint. On a lesser scale, they can be sexually manipulative and exploitive within relationships.

Brokenness in human sexuality can be healed with a willingness to embark on a therapeutic journey that includes long-term psychotherapy and touch therapy. Somatic psychotherapists specialize in treating this type of trauma.[8] It is worth the effort. The human system is designed to heal. Choose life. Choose healing.

Healing from Harmful Touch

Sometimes, through neglect or trauma, we lose our natural ability to touch and be touched. We can recover. The process includes acknowledging our loss, grieving it and then consciously restoring touch to our lives. There are several ways to do this. Some we do alone. Others we do with human support.

Acknowledging Our Loss

Adults who were physically and emotionally neglected as children often have difficulty acknowledging their trauma, especially when their material needs were met. They might say, "I don't know why I'm so unhappy. I didn't want for anything as a child." That is to say, "I had all my material needs met, so what could go wrong?" Plenty! Children who do not grow up with the experience of loving touch have a void in their spirit that interferes with all their adult relationships.

According to Dr. Stanley Keleman's research, emotional and tactile neglect alters physical development.[9] The physique of collapse can be recognized by an appearance of folding in on itself. A concave chest is one of the more obvious features of such collapse.

Children who are physically beaten will harden their bodies to the outside world. They shut down their feelings of anger or sorrow when there is no one available to console them. They hide inside themselves and await the first opportunity to escape. Too soon for their years, they bolt to freedom, leaving behind a home they despise. Their bodies are dense, their behavior rigid. They may be high achievers in school or business but their personal lives lack intimacy and expression. Acknowledging this loss is the first step toward releasing the pain and restoring the fullness of life.

Grieving Our Loss

Grieving is a process and grief is not an event. Childhood abuse or neglect occurs over time. Unwinding its resulting pain from the physical, mental, emotional and spiritual body also takes time.

Freedom begins as soon as we set our intention toward it. Next, we begin the process of stating and accepting the historical facts. "My parents did their best, I suppose, but I now recognize that they did a pretty poor job. For whatever reasons, they didn't show me any affection, or each other, for that matter."

As we get used to this realization we will encounter many emotions: shock, disbelief, rage, sorrow, confusion or hopelessness. Often they are so overwhelming that fear sets in, sealing them off for a time. Gradually they will resurface and demand expression. If we lean into the pain and allow the feelings to run their course, healing will be complete. This is a journey we do not take alone. It is far too painful. Instead, we walk beside a skilled listener who refrains from giving advice, one who encourages us to go through the darkest valleys. This is choosing life.

Original nurturance is a need that can never be replaced, because we cannot go back and change our life. Coming to grips with this fact is a terrible blow to the human spirit. It is like a death. We can mourn our loss exhaustively while being supported by close friends and a trained professional.

An amazing aspect of being human is that when we let our hearts break completely, emotional and spiritual health emerges. Along with it comes a softening and elasticity of the physical body that is quite obvious. The mind begins to clear. We once more become creative. Ideas and solutions appear. Our sense of humor creeps back. The painful loss becomes a sad memory rather than a living presence. By choosing to walk through the valleys, we earn the energy to climb the highest pinnacles of living experience.

The most regularly neglected aspect of this healing pilgrimage is touch. Emotional pain is imprinted in the tissues of our bodies. Only through newly inscribed touching impressions can we heal completely. We must be touched with care and tenderness. This is how we learn to love and be loved. To touch is to be touched.

Restoring Touch to Our Lives

Tactile sensations will relax the body, soothe the mind and heal the spirit. There are a variety of ways that we can consciously and intentionally restore touch to our lives.

Therapeutic Massage

Nurturing oil massage, given by a sensitive professional, encourages the body, mind and spirit to relax. While in this relaxed state we can receive touch at a deep and profound level. It is as if the cells themselves say, "Ah." Enough of these "Ahs" will eventually replace the screams or yearnings of physical abuse and neglect.

Esalen Swedish oil massage is an especially soothing method because of its slow connecting strokes. It is important that the massage therapist be a specialist in this field in order to pace the work appropriately and interpret any nonverbal responses.

Acupressure and other systems of bio-energetic bodywork help a person to relax without direct skin contact. They are given with the clothing left on, or under a light cloth sheet. Early in the therapy, these may be the preferred approaches. Gentle rocking movements mimic the environment of the fetus and young infant. When we are asking the physical form to reorganize it is important that we coax it forward from the earliest stages of life.

People dealing with the aftermath of physical abuse, sexual abuse or neglect need a safe environment in which to receive their massage therapy. This will become a journey of transformation born out of trust. Sensory stimulation such as sounds, smells and lights are minimized so that touch becomes the focus.

A skilled massage therapist applies slow, evenly paced repetitive strokes with the palm of the hand. This instills a message of gentle, firm, consistent contact. It's just what the neglected child did *not* receive.

Skill also means being sensitive to nonverbal feedback such as stiffening, shallow breathing, skin cooling and shivering. These responses say, "You are being intrusive." The massage therapist must be able to read these messages and immediately adapt to them. Given time and encouragement, clients will learn to respond verbally to pleasing sensations and say "no" whenever they want to. These are important steps in the healing process.

A trusting relationship between client and massage therapist may take many months to develop. The client will first learn to feel and accept the touch, confident that it will not be intrusive. The next phase involves being receptive to sensations of well-being that accompany the endorphins flooding through the body. This may be surprising, frightening and emotional. The massage therapist should be prepared to understand and support these feelings.

When choosing a massage therapist, it is important to ask questions about their specialties. If physical or sexual abuse is not mentioned, you should look further.

Physical nurturance is a profoundly direct method for healing spiritual and emotional pain. Clients should simultaneously seek counseling with a psychotherapist who understands the drama of tissue memory and can safely guide them through the multitude of behavioral changes that ensue. Therapeutic massage can hasten healing on many levels if the relationship is right. Choose carefully.

Relaxation Massage

All massage should be therapeutic. The recipient wants to feel better than before, and deep relaxation accommodates that need. Anxiety fades. Muscular aches and pains diminish. The brain responds by flooding the system with pleasing hormones. For those who are able to receive this gift of touch, massage is one of the most delightful ways of choosing life.

Depending where you live in the world, the typical massage you receive will be very unique. European massage works deeply into the muscles with a vigorous oil treatment. The Swedish style of European massage adds tapotment, which means percussion. This invigorating technique uses light, brisk tapping with the fingers or hands. It stimulates the blood and lymph circulation and leaves the person feeling energetic and relaxed. A method called cupping, where the hands form the shape of a cup, is an established therapeutic practice that has been employed for centuries. The therapist taps the sides and back of the body with cupped hands to loosen mucus from the lungs and respiratory tubes. It can be live-saving to people with chronic respiratory conditions.

Middle Eastern massage is also energetic and used more as a medical therapy than for relaxation. The Middle and Far Eastern medical sciences consider the human body to be an energy form. They describe a sophisticated system of bio-energy fields within and surrounding the physical body. Balancing this system is the goal of hands-on therapies.

Acupressure is one such method. Here the practitioner places the fingers lightly over strategic points and waits until the pulses attain a rhythmic duet. Shiatsu utilizes a similar system, but the technique is very different. The practitioner presses into many strategic points to stimulate the flow of blood, lymph and life energy. Each modality is deeply relaxing.

Other methods incorporate cradling and rocking the body, sometimes under water. Some systems use sequences of holding where the practitioner places the hands on the client's body in very specific locations and directions.

Whatever the method, it seems that accepting touch as a healing force is indigenous to human nature. Much of its success has less to do with technique and more to do with the relationship between practitioner and recipient. Certainly, skill is involved, but skill without personal presence and trust converts the process to a mechanical one. Results are what count. We can make our conscious choice to choose this life-giving experience with or without hard data to prove its efficacy.

Handshaking

One way to become a life participant is to embark on some social reform in the area of touch-deprivation. We will begin with handshaking because it is permissible in the Western culture. Bystanders do not take advantage of this little ritual, but participants do. Handshaking is simple and acceptable.

You can begin by establishing your intention to add a handshake whenever you say, "hello," or "good-bye." It will soon seem as natural as making eye contact, smiling or nodding, which are the routine gestures we use. Most people like to be touched and you, too, will find it mutually pleasing. One study shows that waitresses who touch their patrons briefly while serving their food to them will receive larger tips than those who don't. This demonstrates the wordless power that touch can evoke.

Next, you can begin to elaborate on the handshake itself. Extend the connection time just a little as you make eye contact. If you are trying to recall where you have met this person before, keep shaking the hand as you search your memory. When you locate the association, add a brief touch to the arm with your other hand, or cover his or her hand with your free hand. Each of these moves adds a touch of intimacy and friendliness. Once you are comfortable with these contacts you will be ready for more.

Some people are ready for a cheek-to-cheek press or a kiss on the cheek. If you follow the European tradition, a kiss to both cheeks is delightful. Until you know your recipient, it is a good idea to ask permission for such a gesture: "May I offer you the European greeting?" Soon you will be able to read the encouraging signals for this gentle acknowledgment.

Learning to recognize and withdraw is key to this process. We must remember that we live in a touch-deprived society. People are suspicious about physical advances. The typical rejections include pulling away, stiffening or palm-sweating. You will of course, honor these by gently breaking physical contact. Your ability to engage in these little touching customs requires nothing more than a genuine desire to touch and be touched. With a little practice, you can expand your daily quotient of touch to a healthy level. This is choosing life.

Contact Sports and Games

Rough and tumble play presents opportunities to be touched. So does ballroom dancing. Folk dancing and square dancing are also enjoyable tactile experiences. Water slides resemble the birthing process and are immensely popular. Games, such as *Twister* and *Pass the Orange without Using Your Hands,* are great ways to have people touch each other in play.

Children play *Tag* and *Blind Man's Bluff,* both of which involve touching. These are all healthy exchanges, ways for people of all ages to touch each other in the name of *fun.* We all need an abundance of playful touch to be healthy.

Healing Waters

The touch of water to the skin sends an instant message to the whole system. Warm water says, "Calm down, relax." Cool water says, "Wake up, revive!"

Hydrotherapy has been popular in Europe and Asia for thousands of years. Steam helps the body sweat and eliminate toxins through the pores. Mineral baths are famous for soothing aching joints. Bathing, swimming or soaking are all ways to enjoy water's gift of touch.

Whether we succumb to the pulsing jets of a hot tub or the soothing cascade of a waterfall, the tactile experience of water is one of life's greatest pleasures.

Healing Touch Rituals

The laying-on-of hands is an ancient Christian ritual that combines touch and prayer. In the modern church it is often used at a healing station where an individual kneels or stands. A prayer request is made, and the person officiating places both hands on the head of the receiver while offering an individualized prayer. The act of laying-on-of hands is also used at special ceremonies that mark the beginning of a sacred life journey.

Anointing is another touch ritual that signifies preparation for a spiritual journey. In Christianity, anointing with oil has long been a symbol of grace and blessing. It is a touch that binds both people in common understanding and hope. When people are baptized, their foreheads are anointed with the sign of the cross. *The anointed one,* means a person who has earned favor with God.

A woman with breast cancer sought massage in preparation for her impending total mastectomy and chemotherapy. She talked about her fears, then relaxed into a deep state of consciousness. When the massage was over she asked for a little of the oil. "I want to help them (her breasts) feel as relaxed about this as I do, " she said, as she rubbed the massage oil all over her chest. "I believe in the anointing. Now I'm ready."

To Touch Is to Be Touched

As we consider choosing life, we must add touch to the heart of our living experience. We fill our cup with touch by weaving it into our lives, but we don't stop there. If we are to be participants rather than bystanders, we have a responsibility to touch the untouchable. It is an easy choice to cuddle a beautiful child or a loving grandmother. It is more difficult to extend the hand of friendship to a stranger.

You can learn a great deal about another person by the way they respond to your outstretched hand. Some stand transfixed as if they can't believe it is happening. These are the disenfranchised of society. Their library of touch is empty. They need you. Others reluctantly offer a limp set of fingers. They need you too. Their future is undecided, their present is confused. Still others willingly give you a cold and clammy hand. These are the anxious ones. They need the sure-handed connection of someone who cares enough to reach out.

Warmth comes from the heart. It reaches out to others via our smile, our eyes and our hands. The next time you are standing beside an elderly person, put your arm around him or her and give that shoulder a little squeeze. It does wonders for the human spirit. You both will be rewarded with a flood of good feelings that transcend words.

As you develop your sense of touching, you will be presented with a dilemma. You will come to know the tenderness of a warm embrace, the tranquility of a deep massage and the happiness of a hug when you are sad. You will feel the softening of an aged shoulder, and see the perplexed look of a total stranger. These experiences are real and they are yours forever. The dilemma is this: Is it better to touch or be touched? Choose life and spend the rest of it finding out.

Chapter Thirteen
Music

> *"Music is the mediator between the spiritual and the sensual life."*
> *—Ludwig van Beethoven*

Imagine it's the Christmas season. You're looking forward to some relaxation after a hectic workweek. You pop a new CD of Gospel music into the player, then sit down to enjoy your neighborhood deli's specialty: a juicy pastrami sandwich. Deep in thought, you suddenly realize your body is swaying to the rhythm of the music. "Go-o tell it on the mou-ountain," sings the choir. You can't stop moving. You are smiling and chewing, chewing and swaying. You feel wonderful. "That Jesus Chri-ist is born."

Most of us don't pay much attention to the connection between music and our well-being. It is just there. It has always been there. For some of us it hovers on the periphery of our lives. For others it is central to our daily moods and activities.

We grow through every stage of our life with a musical accompaniment. Newborns are rocked to sleep with a lullaby. The infant claps her hands in glee to the song of *Pat-a-cake, pat-a-cake, Baker's man*. A small child stops whatever he is doing to join the circle for *Ring around the Rosie*. Adolescents begin their mock attempts to leave the nest through raucous, rebellious sounds that they call "music." [1] Romantic ballads weave lovers together. *Amazing Grace* eases our suffering, and *Blessed be*

the Tie That Binds helps us to say "good-bye." Our physical, mental, emotional and spiritual selves require music.

Universal Language

Music is a universal language that bridges cultures and continents. It touches the human spirit like nothing else. The familiar opening chords of Beethoven's Ninth Symphony vibrate in common human understanding: *Dah dah da DAH, Dah dah da DAH.* We catch our breath. Our pulses quicken in anticipation. We are as one, caught in the rapture of the sound.

A multitude of sounds engulfs us every day. What is it about music that is so enticing? Is it the resonance? Certainly, anyone who has heard Massenet's *Meditation from Thais* knows its calming effect. The melodious song of the violin soothes us. The electrical impulses in our brain have shifted to what is called the *Alpha State.* The entire system relaxes. Conversely, a rousing John Phillips Sousa march moves us to step in time to the rhythm. We can be moved from sedation to stimulation in a matter of minutes.

In an entirely different setting, Tibetan monks chant three times a day to a critically injured snow leopard that gradually and miraculously heals. Or is it a miracle? Perhaps music is the one force that binds together all living creatures. Both clinical research and historical experience teach us that music heals and helps us to relax. It stimulates immune function. It allows us to step lively and to die in peace. How profoundly it influences our lives! Alfred Nietzsche, the German philosopher wrote in 1889, "Without music, life would be a mistake." Choosing life, then, means learning how to appreciate music. [2]

Cultural Considerations

Music has been important to humans for at least seventy thousand years. It was handed down through the generations long before paper and writing existed. Ancient Egyptian cave paintings reveal a variety of musical instruments and stringed bows. Archeologists have uncovered an Egyptian relief from around 2700 BC that portrays a seven-piece group with two people playing wind instruments (probably made from reeds), one plucking a stringed instrument, and four clapping their hands (the rhythm section). Another discovery, an eleven-string lyre, is thought to date back to 3000 BC. An ancient Egyptian medical document, the Ebers Papyrus (1500 BC), describes chants physicians would use to enhance healing.

Other cultures have adopted music as a healing agent. North American Indians still use chanting and drumming to invoke healing spirits. The ancient Hebrew king named Saul was cured of depression when David played his lyre and danced for him. Mothers around the world croon their feverish children to sleep. Soothing music allows the body to rest and restore itself.

In South Pacific cultures, school children learn their history lessons through song and dance. Spain's passionate music resonates around the world and can be heard in each country the Spaniards explored. The strains of bagpipes are familiar to peoples who once were ruled by the great British Empire. In every region of every country, the common people lift their voices and instruments in song. Their stories can be heard, not only in the words, but in the rhythms and melodies as well.

Harmony of the Spheres

For years music was thought to be a link between humankind and nature. Composers and musicians have expressed this passionate relationship through such works as Vivaldi's *Four Seasons*, Beethoven's *Moonlight Sonata* and Debussy's *Claire de Lune*. Ancient Greeks and Chinese believed that trees and wind, as well as the sun, moon and stars, each spoke to living creatures through their own unique musical forms. They held in reverence the life energy and rhythms of all systems and sought to live in harmony with them.

In 525 BC, Greek mathematician and philosopher, Pythagoras, called this musical relationship the "harmony of the spheres." He studied the mathematical ratios between the planets, the laws of music and the vibrations of stringed instruments. What he discovered were some stunning common equations between sounds that are pleasing to the human ear (simple whole numbers) and the length of the strings in a musical instrument. He believed these laws to be the secrets of the universe and that they have a common bond with the human soul.

Pythagoras deduced that musical tones and melodies, which harmonize within these laws of pure tones, send the human body into a healing vibration. His theories are the basis for modern day music therapy. Trained healers use music as a pathway to the deepest part of us. They know that a rosebud unfolds with its own distinctive sound, similar to one of the lower notes on a pipe organ. All living systems emit vibrational tones. The human organism is no exception. When we choose life we hum with an inner harmony. It is essential to our health and wholeness that we learn how to rediscover such a place of balance.

Healing Rhythms

The human organism is one great pulsating symphony composed of many inner rhythms. The heart beats at approximately seventy-five times each minute. Its normal rhythm makes a sound like "lub-dub," followed by a very brief pause. Every tiny cell expands and contracts in a continuous cadence. All of the body tissues are in constant motion, elongating and shortening, expanding and shrinking, widening and narrowing. The body's conductor of this great symphony is the breath. The *in-pause, out-pause* cycle of our breathing sets the whole operation to singing in harmony or scattering in disarray.

The Physical Factor

From a purely physical standpoint, it is logical that vibrational tones would influence the human body. After all, we are composed of organic matter,and, as such, are made up of millions of continuously moving molecules.[3]

Sound vibrations stimulate each of our senses as well as our tissues. As our breathing increases, slows down or remains constant, the other pulses follow. When music relaxes the mind, it relaxes our breathing. The heart rate decreases, digestion slows down, the skin temperature rises, and we feel *grounded.*

Body and Soul, Body and Sound

How music heals relates to vibrations. When sound waves reach the human body, their pulsations resonate throughout the various tissues. The physical body is much like the sounding board of a piano. Not only the ear, but the whole system vibrates in sympathy with the sound waves that strike it. Whether or not these sounds are beneficial to us involves the quality of the vibrational sound and the sensitivity of the receiving body.

Physical bodies have great variations in hydration and texture. The softer and more liquid the human form, the more sensitive it is to sound vibrations. The newborn is supple, barely beyond its semi-liquid state. Musical vibrations course through all of its tissues, affecting the breathing and other pulses.

As we age, the body naturally hardens. Sometimes we have hearing loss, but even so, the physical form will respond to musical pulses. A brain atrophied through senility can still interpret and enjoy music. When people are dying, their favorite music, especially if it is culturally flavored, can be tremendously soothing.

The human ear does not come equipped with earlids, as do the eyes. This is unfortunate. Unpleasant sounds can be partially filtered by putting our hands over our ears, but only after some of the noxious vibrations have already penetrated the system.

This marvelously sensitive instrument, the ear, is capable of differentiating among 1,378 tones that vibrate between 16 and 25,000 hertz or cycles per second. The electromagnetic field of our planet earth resonates at 7.83 hertz (Hz). We don't hear it since this frequency is slower than our hearing range. However, musical compositions that complement the earth's resonance are deeply relaxing to the human organism. In this state we feel spiritually peaceful and richly creative.

The delicate mechanisms of the ear reproduce the vibrations they receive. These travel through the auditory cortex of the brain to be interpreted as tones, rhythms and melodies. Deep in the mid-brain, the pleasure centers of the limbic system happily recognize tempos that harmonize with the heartbeat. The rhythm of a waltz will send a flood of *good feeling* hormones, called endorphins, coursing through the bloodstream. Musical sounds that clash with the natural rhythms have just the opposite effect. They can cause fatigue and pressure headaches.

The brain is a marvelous system, cleverly capable of adapting to its environment. The left side of the brain dominates in language interpretation, whereas the right hemisphere processes musical tones, volume and chords. However, when it comes to music perception such as familiar rhythms, songs and words, the left hemisphere is also involved. Music activates the movement of stored memory material back and forth across the corpus callosum, a collection of fibers connecting the two sides of the brain. The hearing of music is really a whole brain phenomenon. It continues to learn how to appreciate music as long as we live.

Musical training can enhance this function of the brain so that lessons in singing, dancing or playing an instrument will augment whole person healing. Because stored memories play such an important role in our musical pleasure, the prescribing of music for sedation or stimulation includes yet another component, one of personal history and familiarity. It doesn't matter how pure the tones of classical music may be, if we have not learned to like them, they will not help us heal.

Whole Person Health

Healing and Cure

Healing the physical body is complicated with much more at stake than cure. In our fast paced, technological Western culture, we want our cures to come quickly and painlessly. Our aim is the annihilation of symptoms and a speedy return to our former self. As a result, we have created a medical system that reflects this goal.

Cure, however, often eludes us. The increasing complexity of Western society is breeding an increasing mixture of illnesses. There is no magic bullet, no surgery or drug, that can cure disorganizations of the immune system. More and more we are realizing that treatment without lifestyle change is meaningless. Our attitudes and beliefs, which influence how we function day to day, also need to change. We need to start choosing life.

We are learning that we *must* slow down and take seriously our intricate human system. We can stop smoking, eat properly and get enough exercise. We can drink plenty of clean water and breathe clean air. We can have more fun, develop healthier relationships and express ourselves creatively. This formula for good health has been around for a long time. In 400 BC, Hippocrates and his associates, the Society of Aesclepius, said just the same thing. Learning how to choose life, including music, can be part of the design.

Eastern Influence

When there is no Western cure available, we sometimes turn to medical systems of the Eastern world in search of answers. From Asia come theories of *heat and cold, yin and yang,* and the *five elements.* [5] From the Middle East come Ayurvedic medicine, [6] the theory of similars [7] and homeopathy. [8]

These so-called sciences may seem strange to us. They are not based on double blind studies and clinical research. Rather, they are the product of societies where whole person health is a cultural given. It is understood and accepted that within all living things in the universe there is a life force that cycles within natural laws. Illness or disorganization is most likely to occur when a living system becomes unbalanced within itself and in relationship to these laws. All living things must be strong, flexible and cyclical. Music plays an integral part in attaining and maintaining this balance.

During India's golden Vedic civilization, around 1500 BC, classical music known as Gandharva was used to bring about inner harmonies and treat illnesses. This music included the medicinal features of drone, which are repetitious tones that correlate to certain vibrations in the human form. Treatment also included specific applications of harmonics, rhythm harmony, melodies or ragas, form and instrumental color. It was an elaborate system used several times a day for the maintenance of optimum health and the treatment of illness. Many of these practices are still used in India and beginning to find their way to the West.

The *toning* treatment involves expressing a vowel sound as a musical note, which will resonate and bring into balance its correlating energy center, called a *chakra*. According to Yogic philosophy, there are seven such chakras throughout the physical body. Each has a unique relationship with a musical key and a sacred sound. The particular sounds correspond to a color vibration and the pulsation of certain types of body tissues. The physical resonance stirs certain emotional responses within us, calling us to behave accordingly. (Figure 14)

Each of the first five chakras aligns with a natural element of earth, water, fire, air or ether. The higher two relate to thought and light. Levels of consciousness correspond to each chakra. They range from our baser instincts in the lower centers to our more enlightened states in the higher. By toning the sacred sound in the appropriate key, a harmonizing relationship can be recreated within the physical, mental, emotional and spiritual self. The intonation can come from the human voice or pure instrumental sound. Crystal bowls are often used, as are the metallic chimes and bowls created by Tibetan monks. Following a toning session one feels calm and relaxed, alert and balanced.

Chakra and Location	First	Second	Third	Fourth	Fifth	Sixth	Seventh
	Base of Spine	Pelvis	Solar Plexus	Heart	Throat	Brow	Crown
Musical Key	C	C# to D	Eb to E	F to F#	G to Ab	A to Bb	B
Sacred Sound	Uh	Hu TO Oo	Who to Oh	Aw to Ah	Eye to Aye	Ee to mmm/om	Nnn/silence
Toning Sound	UH (Low)	OOO	OH	AH	AY	EEE	EEE (High)
Color vibration	Red	Orange	Yellow	Green	Blue	Indigo	Violet
Physical Tissues	General circulation. Muscular denseness. Hormones. Heart muscle. Large intestine. Reproduction.	Digestion: liver, pancreas, gall bladder. Spleen.	Respiratory system. Nerves. Lymph. Stomach and small intestine.	Urinary tract. BP. Thymus. Heart. Immune system	Bones. Back pain. Thyroid. Throat. Skin. Immune system.	Eyes. Ears. Clotting time. Pituitary. Mental acuity and sanity.	Brain. Life force. Nerves/electrical body. Assimilation.
Emotional Responses	Survival issues. Power. Ability for self-care.	Sexuality. Self-approval. Shyness. Addictions. Fear. Intimacy.	Self-direction. Control and trust. Stubbornness. Depression. Will power.	Giving and receiving love. Intuition. Compassion. Authenticity.	Creativity. Communicate. Connecting. Rigidity. Depression.	Compulsivity. Reason. Judgement. Indecision.	Faith and hope. Attention. Boundaries. Assertiveness. Confidence.
Elemental State	Earth	Water	Fire	Air	Ether	Thought	Light
Level of Consciousness	Physical/Sensual.	Emotional.	Mental. Intellectual.	Causal. Lower creative.	Causal. Higher Creative.	Intuitive.	Knowing and Oneness.

Figure 14. Chart of Chakras with multiple levels of relationship.

Applications in Western Medicine

Music for physical healing is an exciting addition to the holistic health model and the self-empowerment health revolution. Neurological disorders, such as Parkinson's Disease, Alzheimer's Disease, and autism all show promising response to music. Musical rhythm, using flat hand-held instruments, helps people with some dementias, including the Alzheimer's type, to organize their time and space. They can also dance and move in rhythm to familiar music.

The same is true for severely psychotic patients.[9] It is fascinating to note that when those parts of the brain controlling cognition, language and judgment begin to degenerate, the parts that respond to music remain intact. If people with dementia could communicate with us, they would say, "Speak to us through music. That is how we can understand you."

In some cases, patients with Parkinson's Disease relax their rigid muscles in response to musical tones. Their hands will roam over the keyboard of a piano even though they are frozen when attempting to feed or dress themselves. Creating sounds on the piano fills them with well being and their usually sad countenance blossoms into a smile.

This can be a frustrating experience, too, especially if the patient was once proficient in piano playing. However, the risk is worthy because of the miraculous response for those whose spirits are uplifted through the music. For a few precious moments, they regain their wholeness and dignity.

Many autistic children have learned to speak through music therapy. Their difficulties in verbal expression are thought to relate to a dysfunction in the left side of the brain. This is the last of the two sides to develop and the one that controls language expression. Building on an autistic child's ability to mimic, the music therapist creates a bridge into the child's consciousness by mimicking their sounds. In the next stage of this slow and deliberate process the teacher bridges *their* sounds into whole notes. Once the child can mimic the musical tones, the transition is made to word sounds.

In the treatment of illness, music is gaining more and more credibility as the research continues.[10] There is a story about Pablo Casals, the great cellist who used the piano as a therapeutic intervention. Each morning he awoke, wheezing from emphysema and stiff with arthritis. With swollen fingers he laboriously dressed himself then sat down at the keyboard.

As he focused on his music, Bach, Brahms or Mozart, he would feel his body tuning itself to the pure sounds of the piano. Gradually his fingers unlocked, as did his spine, his arms and his legs. His breathing deepened. Soon he was able to stand upright and go for his morning walk. Upon his return, he was ready for his beloved cello. Only from this place of physical, mental and spiritual tone could he achieve what he did with the cello.

Pain Management

Music is known to be highly effective in pain management. There is a principle of physics called *entrainment* whereby two pendulums will gradually fall into parallel motion. This phenomenon seems to work in the human body as well. Some of the body's rhythms will gradually synchronize with the rhythms of the music. Changes most commonly measured are the breathing, heart rate and blood pressure. These rhythms increase when we experience pain and decrease when we interrupt its perception or its cause.

In order to reduce the perception of pain, we begin with familiar music that seems to equal the passionate intensity of the pain. The choice can be classical, jazz, pop hits or Country Western. Any type of music is suitable as long as we feel that it echoes the pain itself.

This part of the experience can involve listening, singing or playing a musical instrument. If your head is pounding with pain, and you like Strauss waltzes, you might begin with the *Blue Danube*. Raise the volume so it reflects the potency of the pain. Gradually lower the volume so the entrainment principle can occur. It is a matter of first matching the vibrations of the music to the pain, then slowing and softening them. The throbbing vibrations of the pain will correspondingly diminish.

You can add visual imagery to the process by closing your eyes and watching a river shift from a raging torrent to a tranquil current. If you are a classical music lover you might begin with Suppe's *Poet and Peasant Overture,* loudly at first, then gradually reducing the volume or switching to a Chopin Nocturne. Sensations of music and pain are both processed in the mid-brain. Perhaps this is why entrainment is so effective for pain control.

Music has also proven a healthy distraction from pain. By focusing intently on each note, or tapping out the rhythm, we can keep our mind busy. We have the ability to literally tune out the pain. This is a very difficult process for some people. Those who have applied themselves in other life disciplines such as martial arts, sports, dance, or painting find it much easier. The same skills of concentration apply.

Taking a Tonic

We can also learn to recognize the tonic or ending chords in the music we listen to. Musicians joke about taking a tonic. Compositions by Mozart and Bach or Gregorian Chant are filled with pure, whole tones and tonic chords.

To learn how to *take a tonic chord,* begin by breathing deeply as you listen. Purse your lips and exhale through your mouth with an audible "puff." Do this each time a phrase comes to conclusion. You will soon hear the tonic chords. They are like the periods on a sentence. They will simultaneously round off the musical phrase *and* the sharp corners of your pain. Mozart's sonatas are especially effective for this practice. The pleasing and relaxing effects of the music will reduce muscle tension and increase the flow of the body's natural pain suppressers.

Depression

By soothing the human spirit, we know that music inspires people recovering from a stroke. Depression and discouragement are common during the long rehabilitation phase. One woman said, "It was that bouncy music they played in Physical Therapy that helped me to try and try again."

Situational depression that is linked to feelings of helplessness can be relieved by music with tonic chords. The music resembles problem-solving. Over and over again, it moves up and around a theme. Over and over again, it concludes in a tonic chord. It seems to minimize chaotic thinking and stimulate creativity. People working in the creative arts use such music as they write, paint or sculpt.

The Relaxation Response

Listening to music also decreases the lung's resistance to the flow of air. This is another reason why Pablo Cassals played the piano; it loosened his contracted joints and relieved his shortness of breath.

Music has been shown to raise or lower blood pressure. It can change the electrical conductivity of the skin as demonstrated in the technique called biofeedback. Music is also used to reduce anxiety during dental work and to relax a woman during labor. It also helps minimize the discomfort of nausea associated with chemotherapy and to relax people before and during surgical procedures.

One study demonstrates that musically sedated patients require up to fifty percent less anesthesia during their surgery. Another indicated that when seriously ill patients in coronary care and intensive care units listened to meditative music they were less agitated, slept more soundly and needed less pain medication.

Spiritual Health

Spiritual health reflects our ability to feel centered in our bodies, connected to others and in harmony with the universe. For some this means sensing God's closeness. Others feel a transpersonal connection to nature. Many believe they are spiritually healthy in the giving and receiving of love. Some perceive a co-existing calmness and exhilaration.

Whatever our personal experience of spirituality may be, music serves as a profound catalyst for its fulfillment. We meet it in a great cathedral where the sounds from a massive pipe organ sink into our viscera. We may find it in the hush of a redwood forest where the pure pitch of bird-song reminds us that we, too, are pure. We may feel it in the musical laughter of a delighted child. The sacred music of the ages or the simple sounds of a Taizé chant may move us to spiritual ecstasy. Certainly, these are some of life's peak experiences. Why not include them in yours?

Choosing Music, Choosing Life

Music is a gift of the universe that heals us, motivates us, calms us and softens us. It keeps us company. It helps us to grieve and to rejoice. Participants selectively use music to enhance life. Bystanders haven't given it much thought. Because music is such a powerful force, we need to be conscious about it. Not all music is good for us.

Sounds can make us sick. Insipid music nauseates the system. It is otherwise called, *elevator music.* Too much Country Western music fills the mind with negative thoughts: "the dog died, the woman left, the man cheated, and the heart is broken." Music has been used to express all manner of pain and suffering. Be judicious in your choices of popular music. Many lyrics expose life's darkest side. Catchy, repetitive tunes can run around inside your head for days, making focus difficult. It is important to avoid these vibrations that poison the system. We cannot tune music out the same way we can tune out conversation.

Rigid people find jazz too disorganized. Others find it relaxing. Our taste begins at *point A* and will stay there unless we do something about it. We can experiment with sounds that seem strange at first. If they match our personal rhythms we will know it, for a feeling of well-being soon comes over us. We can enhance our repertoire of pleasure music by consciously listening to unfamiliar composers. We should give new sounds a chance. It may take another person to help us hear the rhythm or phrasing. Getting to *point B* is part of choosing life.

Peppy music will help you get the chores done. Soothing music will let you relax. Whatever you are choosing to do, be it work or play, music can enrich the experience. There is music in all of life. The sounds of the ocean are music to some, while the rhythm of a cat's purring will lull another to sleep. Music will both heal and entertain.

There is a wonderful story in the Old Testament of the Bible. It concerns a fellow by the name of Job whose life was in a mess. Moreover, Job had a bad habit of whining and complaining about it to God.

As the story goes, God got fed up with Job's attitude and took him to task. In essence, He said, "Now see here, Job, what gives you the idea that you know so much about how things should be? Were you there when I created the earth? Were you there 'while the morning stars sang together, and all the angels shouted for joy'?"

Sometimes we are much like Job. We complain about our circumstances rather that choosing a means to change them. We can learn to choose life in many ways, music being one of them. If we live consciously and set our intention toward fresh beginnings we will hear the morning stars. We will have chosen life.

Chapter Fourteen
Beauty

Life is too short to drink from ugly cups.

What comes to mind when you hear the word, *beauty?* Is it music, art or poetry? Do images of nature appear before your eyes: rolling surf, a pristine lake, a rushing waterfall? Or do you think of the beauty found in relationships: tenderness, wordless intimacy and kindness? If you were to make a list of the beauty in your life, how many pages would it fill?

So much of life is beautiful, and we need it more than ever before. Increasing economic complexities in most societies leave people gasping to keep abreast of change. Daily survival absorbs our bodies and minds, stealing time to such a great extent that we forget about beauty and the joy it brings. Beauty adds abundance to our spiritual reserves. Beautiful memories help soothe us when we are sad. They offer hope when we are confused. Beauty charms our present and quickens our anticipation of the future.

In choosing life we take steps to increase our awareness of the beautiful. Sometimes it is right under our noses, and we fail to notice it. Age, wrinkles or deformity may disguise it because beauty may be hidden, waiting for discovery. Arrogance precludes it. Innocence accepts it. Beauty is a personal experience. We perceive something as beautiful when it pleases us. How do we develop this sense? Some of it is a natural process, and much of it is learned.

Suppose we are walking down Ocean Avenue in Carmel, California. We pause in front of a gallery to gaze at an oil painting. We are not impressed. Suddenly someone comes up behind us. We hear an appreciative, "ahhh." Eager for an audience, the admirer begins to point out the painting's interplay of line and color, notions that hadn't occurred to us. He then goes on to talk about the artist, where she grew up and how her fond childhood memories had inspired this work. As we listen, something mysterious begins to happen. The scene before us comes into focus, coaxed there by the words of the speaker. Now we see the beauty in it: the shapes, the shades and the story. Transfixed, we realize we are silently communing with the artist. We are in a relationship with a person we may never meet. Our lives will never be quite the same.

Beauty feeds the senses, but more than that, it nourishes the human spirit. We pause and are reborn each time we absorb a lovely sound, a splendid sunset or a graceful curtsey. Life offers so many forms of beauty: exquisite flavors, dramatic designs and seductive smiles. Each arouses our appreciation for living. Our task then, in choosing life, is to broaden our awareness of the beautiful. We must step out of our ego cages and become receptive, even reverent of the beautiful in life. So often we try to dominate our senses by fitting them into preconceived judgements. A better choice is to remove the lenses of opinion based on other people's likes and dislikes. Because of its timeless and temporal qualities, beauty is everywhere.

Visual Beauty

Light vibrations enter the eye where they travel along the optic nerve to the brain. There they divide. Some determine the body's sleep/wake rhythm. Others interpret light and dark, color and image. As with any information gathered by our senses, visual data translates into human experience. Seeing is believing. Believing is the basis for behaving. The manner in which we behave demonstrates to others who we are. People usually respond to us according to our behavior.

This influences the development of certain characteristics and the diminishing of others. We might say, "Seeing is becoming."

Everything we see may be interpreted as beautiful, bland, or ugly. Line and color, shape and design, sillouhette and shadow, all become fixed in our consciousness as pleasing, dull or offensive. Mental conditioning is largely responsible for these translations. It occurs gradually as our sphere of influence expands.

The eyes continue to grow and develop during the first six years of life. Little babies become animated when they can differentiate between black and white. It's as if they say, "Aha, I've learned something and isn't it exciting?" The cells in a baby's brain are immature and cannot interpret beauty. This comes later. As they grow they begin attaching visual language to feelings. When feeling good about Mommy they will say, "Mommy, you're bootiful." When they've been scolded they are quick to say, "Mommy you're ugly." The words have nothing to do with visual perception. They mean, "I feel badly, and since you are supposed to be in charge, and you're not stopping me from having these bad feelings, you are to blame. You are ugly."

When a parent says, "Oh, look at the pretty flower," the young child will repeat, "Pretty flower." If the flower is yellow, an association will be made that yellow is pretty. Later, when asked, "What is your favorite color?" this child will triumphantly respond, "Yellow." A positive association has been made between mother, child and the flower. It includes feelings and behaviors. As long as no life circumstance interferes with this initial interpretation of yellow, that is, nothing dramatically negative happens where yellow is involved, it will continue to be a favorite.

Temperament also contributes to our opinions about what is beautiful and what is not. We may be able to convince an amenable child that the brown dress from Aunt Mary is lovely, but a strong-willed child will want nothing to do with it. Both children may dislike the color. Temperament determines which child will be induced to wear it and which will not.

Colors are light vibrations of varying lengths and frequencies. They influence, and are influenced by the myriad vibrations and pulsations within the human body. Some complement our uniqueness, others do not. The less we are taught about which colors we are supposed to like, the more we will discover which colors are good for us. By surrounding ourselves with pleasing colors we improve our well-being and reinforce our own personality.

Children see through the eyes of those who influence them the most, usually their parents. Authorities sway our opinions throughout life, but never more than during these first five years. The way we appear to others is intricately involved with the way we feel. The ability to notice life around us is linked to our satisfaction with ourselves. When we are content with who we are we need not spend time being concerned with, "Am I good enough? Am I smart enough? Am I likable?" Children who get off to a good start have time to observe the world around them. Children whose parents encourage this role of observer are fortunate indeed.

Young children, eager to please, mimic those around them. Andrew swaggers around in Dad's baseball hat. Mommy offers, "You look handsome, Andrew." Andrew already knows he is handsome because he has the hat to prove it. Hearing Mommy's words reinforces what he knows. Good-feeling endorphins surge through his little body leaving behind a memory of confident conviction. Molly loves to stagger around in Mommy's shoes. "How's my princess today?" Molly knows she is beautiful. Daddy's beaming face says it all. She will remember that look and watch for it in future admirers.

An important aspect of childhood should be learning to appreciate the visually beautiful around us. Nature, buildings, shapes, forms, sounds and textures can be called into awareness when children are as young as two years of age. They will quickly develop their senses and come to know what pleases them. Christine at age four knows she likes her green socks best and will make a fuss about wearing any others. Aaron wants to wear only his blue soccer shirt. Neither one cares about matching or coordinating. That comes much later. A wise mother will let them choose their own clothes with comfort in mind and be glad they want to. Children feel confident when they are wearing their favorite colors and textures. It signals to the world, "See how grown up I am? I'm dressing myself." (As if we didn't know!)

Children can overcome fears by using their senses. A child who is afraid of the dark can be taught to value the texture of a piece of deep blue velvet. A correlation can then be made between soft, gentle dark and nighttime. "See how beautiful is the night sky? It covers the earth with a lovely blue velvet blanket just like yours. Nighttime's blanket has holes in it to let the moon and stars peek through."

Associations of feelings, language, colors and shapes continue to develop until adolescence only to be tossed aside and replaced with newer definitions. During this stage it is the adolescent's job to sample extremes, the different, even the strange. They become confused about what is beautiful and often lose sight of their own beauty. Teens can be harshly critical of family members and familiar role models. The world appears ridiculous to them so they adopt clothing and colors that reflect their inner chaos.

Leaving adolescence behind, young adults can rekindle childhood memories of feeling beautiful. Suddenly it is important to look physically attractive. They bathe, shave, get a makeover and have their *colors done.* Looking good gains an added dimension of feeling sensual. Beauty takes on a delightful new dimension through this sensory awareness.

As we grow up, media, movies and marketing exert tremendous influence on our ideas of what is beautiful. They satiate our senses with images of everything from clothing to cars. They define the latest in beautiful items for us to purchase. They even tell us who the beautiful people are. We become inculcated with how we should look, speak and act.

The advertising media targets adolescents and young working adults. Both are driven to the marketplace by blossoming sexual desire. Mom's ideas of good taste are swept under the rug to be replaced by the latest craze. Fads spread like measles throughout the group. Insistent messages say, "Sexy and slim guarantees true love." This potent medium has the power to reshape reality. Dressing for conformity can be very unbecoming. An olive-skinned female who looks almost moribund in chartreuse will wear it anyway if it is the latest spring color. A healthy degree of nonconformity can be wise.

Fashion influences that define the *beautiful look* will compel young people to comply. Inner conflicts often arise costing many their self-esteem. If people don't have the means to purchase trendy clothing, they feel left out. If their body doesn't look good in the latest fashion they feel ugly. When they are heavy or round in shape, they can't compete with the ubiquitous models.

Feelings of insecurity can cost many a young woman her health. If her *thin image* leads to bulimia or anorexia, it may cost her a life. The basic human need of feeling good enough can so easily be met within the formative first five years of life. When it isn't, its price tag goes up. Today's society doesn't offer much to young people when it comes to building self-esteem. Too many little boys don't get to share Daddy's baseball hat, and too many little girls miss out on Mommy's high-heeled shoes.

During the 1700s, artists depicted beautiful females as round and voluptuous. The mother figure with large, soft breasts and wide hips was the epitome of female allure. Contrast this with today's Western rendition of the beautiful female: long, slender torso and narrow hips, a feminine version of the male body. Are we so programmed by Madison Avenue that we fail to see beauty in softness and grace? I once heard a gentleman say, "There is nothing more beautiful than a pregnant woman. To me it's an incredible turn-on." This was a married man with children of his own. He went on to explain that each time his wife was pregnant she felt beautifully feminine and sensual. These were the most intimate periods of their marriage. Beautiful feelings implant a beautiful self-image, which in turn fosters intimacy and love.

Partners need to express what they find beautiful about each other. Men like to hear that they are handsome and will usually believe it. "Beautiful" is more believable to a woman than being told, "You're so pretty." Prettiness is a genetic accident while beauty is a cultivated mixture of confidence and self-care. A woman will accept the words when she sees a genuine expression of admiration in her partner's eyes.

It is important that our culture begins redefining feminine beauty, and men have the power to do it. When a woman is told she has a lovely smile, she hears, "I am lovable." When he says, "You are so soft, so beautiful," she hears, "I am sufficient and I am lovable." If he says, "You are beautiful when anger flashes in your eyes like that," her interpretation is, "I am safe and I am loved no matter what." Women are harshly critical of their appearance. They will leave the house without breakfast but never without lipstick. A woman will love you forever and forgive you almost anything, if, on a *fat day* or a *bad hair day,* you say, "You may not know this, but you are absolutely beautiful."

Women sometimes forget that men need compliments too. "Great tie," with a little smile and a raised eyebrow is a nice but rather modest tribute. He may wonder, "Well, what about the rest of me? I know it's a great tie." "You look great in that tie," says "You are a handsome guy, and that tie amplifies the fact."

Human warmth and kindness will offset the most unpleasant physical features. However, good looks will not offset a sour personality. We must guard against the distractions of physical beauty or the lack of it. A beautiful spirit can be found inside a peculiar body. It can even be buried under a cantankerous attitude. Sometimes we have to look below the surface to find it. Appearances can deceive the emotional heart.

Much of what is pleasing to the visual eye relates to our mood and emotional needs. If a color is visually pleasing, chances are it will please us emotionally as well. Colors influence our moods. Short spectrum or warming colors such as reds, oranges and yellows, appear to extend time. They stimulate brain activity possibly because they have the lowest photon frequency but the highest intensity. Red is a popular color for restaurant interiors. It creates an illusion that considerable time has gone by so the patrons won't linger. Turnover equates to profit.

Long spectrum or cooling colors like blues, greens and violets, have the opposite effect on one's sense of time and mood. They are applied in work settings because they make time appear to move more quickly while exerting a calming effect on the workers' emotions.

Our homes should be places of beauty; sensual reflections of ourselves that remind us of our passions and delights. The ancient Oriental science of Feng Shui elevates interior decorating to a spiritual level. It blends the wisdom of geometric design with human traits in order to create pleasing and healing environments. At the core of this philosophy lies the mystery of Chi, or, life force energy. Today we know it to be electromagnetic in nature. Chi or electromagnetic fields traverse all living forms as well as the earth. Eastern thought emphasizes the importance of balancing the relationships between humankind, the earth and the heavens. It applies to all areas of life, health, wealth, creativity and work. Chi is the force common to them all and therefore considered sacred. Architecture and interior design are aspects of life that must harmonize with the Chi of the earth and the people who live there.

A few years ago, while vacationing in Tahiti, I called upon a local physician. My goal was to gather information about the health of the islanders for an article I was writing on longevity. He agreed to the interview and introduced me to his strikingly beautiful wife. She wore a native Tahitian costume, a sarong tied at the waist. Her torso was bare. Bright orange hibiscus flowers nestled behind one ear. She was tall and regal, a stark contrast to the crude shelter that was their home. As she brewed rich, strong coffee, my eyes scanned the room. The ceiling was a corrugated tin roof. Lavish sprays of feathers and dried fern fronds ameliorated the crudeness of the beige mud walls. A piece of bright floral cloth casually framed an opening in the wall, the room's only window. Gracefully she served our coffee while speaking in a sultry French accent. We might have been in a parlor at Versailles for all the elegance found there. That which was plain and ugly paled beside the beauty she had created.[1]

Beautiful Sound

Sound vibrations can soothe, annoy, please, irritate or stimulate the nervous system. Music can evoke memories and shift moods. Sounds are beautiful when they alter our brain wave rhythm in a manner that is pleasing. If we are anxious, sounds can help us relax. When we are depressed, sounds can raise our spirits. Passionate people choose passionate music because it vibrates with their deepest sense of themselves. It reminds them of who they really are. Calm people choose gentle music because it helps them get in touch with their inner peace, the place they feel most familiar and secure.

Sound waves travel through the external ear to the inner ear and then to the oldest part of the brain. They are intricately linked to our instinctive fight or flight responses. Sounds warn us of danger. They are the first of the senses to develop and the last to leave. An eighteen-week-old fetus will alter its heartbeat with a change in sounds. A person who has had a stroke and cannot speak will smile at a familiar song. A dying person will visibly relax when he or she hears the words, "Just breathe and let go. Stop trying so hard to hold on. Relax."

Some people like loud sounds while others like them soft. Some people like ocean sounds and others prefer birds. Sound is beautiful to us when its pulsations harmonize with our own. From a very early age we learn to recognize certain sounds and surround them with memory. There are some universally disliked sounds: the screams of the dentist's drill, fingernails on chalkboard, gunshots and the thudding of a blown-out tire.

Beautiful sound evokes pleasing memories and harmonizing vibrations. If you want to get to know someone, just ask, "What are your favorite sounds?" Does a crackling fire and soft music remind you of romance? What do humming engines or buzzing saws make you think of? What happens to your appetite when you think of potatoes boiling, dishes rattling and knives chopping? Every young mother knows the baby sounds of gurgling and suckling. The refrain of a lullaby brings comfort and so does the purr of a car engine turning over on a frosty morning. The cracks of ball on bat, a national anthem and the swish of skis on snow are sounds that thrill. There are happy sounds: a child's laughter, a lilting voice and a jackpot of silver dollars. Sounds such as these are healing to the human spirit. We should stop and savor them.

Sound waves alter the body's rhythms. Breathing, cardiac rhythm, intestinal pulsation and all the other pulses will quicken or lessen in response to sounds. Just as pleasant sounds create harmony, agitating sounds create dissonance, which can result in irritability, insomnia and headache. Snoring is harder on a marriage than a bad habit. Because sound is directed to the oldest part of the brain, it is difficult to ignore. We may think we are ignoring it but pulsation enters the brain regardless of what we believe.

There are many environmental sounds we cannot control: airplanes, traffic, leaf blowers and thunder. To choose life we must first become aware of sounds we can control and take steps to alleviate the culprits. We can choose music carefully. We can wear earplugs. We can turn down the volume. We can use white sound machines to interrupt noise. An oscillating fan is an excellent way to soften grating sounds and introduce a rhythmic pulsation. Most importantly we can acknowledge that sound affects us. If we have been blessed with the gift of hearing, we ought to value it and care for it. Life without sound loses much of its beauty. Life with sound can be more beautiful than we have ever imagined. Choose your sounds wisely. Listen to the rhythms of your body and learn to work with them.

Tactile Beauty

So much of our daily existence involves touch that we may fail to notice the beauty it brings. It, too, is an experience of personal preference. Our response to touch begins with our earliest tactile imprints. The birthing experience of rhythmic compression is vitally different from the warm, wet environment of the womb. We are fortunate when our first dry contact with another human is firm and gentle. Subsequent swaddling and bathing gives us immediate clues about the trustworthiness of other humans. Once we've left the safety of the mother's womb, we instinctively fear falling. Beautiful touch that comforts and reassures helps to assuage this fear.

During the first few months of life we continue to be exquisitely sensitive to touch. The manner in which we are bathed, cleaned, diapered and held leave indelible sensations on the body and lasting memories in the mind, spirit and emotions. A beautiful tactile beginning is a true blessing.

Our sense of touch develops with the rest of our physical growth. The ways we are played with, soothed or punished will all stamp impressions into our personality. They will have associated thoughts and feelings that remain there until a new experience replaces them. The frequency, intensity, severity, and associated emotions of early touching will influence the extent of their impact. Children who are tickled affectionately continue to view this activity as loving. Children tickled mercilessly carry an angry and fearful remembrance with them into adulthood. Can such an adult ever enjoy a beautiful experience of being tickled? The answer is "Yes." We can re-program our responses to touch through awareness and fresh experience. Beautiful touch heals our brokenness.

Our response to touch is also influenced by bodily composition. The distribution of three basic types of tissues, ectoderm, endoderm and mesoderm, help to determine what type of touch feels good to us. The combined relationship of these three tissues stays with us throughout our lifetime. We can cover them with fat, enlarge them with steroids or emaciate them with starvation, but our physical composition remains what it is.

People who have long flat bones and a large skin surface per overall body volume are extremely sensitive to touch. Earlier, we called this body type ectomorphic or ecto in the abbreviated form. Beautiful touch to an ecto includes fabrics that are lightweight, soft and cozy. They love to have their backs scratched. Ectos appreciate gentle, contactful touching. Pressure that is too light will irritate them. Pressure that is mildly deep will send them into spasms.

The mesomorphic body type has sturdy squarish bones and dense muscle fibers. Beautiful touch to a meso presses deeply into their muscles. They like big hugs and close encounters, pulsating showers and gusts of wind. Mesos feel absolutely beautiful when they have worked hard enough to glow with perspiration.

It is the nature of the more rounded body type, the endomorph, to love all manner of touch. Their life is feeling-oriented so they trust their *gut* response in most situations. Touch that engenders emotion is the most beautiful to them.

Most of us find beauty in a soft summer breeze, a firm handshake, a lover's skin and the touch of silk. Some like soft fabrics: velvet, cashmere or camel hair. Others prefer crisp cloth: starched cotton, linen or poplin. Still others find beauty in stiff, even rough material: sailcloth, tweed or burlap. The clothing we wear is cut from the same cloth as our personality. It tells a great deal about who we are.

People who give and receive enough touch, sexually and otherwise, know they are beautiful. They are confident and assured. Bring beautiful touch into every day of your life. It will release the inherent beauty of your human spirit. You will radiate confidence, self-love and compassion. Everyone who comes near you will be influenced by your powerful presence.

Beautiful Tastes

Flavors and aromas, textures and temperatures add so much to living we cannot even imagine life without them. From basic survival to social embellishment, the creation of culinary art has been central to our humanity. Foods and beverages have the potential to heal, comfort and entertain.

They can stimulate or sedate our thinking. They seduce us when we are emotionally weak and boost our energy when we are tired. They are a channel for creative expression and the agent of hospitality. The partaking of nourishment is one of our earliest activities. The minute we stop it in earnest, we begin to die.

Choosing life is not about surviving but about building upon dreams. We can survive on very simple foods. The peasant diet of rice, beans and fruit would provide most of our daily requirements, but adding beautiful tastes into daily experience enriches our life and increases our zest for living. Flavors and aromas are everywhere. We can choose to expand our repertoire of them in myriad ways.

We may forget words, but we rarely forget the impression of a flavor. It is an encoded experience that lasts a lifetime. Some of our taste acuity fades with aging, but that favorite tapioca pudding will still bring a smile to an ancient face.

Before biting into an apple we conjure up its anticipated flavor and texture. How shocking to expect sweetness and be greeted with sourness! Our whole body recoils. Hair-like gustatory nerves located in the tongue produce some of the most dynamic responses we know. These highly specialized flavor centers are known as *taste buds.* Their influence strikes at the heart of our body, mind and spirit.

Our native constitutional gifts include six distinct tastes: sweet, sour, bitter, salty, pungent and bland. Each of them has variant subtastes: semi-sweet, semi-sour, tangy, hot and spicy and astringent. Tastes are affiliated with smells, and this adds to their pleasing qualities. Plants provide us with thousands of flavors from the distinct to the delicate. In food and beverage preparation we learn to blend them, bringing out certain qualities while diminishing others. Developing the palate is another way of choosing life. Anyone can distinguish between the six basic tastes. We add beauty to living when we fine-tune our senses so we recognize and enjoy a variety of flavors and gustatory textures.

Most people like a sweet taste. A salty taste is the next favorite, followed by pungent, sour, bitter and bland.   Texture enhances the pleasure of tasting and is highly personal in preference. Some like the crunchy feel and sound, others prefer smooth and silky. Some just enjoy them all. We have very early memories of taste. They are intricately linked to our first experiences of living: that of suckling and contentment. This is where the taste pleasure begins and it is one we carry throughout our lifetime.

Eastern philosophy and medicine view the six basic tastes as a corollary to health. When we have a craving for a particular taste, it does not mean we need it. Rather, it is a symptom of imbalance in the system. We can balance our taste receptors by gradually introducing all six basic flavors. Each has a place in our nutritional requirements and should be part of our daily diet. Western taste is skewed by the degree of sugar and salt added to foods and beverages. It is so pervasive we have evolved into a species that craves them. Coffee and pure chocolate provide a bitter taste to our diet helping to equalize this primal sense. We have come to crave them as well.

The tongue, nose and palate are all involved in flavor appreciation. Foods and beverages should be savored and relished. When taken in small quantities their full sensation can be experienced. There are three phases to consider when eating or drinking. The first is the anticipation phase. It includes memory recall, visual admiration and inhaling the aroma. When you go to a restaurant do you read the whole menu? For some, this is a scintillating ritual. The next is the tasting, chewing experience. Food should be chewed to a fine paste for the benefit of good digestion. It also allows enough time for all the taste buds to be stimulated. Finally, the swallowing and after-taste aspect of the experience provides fullness and satisfaction.

Choosing life involves our participation in all three phases. Beautiful taste is ours when we slow down and truly enjoy what we have. Once we master this art we can expand our repertoire of flavors and aromas, a few at a time. Life becomes richer when we gently nourish this wonderful gift, our sense of taste.

Beautiful Scents

Beautiful fragrances emanate from many forms of life and are central to all living systems. Plants contain aromatic essential oils that regulate their cell life and serve as a communication device. Specific insects and birds respond to the call of these unique smells. They land on the flowers and while busying about, manage to get pollen all over their bodies. They then fly off to the call of another scent wafting from the female of the same species. Some plants are more sophisticated than others in summoning their couriers. Orchids have one of the highest contact rates.

Insects, birds and animals depend on their sense of smell for survival. It warns them of danger and leads them to food. Humans don't usually bother to cultivate their sense of smell, being satisfied with what they have. But fragrances add more to life than pleasure, for they have medicinal properties as well. Essences enter the blood stream and are transported to tissues that respond to them. Some stimulate while others sedate. Some act as anti-inflammatory agents and others as antibiotics. Some soothe anxiety while others diminish depression. Some essences kindle sexual desire, and yet others calm the nerves. Plant essences are one of nature's most beautiful gifts. We can learn to appreciate them and, in so doing, choose a fuller, richer life.

Humans are odiferous creatures. We smell! Some of these odors emanate from the body's elimination systems of bowel, bladder, breath and sweat glands. Depending on the health of the individual, these odors and can be sweet, pungent, sour or quite toxic and unpleasant. They rarely qualify as beautiful. There is, however, a subtle aroma produced by specific glands that serves another function, that of propagating the species.

All mammals emit aromas that are actually sexual signals called pheromones. These are hormones produced by one creature that are perceived only by another of the same species. Bears are attracted to other bears by way of pheromones. Tigers are not attracted by elephant pheromones, only by those of other tigers. Pheromones are unique in that they have the properties of producing a change in the sexual or social behavior of the recipient. They are the earliest signals of interest from one mammal to another.

Scent, therefore, plays a significant role in the physical attraction of one person to another. Both genders have within their normal anatomy, highly specialized scent-producing glands that are part of the sex drive. They are located in the regions of the genitals, chest, and abdomen. These glands go into action whenever one individual becomes interested in another. When the chemistry is mutual, the pheromone production increases, causing a powerful urge to speak, to connect and to flirt. Naturally, humans vary widely from one to the other in any hormone production with this one being no exception. Chemistry can repel as well as attract.

Nursing mothers produce pheromones around the nipples. Research demonstrates that newborn babies can identify their own mothers by smell. Young children find comfort in cuddling a blanket that has their mother's scent. Amniotic fluid, which surrounds the fetus inside the uterus, has a musk-like smell. Interestingly, musk is a universal favorite in colognes, after-shave lotions, massage oils and perfumes. Its essential oil comes from the seeds and roots of the angelica plant. It grows natively in northern Europe and has revitalizing medicinal properties. It is one of life's most basic and beautiful scents.

The sense of smell is sometimes referred to as *The Gateway to the Soul*. There are two reasons for this. First, the olfactory cranial nerves are directly linked to the limbic or most primitive part of the brain. It may even be considered an extension of the brain by way of location. The limbic system regulates three basic drives: thirst, hunger and sex. When the sense of smell is activated because of hunger in any of these areas, the urge for satisfaction is profound. It is a reactive request that doesn't involve the reasoning mind. This is why cravings in any of these three areas are so difficult to manage behaviorally.

The second reason we refer to the sense of smell as the Gateway to the Soul has to do with memory. Powerful associations are made between smells and feelings. The memory of feelings associated with notable situations are stored. They can sometimes be traced to very early periods in our lives.

One gentleman tells about a beautiful feeling of tenderness that came over him whenever he was exposed to a particular fragrance. He could be walking down the street, and just catching a whiff of this certain scent would be enough to shift his mood. He assumed the fragrance came from a woman's perfume, and, although the sensation was pleasing, it was also a little unnerving. Eventually curiosity got the better of him and he began a search to trace the fragrance. He started at a large department store and, after much sampling, he settled on a name. Further research produced a composite of the kinds of women who wore the perfume and its era of popularity. Through some diligent work and a little luck he was able to get to the bottom of the mystery.

It seems that when he was born, his mother developed a severe infection and had to be isolated from the obstetrical unit. She was kept in the hospital for three months. As a newborn, he remained in the hospital nursery until an aunt could come from across the country to take care of him. It was this aunt who wore the beguiling perfume. She and her fragrance were his earliest associations of mothering. There was no more beautiful scent to him than that one.

What are your most beautiful scents? Are they found in nature, like roses or rain forests? Do they come from the kitchen, like freshly baked bread or chocolate chip cookies? Are they associated with work, perhaps engine oil or fresh sawdust? Is it the perfume of a lover or the sweet smell of a baby? Can you imagine life without them? Bystanders take them for granted. Participants cherish their favorites and are alert to discovering new ones. You can develop your sense of smell by experimenting with aromas in all walks of life. Be sure to nourish your spirit with those that comfort and refresh you. Breathe deeply, letting the fragrance and the memories flood you with pleasure. This is choosing life!

Kinesthetic Beauty

Movement offers a special form of beauty that engages the senses. Children are intrigued with moving things. They delight in some of the simplest moves made by the smallest of creatures: ants on the march, a bug curling itself into a ball, a butterfly manipulating its tiny legs on a flower. The antics of pets resemble a daily parade of entertainment: "Mommy, you know what I saw Buffer do? He dugged and dugged till he made a big hole and there was a bone in there!" Adults recapture an appreciation for living when they wake up and look at the world through the eyes of their children. Life is so much more enjoyable when you are a participant.

Nature is constantly on the move offering a wide variety of kines- thetic spectacles. For sensitive souls there are cascading waterfalls, gentle waves and undulating tides. For those who like action there are exploding rapids, crashing waves and thunder storms. A falling star makes us sigh. A blitz of chain lightening catches our breath. How many of us have waited to capture that last bit of sunlight against a horizon or watched fluffy white clouds float across an azure sky? Beautiful movement has a special appeal to the poet in each of us.

Humans love moving their bodies to musical rhythms because it lifts the human spirit. Little children dance instinctively. Ancient peoples used dance to invoke healing spirits and to talk with the gods. Egyptian hiero- glyphics depict bodies swaying to the rhythm of simple instruments. Each society uses dance as an art form. It combines grace and power, a para- doxical union that stimulates the senses. Admirer and participant experience beauty through this expressive medium.

Watching athletics allows us to vicariously enjoy movement. As the thrill of the contest mounts, so does our excitement. It's as if we are on the field, poised for action. To be caught up in this type of stimulation is what we pay for. We can easily overlook the kinesthetic beauty of the players in exchange for our own tingling pleasure. The game of football is a prime example of this type of involvement. Amidst crashing limbs and colliding bodies, one could easily miss the athletic grace to be found there.

The first time I noticed it was when I witnessed a wide receiver run all the way into the end zone for a touchdown. He did a little dance that demonstrated outstanding strength and agility. In order to slow his speed he leaned back at a forty-five degree angle while still moving forward. His body undulated, high-stepping knees and springs in his toes. It was brief and remarkable. For the first time I saw the beauty of an athlete whose body did exactly what his spirit demanded. It was an expression of sheer joy.

Dancers who stir our emotions are clearly responding to some source of deep inner beauty. Body and soul merge in flawless expression. Musicians with hands flying over a keyboard or fingers caressing a bow appear somehow detached from their physicality. Their faces hold an expression of being in love.

Movement captivates the human spirit in ways that static beauty cannot. Watch the face of a father as his newborn wraps a tiny fist around his index finger. There are no words to describe the beauty of that act. Observe a young child shaping a letter of the alphabet for the first time; his whole body is engaged: pencil clutched, head bowed, tongue protruding. It can bring tears to the eyes. Whether the movement is a first occasion or the result of arduous practice, it can enrich our lives as nothing else can. Take heed of beautiful movement. It will bring you untold happiness.

Beautiful Gifts

Some of life's most beautiful gifts are not gift-wrappable. They involve the things we do and the words we say that let others know we care about them.

Gestures of kindness, especially when they involve personal risk, are among some of life's most beautiful gifts. I once heard the true story of a gentleman, an amputee, who was riding on the back step of a crowded cable car. He clung to the safety pole as the car jerked and swayed its way up one of San Francisco's historic inclines. During a particularly violent lurch, the man's prosthetic leg loosened, slipped out of his pant leg and began rolling down the hill. Passengers yelled, "Stop! stop!" It was an odd request for the sacrosanct trolley-car conductor whose better judgment precluded such an act on such a hill. Brakes screeched as the car ground to a halt on its breathless perch. In a brave and beautiful gesture of kindness, a lady passenger said, "Would you like me to go and get your leg?" The man nodded numbly. After some delay, the prosthesis was retrieved and safely clipped into place (which the man had previously neglected to do). After one giant lurch the little trolley began inching its way up the hill. The lady who volunteered to fetch the prosthesis exceeded kindness. Anyone who knows San Francisco traffic or cable cars will agree.

Smiling is a beautiful gift, as is saying, "hello." We teach our children not to talk to strangers and then forget that as adults we should. We live on a very small planet and need as many beautiful gifts as we can find. An elderly couple being affectionate gives us a gift by reminding us that love is never too late. A remorse-filled apology is a beautiful gift as is a "thank you." There are so many courtesies directed toward us each day. How fully do we receive them? In choosing life we learn to pause and absorb these offerings of human good will. They warm the spirit and invoke reciprocation.

Ecstasy

There are occasions in life where beauty exceeds even itself. These are epiphanies, breath-catching experiences that impress the body, mind, spirit and emotions with unmistakable beauty. They stay in our mid-term memory, ever ready for quick and easy recall. At times they pop into our present without any apparent provocation, flooding us with warm, happy feelings.

Ecstatic beauty is like a rare and precious gem. When we experience it we feel as if we have received a marvelous gift. New parents taste the ecstasy of creation when they cradle their newborn child. Couples who have fallen out of love and fall back in again share the rapture of a healed relationship. A mountain climber surveys his vista with triumphant joy. The gold medal winner savors a surge of pride born from arduous practice, discipline and sacrifice. A faith community resonates with the harmony of an inspiring worship service. Tears of joy overflow when someone dear has been healed or something precious has been found. Life hands us all the struggles and the rewards that require exceptional response.

When we choose life and are fully alive we experience ecstasy time and time again. These are some of life's profound gifts, often but not always earned. They are pivotal points in our existence.

Paradoxical Beauty

Every child should hear the story of *The Ugly Duckling* by Hans Christian Anderson. This is a fable about a young bird that is hatched into a family of ducks. He doesn't look anything like the others so they tease him and call him ugly. His reassuring mother does her best to assuage his hurt feelings but to little avail. It is a touching story that captures the pain children feel when they are teased and labeled as *different*.

This story has a happy ending. One day the ugly duckling sees himself mirrored on the smooth surface of a pond. In astonishment he realizes that he is not a duckling at all, but a beautiful swan. The story teaches that things are not always as they seem and we must believe in ourselves no matter what others say about us.

What is beautiful to one person may be ugly or uninteresting to another. Organized people see the beauty of order and predictability. They love to watch patterns falling into place; the mathematician sees beauty in an elegant proof; the musician translates note sequences into beautiful sound. Numbers and notes appear lifeless to the uninitiated.

They spring into existence, even into glory for those who can appreciate them.

Others of us are capable of seeing the beauty of disarray: natural wilderness, asymmetrical shapes and the potential of the formless. Healers don't see the disease, they see the cure. Beauty truly is in the experience of the beholder, and we are all so different.

To be fully human means embracing life's paradoxes. Discovering the beautiful in something offensive expands our humanity. It stretches our understanding and teaches empathy for others.

There is pain in relinquishing the familiar, even if it is harmful to us. However, through the suffering of letting go comes the beauty of growing and learning. We doggedly hold on to the accustomed way of doing things. Finally we let go, and when we do we heal as we grieve and become better people. It takes adequate support and an intention to do so. This is a choice.

When we isolate ourselves from others by stubbornly justifying our bitterness and resentment, we remain stuck in angry victim behavior. It's really difficult for others to love us when we are like that. By becoming vulnerable and asking for help we open a door that lets in advice, opportunities, suggestions and compassion. A pained stoic will suffer in silence and believe it is good to do so. However, from the ashes of human suffering can come profound intimacy.

Contradictions, inconsistencies and reversals are all part of living. We can face them alone or with another. We can deal with them or avoid them. Participants choose to live through them with support. They can surrender to receiving the tender and unexpected prizes that come from admitting, "I don't know how to get through this." With the divine in our heart and a friend to count on, we can overcome anything. Beauty is everywhere.

Beautiful Relationships

There are three types of relationships: the one we have with our-selves, the ones we have with other individuals and those we have with corporate systems. The ultimate and unique corporate relationship is the one we have with God. The one we have with ourselves involves our self-image, self-control, self-esteem, self-respect, self-confidence and self-love. We learn how to be in charge of ourselves as we grow. One reason self-help books are so popular is that these characteristics seldom develop by the time we leave home. Once on our own, maturation becomes a learn-as-you-go process.

Throughout our lives the relationships we have with other individuals range from casual to intimate, from boring to beautiful. Humans need the love and respect of others. We gain it by learning social skills and risking rejection. Saying "hello," shaking hands, smiling, and nod-ding are healthy ways to build a bridge with people we don't know. These harmless gestures are much more difficult for introverted folks than for those who are extroverted. Sometimes people get labeled as *standoffish* when they are really just happier with solitude. In life's job description for the extrovert it is written, "You shall extend your hand to those reserved types."

Time spent in college, the military or in community service can pro-vide a useful transition period between home and total independence. By the time we are young adults we should have attained three levels of responsibility: economic, social and sexual. These are the requisite build-ing blocks for entering into a career and a long-term partnered relationship. When we have a solid sense of our goodness, a work ethic and a conscience, we are ready for the beauty that comes with love and success. We need to cultivate relationships with others so they may beautify our lives. It begins with our intent to beautify theirs.

As adults we encounter a broad range of people and create a hier-archy of relationships. We may see our favorite bank teller only twice a month, but she contributes to our life. So do all those other acquain-tances: co-workers, friends, relatives, confidantes and partners.

For many people, the longest and most complex relationship is our long-term spousal one. It takes the most tending but can yield life's finest physical, mental and emotional beauty. Intimacy, tenderness, forgiveness, hospitality, sexuality, creativity and compassion are either perfected or compromised within this alliance. The beauty of stretching one's dreams and potential is continually challenged. There is ample opportunity to fully experience and express a wide range of feelings and emotions. A mutual intention to better the self while understanding the other should be built into every marital commitment. Success in marriage is guaranteed when the relationship is God-centered. Not only does it ensure spiritual beauty, it commands an enduring toughness that transcends human frailty. Creating a healthy marriage for a lifetime is not for sissies.

Our corporate relationships involve us with group entities. These may be classified as government, media, organizations of all kinds, legal and medical systems, educational institutions and our own extended families. Our relationship with them differs from the others by sheer distance. Whole systems beyond the family are impersonal and they appear immovable.

We must choose our corporate relationships with care. For example, dealing with health care systems can be harmful to your health. Each type of institution has a personality that reflects the beliefs of its principals. The remote nature of organizations creates a disadvantage for consumers. How can you judge the integrity and character of a CEO? Our corporate relationships should improve our lives. We need to scratch below the surface before we buy and find out how a company treats its employees. Consumerism is power. Participants in life exert it. Bystanders don't bother.

Benevolent work gives meaning to life. We can make beautiful contributions to others by transferring some of our workable skills into community development, youth work, or any charitable organization. Such worthwhile efforts are extensions of the care we give to other individuals and to ourselves. Dealing with whole systems tests our tolerance, patience, faith and tenacity. Progress is slow and the result of our efforts may not happen in our lifetime. There is however, a synergistic beauty that comes from being part of a group endeavor that is unlike any other. Much of the exhilaration comes from the camaraderie of shared effort. The phenomenon of many people moving toward a common goal stretches individual abilities, paving the way for peak experiences. A true participant will choose at least one such venture in a lifetime. You can help to build a house or sand-bag a levy. You may cook for a shelter or paint an orphanage in Mexico. The beauty in giving of your time and talent nourishes the human spirit like nothing else can.

The relationship that transcends all others is the one we have with God. It is difficult for finite minds to expand into the realm of unconditional love and grace. The first step in developing a relationship with God is to pray for help in opening to receive such a beautiful gift. The second is to censor our encounters with the non-beautiful. So often pessimism, sarcasm and negativity creep into our relationships. We begin to know God when we practice tolerance and patience, honesty and integrity with everyone we know. Now we are choosing life.

Beautiful Choices

Choosing life includes nourishing all of our senses. This means discriminating between healthy and unhealthy sensory stimulants. We can sustain life with minimal amounts of food; we thrive by embracing the beautiful. I once met a woman who gave an excellent example of beauty in her life. In her suburban home she had decorated a sitting room with care and elegance. This room was a source of annoyance to her husband because it was seldom used. "I do use it," attested the woman. "Every time I go by it my sense of visual beauty is satisfied."

There is no extra cost in making beautiful choices, just added awareness. We can learn to avoid irritating sights, sounds, tastes, smells and touch. Just as easily we can learn to avail ourselves of those that are beautiful.

There are times when we cannot avoid the nonbeautiful elements of life: the rage of another, the horror of a disaster or the pain of loss. Situations like these are part of life and with adequate support we learn to grieve and survive them.

Even in the midst of the repulsive, we have choice. We can minimize our traumatic response to life's ugliness in a variety of ways. Don't watch television news before sleeping. The visual images will haunt your subconscious throughout your much-needed time of rest. Don't allow yourself to be absorbed by commercial negativity and sensationalism. Adopt a secret of the Buddhists, which they call *soft eyes.* Simply lower your eyelids until you see only what is absolutely necessary. Soft eyes smooth the jagged edges of ugliness.

We must learn what pleases us in both physical and nonphysical ways. We can learn to look for multiple layers of meaning in situations and relationships. We can listen to each other attentively, openly and honestly. There is an old Canadian Indian saying that chides us to reserve judgement about another person until we have walked a mile in their moccasins. A participant will go that distance for the beauty of understanding another human being. They do not fear discord because they welcome the opportunity to negotiate resolution through a type of beauty called consensus.

We all have the potential to seek the beautiful. We can refrain from negative thinking and surround ourselves with positive people. I urge you to find the cups of life that fill you with beauty and drink your fill. Choose life! Make it your goal to be a beautiful person. Your very presence will inspire others to be the same.

Conclusion

W here would you like to be on the continuum of consciousness? Wide awake and living fully? In passionate love with work, play, people and God? I believe that you would move along if you knew, without a doubt, that you could be all of these, and more.

We all want assurances before we risk. We want scientific proof before we believe. A big part of becoming a participant in life is a willingness to step out on faith. No matter where you are, I know you can be better. I have faith in you because I believe in your design. You are designed for greatness.

I realize that living consciously is not always easy. It urges us to selfhood greater than we are. It challenges us to dream beyond our goals and long for more in all areas of living. It invites us to choose life over death and blessings over curses. There are ways to do that if we are willing to walk along the higher road. Trust me, the alternatives are even more difficult.

It is time for you to get serious about choosing life. Here is a little exercise to help you along. Go to the kitchen and take an ordinary spoon from the drawer. Now, look at your face in the bowl of the spoon. Do you see yourself, albeit a little distorted? Is it you, without a doubt? This is one way of looking at yourself, but it is not the only way.

Turn the spoon over and look at yourself from the back of it. Is it you, without a doubt? Have you changed anything about yourself in the last few seconds? Not really. Well, you look very different from this new perspective!

Don't confuse perspective with reality. You have endless possibilities when you set your intention toward your dreams. With enough faith, all things are possible.

If you are feeling stuck, don't lose your concentration. Being overwhelmed is merely temporary unless you choose it as a way of life. Turn the spoon over and right yourself. (The thought.) Take a deep breath and say, "This is going to be a wonderful day. Things will be much easier than I expected. Help will come from some surprising places." (The words.) Then choose a healthy activity. (The action.) Here are suggestions based on each of the previous chapters:

· *Decide right now to become a participant in life. Write it down.*

· *Accept your wholeness. If your body aches, rest it. If your mind aches, listen to some music. If your emotions ache, have a good cry. If your spirit aches, have a chat with God.*

· *Choose a person you would like to know better. Invite him or her for coffee.*

· *Clear out a cluttered area of your home or working environment.*

· *Go through some old magazines and cut out dream pictures. Put them on your refrigerator.*

· *Select something purely creative that you would like to do and take one step toward it.*

· *Take out your list of disagreeable people. Select one. Write down two good qualities about him or her.*

· *Unburden your body by making amends to someone.*

· *Think of something that you believe will **never** be yours: a trip to Paris, an expensive car. Write a positive what if statement about it.*

· *Buy a bottle of bubbles. Keep it in your car. If you find yourself stuck in traffic, blow a few out the window.*

· *The next time you are waiting in line, turn and greet the person behind you.*

· *Have a massage.*

· *Buy a cassette tape of music from another country. Listen to it six times before making a judgement about it.*

· *Visit a museum. Ask one of the docents to show you his or her favorite piece of art and to discuss its beauty with you.*

Above all, don't be a bystander. You will stay lonely, overwhelmed, helpless, rigid, and suspicious. Life is so rich, so filled with opportunity and passion. Be a participant. Wake up, look around, and say, "I will."

Think deeply.
Speak softly.
Love generously.
Laugh frequently.
Give freely.
Work diligently.
Pray reverently.
And dream enthusiastically.

Choose life!

Table of Figures

Notes and Resources

Chapter 1: Participants and Bystanders

Author's note: To assist you on your personal healing journey, refer to *The Choose Life Companion Workbook.*

1. Maxwell, John, *Developing the Leader Within You*, Thomas Nelson Publishers, Nashville, 1993.
2. Chapman, *The Five Love Languages, How to Express Heartfelt Commitment to Your Mate*, Chicago, 1992.
3. DeVoss, Rich, *Compassionate Capitalism, People Helping People Help Themselves*, Dutton, 1993.

Chapter 2: Holism, a Way of Life

1. Software designer Dave Birdsall states, "Quantum mechanics is that branch of physics that concerns itself with very small things, like how the particles that make up atoms behave. At this level, particles both influence and are influenced by each other. An interesting insight on this is the Heisenberg Uncertainty Principle that describes limits on what can be measured. For example, if one wishes to measure the velocity (speed and direction) of a particle beyond a certain accuracy, then it is not possible to measure its position (at the same time). Another way to look at it, is the tool that does the measuring inherently changes what is being measured. Now, there's a wild thought!"

2. Cousins, Norman, *Anatomy of an Illness as Perceived by the Patient. Reflections on Healing and Regeneration,* W.W. Norton, New York, 1979.

3. Shlain, Leonard, *The Alphabet Versus the Goddess, The Conflict Between Word and Image,* Viking, 1998.

4. Kaptchuck, Ted J., *The Web that has No Weaver, Understanding Chinese Medicine,* Congdon & Weed, New York, 1983.

5. Morrison, Judith, *The Book of Ayurveda, A Holistic Approach to Health and Longevity,* Simon and Schuster, 1995.

6. Capra, Fritjof, *The Turning Point, Science, Society and the Rising Culture,* Bantam, 1982.

Chapter 3: Community

1. Covey, Stephen, *The 7 Habits of Highly Effective Families,* Golden Books, New York, 1997.

2. Stanley Keleman is a world-renowned authority on the subject of somatic reality and somatic psychotherapy. For more than forty years he has devoted his professional career to developing an understanding of the organizational relationships of the physical body and life experience. He is the director of the Center for Energetic Studies in Berkeley, California, where he conducts classes and programs open to anyone interested in deepening their quality of life through somatic education and therapies. His prolific writings include such titles as *Embodying Experience, Bonding, Patterns of Distress, Love: A Somatic View, Emotional Anatomy* and *Myth and the Body.* For more information about his books and programs write to The Center for Energetic Studies or to Center Press at 2045 Francisco St., Berkeley, CA 94709.

Chapter 4: Quiet Presence

1. Siegel, Bernie, *Love, Medicine and Miracles, Lessons Learned About Self-Healing From a Surgeon's Experience with Exceptional Patients.*

2. Aldana, Jacquelyn, *The 15-Minute Miracle Revealed,* Inner Wisdom Publications, PO Box 1341, Los Gatos, CA 95031, 1998.

Chapter 5: Wishing and Dreaming

1. The Holy Bible, Old Testament, Book of Genesis, Chapters 27–35.
2. Dave Severn is a successful businessman and mentor as well as a board member of the World Wide Group, LLC.
3. Schwartz, David, *The Magic of Thinking Big*, Simon and Schuster, Fireside, 1987.

Chapter 6: Faith

1. Bunko is a card game where winning relies more on chance than on skill.

Chapter 7: Confession

1. Both Jews and Christians accept that God holds each one accountable for their belief in Him. The reward for this faith is eternal life with God. There are several Biblical sources in the Old and New Testaments that refer to God's *eternal register* of the redeemed as *The Book of Life*. Old Testament: Book of Exodus, Chapter 32, verse 32, Book of Psalms, Chapter 69, verse 28. New Testament: Book of Luke, Chapter 10, verse 20 (quote of Jesus Christ), Book of Philippians, Chapter 4, verse 3.
2. The author believes the terms *confessor* and *confident* are almost interchangeable, but not quite. The religious connotation of confession has a humbling and healing aspect to it that surpasses mere disclosure. Confession in a holistic sense means the sharing of our deepest thoughts and desires. They can be positive and hopeful.

Chapter 8: Forgiveness

1. Matthews, Andrew, *Being Happy! A Handbook to Greater Confidence and Security*, Price Stern Sloan, Los Angeles, 1990.

Chapter 9: Hope

1. Snyder, C.R., Wiklund, Cynthia and Cheavens, Jennifer, Pshychology Department, University of Kansas, *Hope and the Academic Success of College Students,* Presented at the American Psychological Association Covention, Boston, Mass., August, 1999.

2. Snyder, C.R., *The Psychology of Hope: You can get there from here.* Free Press, New York, 1994.

3. Snyder, C.E., Cheavens, J., and Michael, S, (In press.) *Hoping.* In C.R. Snyder (Ed.), *Coping: The Psychology that Works,* Oxford University Press, New York.

4. Snyder, C.R., and Sympson, S., Michael, S., and Cheavens, J., (In press), *The Optimism and Hope Constructs: Variants on a Positive Expectancy Theme.* In E.C. Chang (Ed.), *Optimism and Pessimism,* American Psychological Association, Washington, D.C.

5. Synder, C.R., Harris, C., et al, *Hope and Health: Measuring the Will and the Ways.* 1991.

Author's note: To order these articles, or to obtain a list of others, you may e-mail Dr. Snyder at crsnyder@ukans.edu, or look at his website: http://raven.cc.ukans.edu/~crsnyder.

6. The Holy Bible, Revised King James Version, Old Testament, Book of Genesis, Chapter 13, verse 14.

7. Haas, Elson, *Staying Healthy with Nutrition, The Complete Guide to Diet and Nutritional Medicine,* Celestial Arts, Berkeley, CA, 1992.

Chapter 10: Laughter

1. Cousins, Norman, *Anatomy of an Illness, as Perceived by the Patient.* W.W. Norton & Co., 1979. (Norman Cousins used intentional, regular doses of laughter to heal from a severe illness. In his book he also stresses the importance of attending to the person inside the body.

2. The University of Georgia Centenarian Study report to the 1997 Medical and Health Annual, Encyclopedia Brittanica, Inc., *Who*

Will Survive to 105?, by Leonard W. Poon, Ph.D., Phillip A. Holtsberg, J.D., M.B.A., Mary Ann Johnson, Ph.D., and Peter Martin, Ph.D. For a complete listing of publications from the Georgia Centenarian Study, from 1990 to present, you many e-mail Dr. Poon at lpoon@geron.uga.edu.

Chapter 11: Hospitality

1. Hurley, Judith Benn, *Savoring the Day, Recipes and Remedies to Enhance Your Natural Rhythms*, William Morrow and Company, Inc., New York, 1997.

Chapter 12: Touch

1. Montagu, Ashley, *Touching, the Human Significance of the Skin*, Harper and Row, New York, 1997.
2. Field T., Schanberg S., Scafidi F., et al, "Tactile/kinesthetic Stimulation Effects on Preterm Neonates," *Journal of Pediatrics* 77(5): 654-658, 1986.
3. White J.L., LaBarba R.C., "The Effects of Tactile/kinesthetic Stimulation on Neonatal Development in the premature infant," *Journal of Developmental Psychobiology*, 6:569-577, 1976.
4. Kuhn C., Schanberg S., Field T.,et al, "Tactile/kinesthetic Stimulation Effects on Sympathetic and Adrenocortical Function in Preterm Infants," *Journal of Pediatrics*, 119: 434-440, 1991.
5. Field T., Morrow C., Valdeon C., et al, "Massage Therapy Reduces Anxiety in Child Adolescent Psychiatric Patients," *Journal of the American Academy of Child and Adolescent Psychiatry*, 31: 125-131, 1992.

Author's note: Write for reprints of these or other research abstracts and reports to: Tiffany Field, Ph.D, Touch Research Institute, University of Miami School of Medicine, P.O. Box 016820, Miami, FL 33101.

6. Schneider McClure, Vimala, *Infant Massage, A Handbook for Loving Parents*, Bantam, New York, 1989.

7. Dobson, James, *The Strong-Willed Child, Birth Through Adolescence,* Tyndale House Publishers, Inc., Wheaton, IL, 1978.
8. For information on Somatic Psychotherapy, refer to the website http://www.relationshiprescue.com.
9. Keleman, Stanley, ibid Chapter 3, item 2.

Chapter 13: Music

1. Brown E.F., Hendee W.R., "Adoloescents and Their Music, Insights into the Health of Adolescents," *Journal of the American Medical Association,* 262(12), 1659–63, Sept. 1989.
2. *U.C. Berkeley Wellness Letter,* "Without music, life would be a mistake," Feb. 1995.
3. Gerber, Richard, *Vibrational Medicine,* Bear and Co., 1988.
4. Author's note: There is a large volume of research underway directed at music as a healing modality in most aspects of health care. Current health newsletters and magazines reflect this. The National Institute of Health has awarded the Institute for Music, Health and Education in Boulder Colorado a major grant to study music in healing. Don Campbell, founder of the Institute has published several books on these subjects.
5. Ibid. Chapter 2, #4.
6. Ibid. Chapter 2, #5.
7. Diamond, John, *Life Energy,* Paragon House, 1990.
8. Horvilleur, Alain, *The Family Guide to Homeopathy,* Health and Homeopathy Publishing Co., P.O. Box 6004, Arlington, VA 22206, 1986.
9. Hamer, B.A., "Music Therapy, Harmony for Change," *Journal of Psychological Nursing,* Vol. 29, No. 12, 1991.
10. To learn more about the medical applications of music, or to investigate a career in Music Therapy, contact the National Association for Music Therapy Inc., 961 Kentucky St., Suite 206, P.O. Box 610, Lawrence, KS, 66044. (913-842-1909).

Chapter 14: Beauty

1. Cameron, Julie, *The Artist's Way: a Spiritual Path to Higher Creativity*, J.P. Tarcher, 1992.

About the Author

Beverly Breakey has been involved in the field of Holistic Health for over twenty years. She is a Registered Nurse, educated in Canada with a specialty in pediatrics. More recently she graduated from John F. Kennedy University in Orinda, California, with a Masters degree in Clinical Holistic Health. She went on to obtain her California license as a Marriage and Family Therapist and is the clinical director of the InterGenerational Health Center in San Jose, where she also has a holistic counseling practice.

Breakey has been an educator since 1980 teaching continuing education classes to health professionals on the subject of Holism. She is presently among the faculty of the Touching For Health School of Professional Bodywork in Stockton, California, where she writes curriculum and teaches the interrelatedness of emotion and the physical form. She is also adjunct faculty for the John F. Kennedy University's Department of Holistic Studies. She and her husband, Richard Russell, live in San Jose.

About Ashar Press

Ashar is an ancient Hebrew word which means *to be blessed with happiness*. We at Ashar Press hope that the information in this book and our other products may inspire you to grow and be filled with ashar. We invite you to visit our website (www.asharpress.com), where you will discover more thoughts, words and actions to help you Choose Life!

Index

313

QUICK ORDER FORM

Fax orders:	(408) 371-7960
Telephone orders:	TOLL FREE: (877) 342-7427
E-mail orders:	books@asharpress.com
Postal orders:	Ashar Press
	PO Box 54130
	San Jose, CA 95154-4130
Website orders:	http://www.asharpress.com

Please send the following Books/Products to the address below. I understand that I may return any of them for a full refund for any reason—no questions asked.

☐ *Choose Life! Living Consciously in an*
   Unconscious World..$ 19.^{95}
   Canada .... 24.^{95}
☐ *Choose Life Companion Workbook*...................................$ 12.^{95}
   Canada .... 17.^{95}

Sales tax: Please add 8% (varies) for products shipped to California addresses.
Shipping: U.S. $4.^{00} for the first book/product and $2.^{00} for each additional book/product. International: $9.^{99} for the first book/product and $5.^{00} for each additional book/product

Name:_____

Address:_____

City: _____State: ____Zip:_____

E-mail address: _____

Please send information on:
☐ other books   ☐ other products   ☐ consulting
Payment: ☐ Check   ☐ Credit card   ☐ Visa ☐ MasterCard

Card number: _____

Name on card: _____ Exp. Date: _____/_____

Signature:_____

For the most current listing of our books and products, please take a spin in our web: http://www.asharpress.com